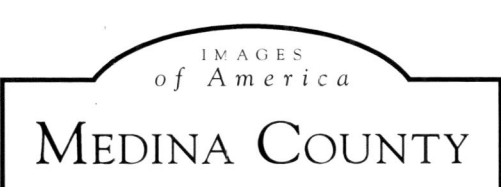

ON THE COVER: Citizens of Medina County enjoy an outing in their new automobile on a Sunday afternoon drive in the late 1800s. Standing on the left is Adolph Ihnken with his mother, Marguerite Droitcourt Ihnken; on the right is Albert Ihnken. The young man's father, John Ihnken, is supposedly taking the picture. (Courtesy of Bonnie and Lester Ludwig.)

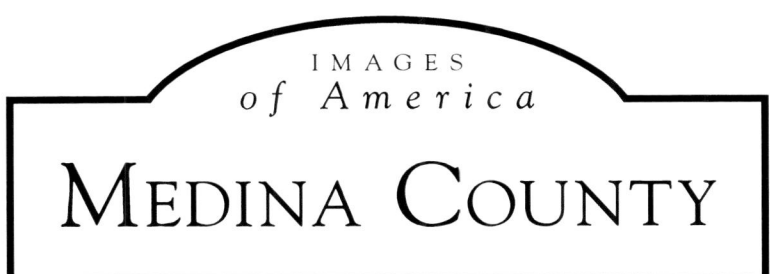

Priscilla DaCamara Hancock

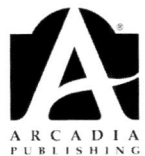

Copyright © 2011 by Priscilla DaCamara Hancock
ISBN 978-0-7385-7989-4

Published by Arcadia Publishing
Charleston, South Carolina

Printed in the United States of America

Library of Congress Control Number: 2011920841

For all general information, please contact Arcadia Publishing:
Telephone 843-853-2070
Fax 843-853-0044
E-mail sales@arcadiapublishing.com
For customer service and orders:
Toll-Free 1-888-313-2665

Visit us on the Internet at www.arcadiapublishing.com

Contents

Acknowledgments 6

Introduction 7

1. Famous Roads, Indians, Early Colonizers, and Churches 9
2. Towns, Railroads, and Schools 55
3. Agriculture, Industry, Medina Dam, Golden Medina Valley Farms, Happy and Sad Times 81
4. Memories of a Few of Medina County's Patriots, and Hondo Army Air Field 111

Acknowledgments

This book has been made from photographs culled from many sources and represents a glimpse into the vast history of Medina County. The Medina County Historic Museum was founded in 1970 by the Hondo Garden Club. Administrator Steve Lapp and director Frances Guinn were very helpful, allowing the museum's photographs to be used for this book. Many pictures were also used from the De Montel collection and from individuals, including Laurel D'Osogna, Charles Suehs, Mabel Burel Suehs, Mary Ann Pringle, Dorothy Ott Suehs, Myrtle Schulte Schneider, Paula Mangold, Clif Eissler (Castroville airport manager), Medina County judge Jim Barden, and Devine's Mary and Henry Briscoe family. Yvonne and Lester Ludwig were more than generous with their large pictorial collections and with their vast knowledge of the history of the area. Many other pictures were donated by family descendants and by the Castroville Library. The mayor of Natalia, Ruby Vera, was a valuable asset, finding pictures from the golden-valley years after the Medina Dam was built. There are many other families that influenced and solidified the county whose stories have yet to emerge and are not told on these pages.

I want to thank my understanding family—my husband Robert, daughter Dolly Hancock Armstrong, and my sons Robert and Brad Hancock—for their advice. Charlie Limones was invaluable as a scanner, and Al McGraw, archeologist for Texas Department of Transportation, provided valuable insight and assisted with historical maps. This book would not have been possible without the encouragement and love of history of all of these people.

Unless otherwise indicated, images appear courtesy of the Medina County Museum.

Introduction

Before European feet touched the land called Tejas, indigenous Indians roamed and ruled the county called Medina. Just west of the large city of San Antonio, inhabitants of Medina County have withstood droughts, floods, and many unforeseen challenges, including conflicts with Indians. According to Damien Mazanet, in the late 1600s, the Medina River was known as Penapay (or Panapay) in the Indian language of Coahuilteco. In 1690, New Spain's governor of Coahuila, Mexico, Alonso de León, led an expedition of soldiers and priests through the area and named the river Medina on the day after Easter, April 11, 1689.

De León probably named the river after Pedro de Medina, a 16th-century Italian astronomer whose navigational tables were used by de León and his contemporaries. De León's expedition arrived on the Medina River on Lunes de Pascua (Easter Monday) but should have arrived a day earlier, on Easter Sunday. His expedition had spent a miserable day to the southwest attempting to recapture a stampeding horse herd.

In the 18th century, the Medina River, in modern Medina County, included the pass or ford for a colonial route to the headwaters of the Nueces River (el Cañon). Medina also contained a Spanish mission—San Lorenzo de Santa Cruz—established to spread the Christian doctrine among the Apache. Following the same point from Castroville along the Medina River, northward up the stream valley, also led near Bandera Pass, which was once an entrance to the Apache stronghold of el Cañon del Ugalde.

In the late 1700s, the Medina River formed the political boundary between the Spanish provinces of Coahuila and Texas. Historical crossings along the river, which deserve further study, were used to establish the early settlement at San Antonio as a waypoint to build and supply settlements at Nacogdoches and the East Texas missions as well as the Spanish capital of Texas, Los Adaes, which was located in present-day Louisiana. From about 1800 to 1870, the route was traveled by almost anyone with business in the administrative centers of Monclova, Mexico City, or Saltillo.

In the early 19th century, the Medina River was the setting for the 1822 war between the Lipan Apache and Comanche in Texas. The two groups were to join forces as allies and jointly negotiate a treaty with the Mexican Republic. However, the Apache abandoned their newfound allies, and without waiting for the arrival of the Comanche, traveled alone to Mexico City to negotiate a separate peace. The subsequent Comanche attack on the Lipan camp precipitated hostilities that lasted throughout the early 1800s.

During the Mexican Republic period, the region remained wild and untamed, inhabited only by American Indians, herds of buffalo, antelope, deer, bears, cougars, wildcats, and other indigenous animals. Several changing routes of the historic Camino Real crossed Medina County. In South Texas leading toward San Antonio, the Camino Real consisted of three distinct regional routes that crossed the Rio Grande near the modern town of Guerrero, Coahuila. The regional routes between San Juan Bautista on the Rio Grande and San Antonio were known as the Camino Pita, Upper Presidio Road, and Camino de en Medio, also known as Lower Presidio Road. The first two of these routes crossed Medina County. The Lower Presidio Road crossed the Medina River downriver in modern Bexar County. South of San Antonio, the Camino Pita and the Camino de en Medio were roughly parallel but crossed the Medina River at different locales. In addition but separate from the river crossings near Guerrero, several trails of the San Antonio–Laredo Road crossed the Medina River in neighboring Atascosa County.

About 1870, the Upper Presidio Road, which was used by Santa Anna in 1836, was established. The third road was Gen. Adrian Woll Road, a smugglers' trail used by General Woll as he attacked San Antonio and the Alamo in 1842. Another important road is the Chihuahua Trail, which in the post–Civil War era carried more commerce than did the better known Santa Fe Trail. There is also the old Fort Ewell Road in southeastern Medina County.

During the Republic of Texas period, land grants played an important part in history. *Empresario* (Spanish for entrepreneur) Henri Castro brought settlers from the French providence of Alsace-Lorraine (along with a sprinkling of other Europeans) to the area and founded Castroville, Quihi, Vandenburg, and D'Hanis. These were the first settlements west of the village of San Antonio. In a memorial presented to Congress some time before January 14, 1841, a law granting land to immigrants was passed and was the basis for all empresario grants made under the Republic of Texas. San Antonio needed a buffer from the Indians who roamed the Comancheria (Indian lands around and beyond the Medina River), and the unsuspecting immigrants came and faced many challenges. Castro's colonists had altercations with the Indians for the first 25 years of their settlement. Castro, second only to Stephen F. Austin in the number of families he helped to settle, spent more than any other single individual in furthering the colonization of Texas. He spent over $100,000 of his own money, yet he died poor and neglected.

Farming, the first the main occupation in the early settlements, gave way to ranching (cattle and sheep) by the Civil War. In 1911, when the Medina Dam project was initiated, irrigation was introduced. Many new settlers came from the Dust Bowl, finding a new way of life. In 1936 and 1937, two large railroad systems came through the county. The Missouri Pacific passed through the southeastern end of the county, serving Devine, Natalia, and other communities on its way to northern Mexico. The Southern Pacific crossed the central part of Texas, serving the towns of LaCoste, Pearson, Noonan, Dunlay, Hondo, new D'Hanis, and Seco, and connecting the east to the west just as the Camino Real had done many years before.

During World War II, Hondo Air Base was constructed to teach aviation and navigation to brave young Americans who would later fly combat missions defending our nation. As a result of the base, the small town of Hondo (the county seat) blossomed and businesses grew. In the following years, with the access of great highway systems, people from Medina County could work in San Antonio while retaining their farms and ranches in the county. The challenges have changed, but the early settlers' heroism and tenacity are cemented in Medina's residents to this day.

One
Famous Roads, Indians, Early Colonizers, and Churches

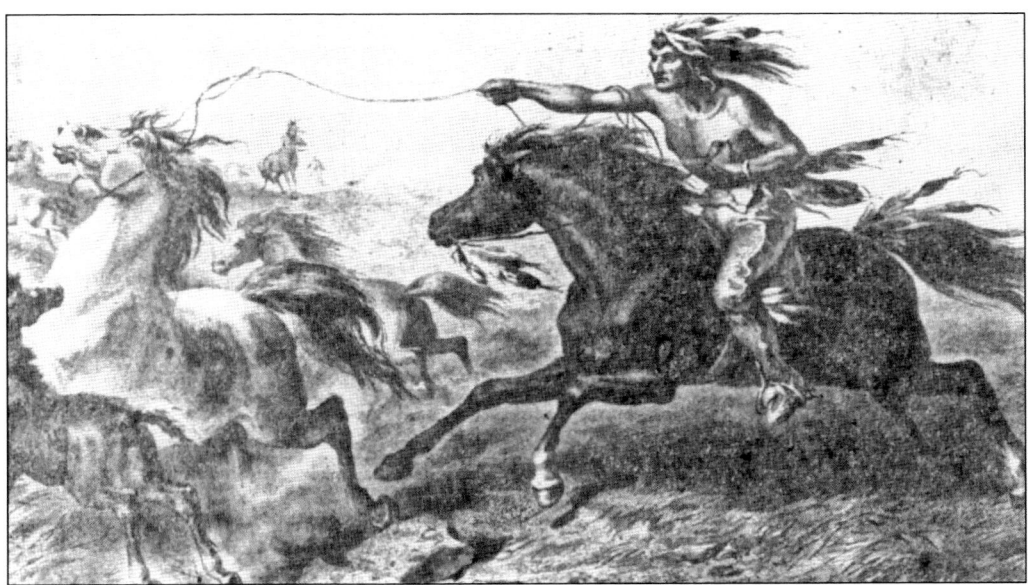

Before Europeans arrived to settle in Medina County, the Comanche Indians moved out of New Mexico. Pressure from the Ute and Navajo in the west pushed the Comanche eastward into central-west Texas. The Lipan Apache (who were no match for the Comanche after enduring much warfare) moved into Webb County around Laredo. The Kickapoo moved north to the Dallas area. The Cherokee and many other tribes moved as the Comanche wrecked havoc, with the plunder of horses and slaves as their goal.

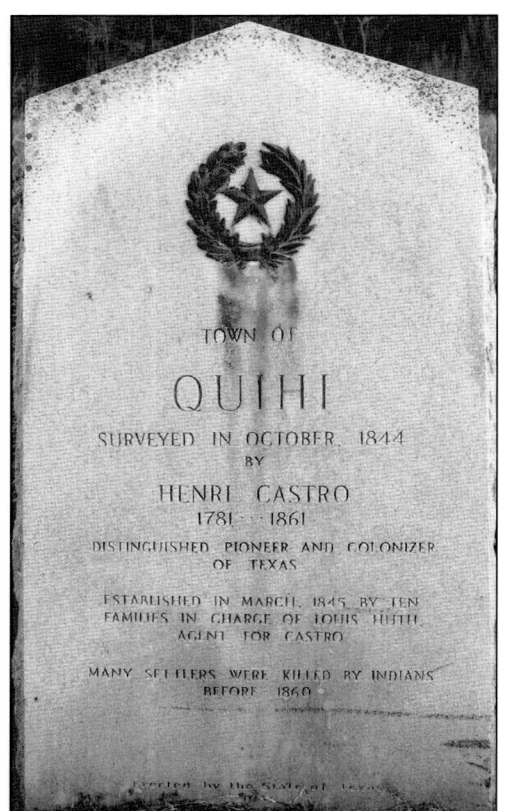

Quihi, along the Quihi Lake, seemed an ideal place to settle. However, it had long been a watering spot for tribes of the area. The settlers knew nothing of this, nor did they have guns to protect themselves. This Texas historical marker tells the tale.

This drawing, from the *Hondo Anvil* newspaper, depicts an Indian stealing a child. Children were kidnapped frequently, and many were never recovered. Two boys in nearby Boerne did escape and return to their families to tell the tale of their capture and lucky escape.

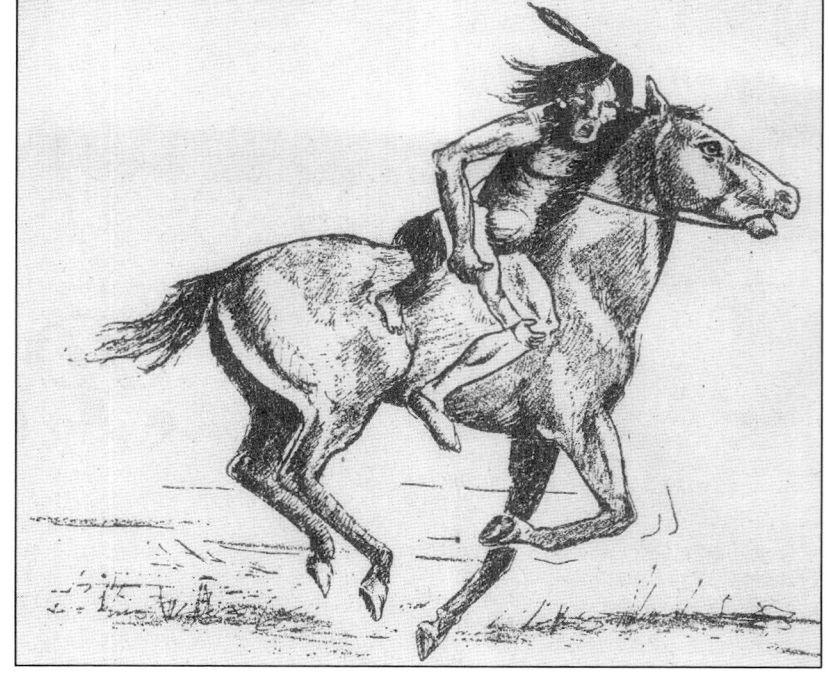

The routes taken through Medina County varied depending on weather and Indian raids. The road shown on this map is the route taken by the French general Woll and his Mexican soldiers when traveling toward the second siege of the Alamo.

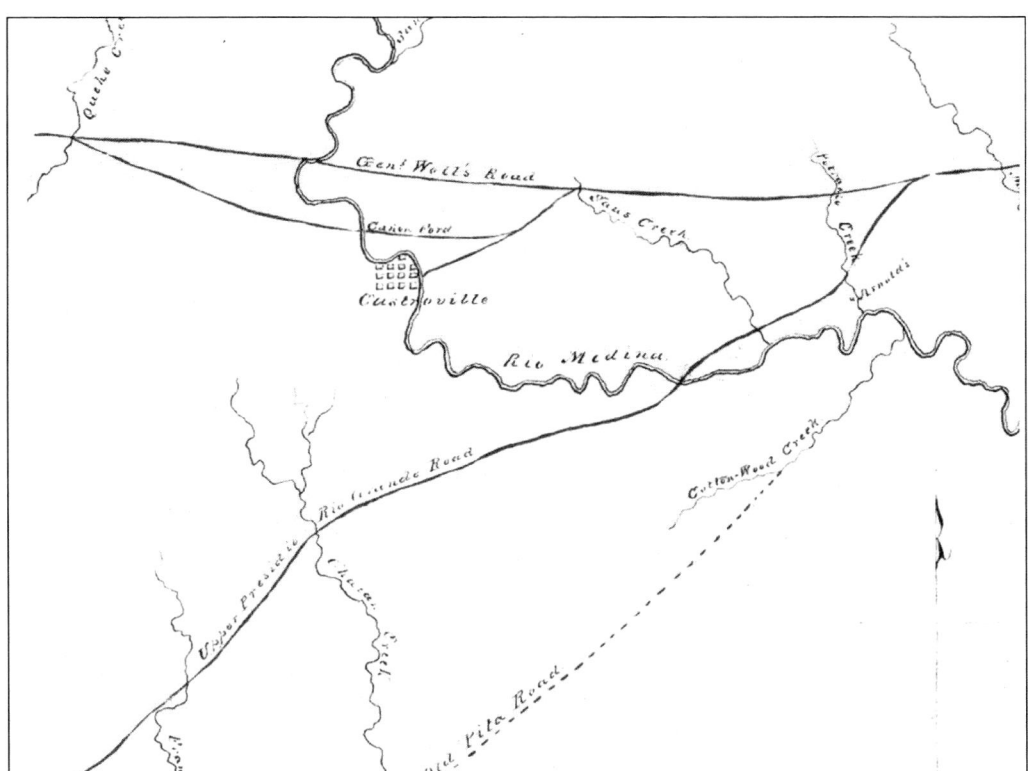

GENERAL WOLL'S ROAD

IN 1842, THERE WERE TWO MAJOR INVASIONS INTO THE REPUBLIC OF TEXAS BY MEXICAN TROOPS. ACTIVE BRIGADE GENERAL ADRIAN WOLL WAS ORDERED TO LEAD THE SECOND OF THE TWO EXPEDITIONS INTO TEXAS IN ORDER TO CAPTURE SAN ANTONIO. WOLL ORDERED BREVET COL. JOSÉ MARÍA CARRASCO TO CONSTRUCT A NEW ROAD THAT AVOIDED EXISTING ROADS AND TRAILS, IN ORDER TO REACH THE CITY UNDETECTED. TRAVELING ON THE ROAD WITH GENERAL WOLL WOULD BE HIS STAFF OF AT LEAST TWENTY OFFICERS, 850 INFANTRY SOLDIERS, ARTILLERY, AT LEAST FIFTY SUPPLY WAGONS AND CARTS, AND A LARGE HERD OF LIVESTOCK. THE INVASION AND ROAD CONSTRUCTION BEGAN ON AUGUST 24, 1842, WHEN WOLL'S FORCES FORDED THE RIO GRANDE AT THE NOGAL CROSSING, APPROXIMATELY TWENTY MILES DOWNRIVER FROM PRESENT-DAY EAGLE PASS, NEAR THE RIVER'S CONFLUENCE WITH SAUS CREEK.

GENERAL WOLL AND HIS TROOPS PASSED THROUGH THE QUIHI AREA ON SEPTEMBER 9, 1842. WOLL ATTACKED SAN ANTONIO AT DAYBREAK ON SEPTEMBER 11 AND TOOK THE CITY IN JUST TWO HOURS. HIS FORCES KEPT THE CITY CAPTIVE FOR SEVEN DAYS. THE INVASION WAS THEN STOPPED DURING THE BATTLE OF SALADO CREEK BY 225 TEXIAN VOLUNTEERS LED BY CAPTAINS MATTHEW CALDWELL AND JOHN C. HAYS. DURING THIS BATTLE, TEXIAN CAPTAIN NICHOLAS M. DAWSON'S VOLUNTEER COMPANY WAS INTERCEPTED 1.5 MILES FROM SAN ANTONIO AND MOST WERE KILLED BY WOLL'S TROOPS. THE FIFTEEN TEXIAN SOLDIERS THAT SURVIVED WERE TAKEN PRISONER.

FEARING ANOTHER ENCOUNTER WITH TEXIAN FORCES, WOLL RETREATED FROM SAN ANTONIO DURING THE NIGHT OF SEPTEMBER 19, ALONG THE ROAD THAT HAD BEEN CONSTRUCTED JUST DAYS BEFORE. THE TROOPS PASSED THROUGH THE QUIHI AREA AGAIN ON SEPTEMBER 20, AS THEY MARCHED BACK TO MEXICO. THE ROAD CONTINUED TO BE USED FOR MANY YEARS BY MILITARY EXPEDITIONS, SETTLERS AND FREIGHT HAULERS.

(2009)

MARKER IS PROPERTY OF THE STATE OF TEXAS

This marker, placed by the Texas Historical Commission, outlines the invasion by Mexican troops into the Republic of Texas. The Woll Road was constructed secretly so that trails already in use could be avoided.

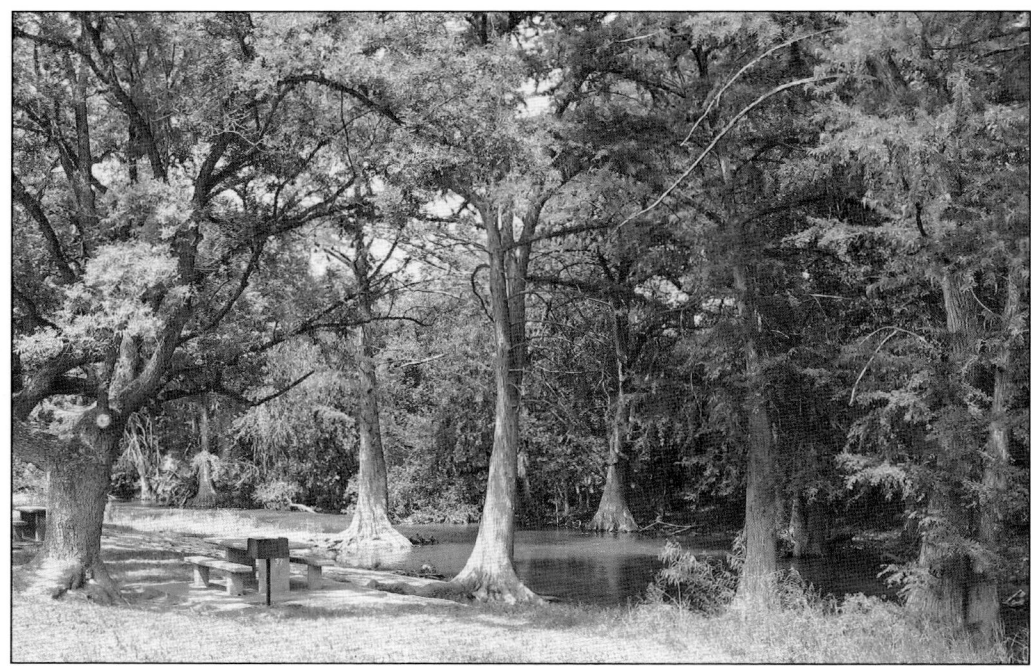

The beautiful Medina River, with its water, marine life, and native pecan trees, has provided sustenance to people and animals for centuries. This meandering, cypress-shaded river became a waterway and irrigation canal in early 1900. (Courtesy of the author.)

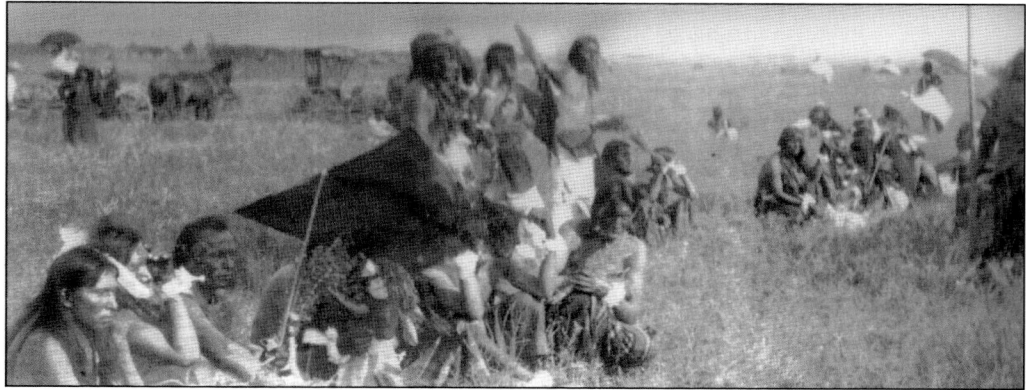

This photograph of some of the remaining Indians in Medina County was taken by settlers at what was called a powwow. A small two-seat carriage can be seen in the background.

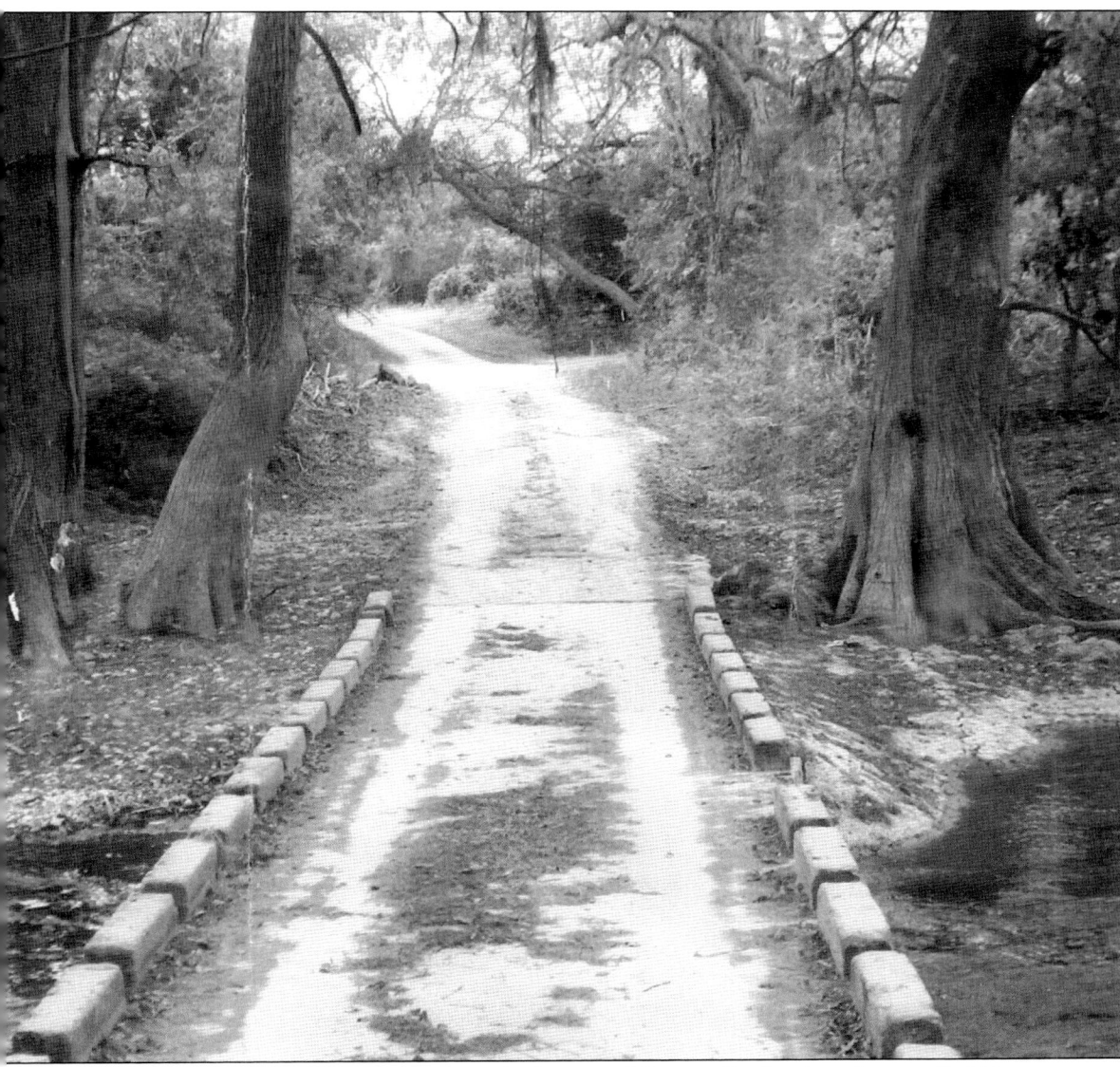
This 1900s crossing of the Medina River, a little west of Castroville, has long been called Flat Rock Crossing. It is rumored to be a smugglers' crossing used to transport goods that would have been taxed by the Spanish government if they were moved by way of the Camino Real. (Courtesy of the author.)

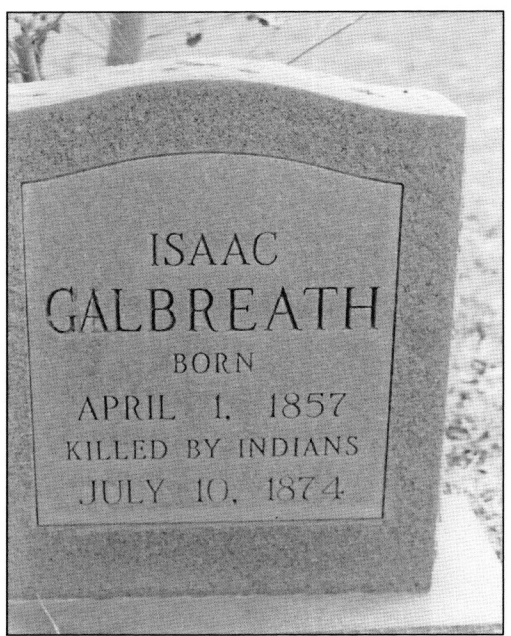

Warfare raged between settlers and Indians from 1844 until 1877 in Medina County. Isaac Galbreath, the 17-year-old son of Texas Ranger Tom Galbreath, was sent from his father's ranch on Chacon Creek to bring in the horses and was "killed by [15] Indians" on July 10, 1874. He died of gunshot, knife, and arrow wounds.

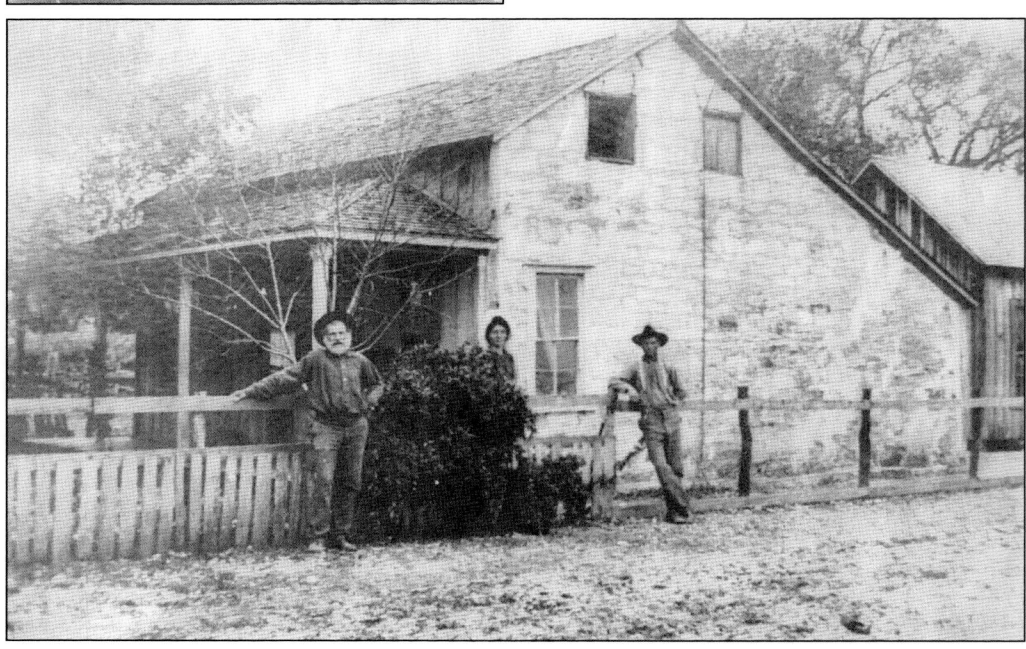

In 1860, Henry Hartman went out with five men to gather a bunch of beeves about 15 miles from New Fountain. Leaving some men with the rounded-up cattle and horses, Henry went out with one man to gather more cattle. They were attacked by Comanche Indians, and Henry's horse was shot, breaking its back and trapping Henry's left leg when it fell. The Indians thought that Henry was dead, but he managed to reach his Winchester and free himself from his fallen horse. He was hit again as he ran through the Indians, sustaining the wound that would make him a cripple for life. Henry is pictured in front of his house in New Fountain in the late 1800s. (Courtesy of Myrtle Schulte Schneider.)

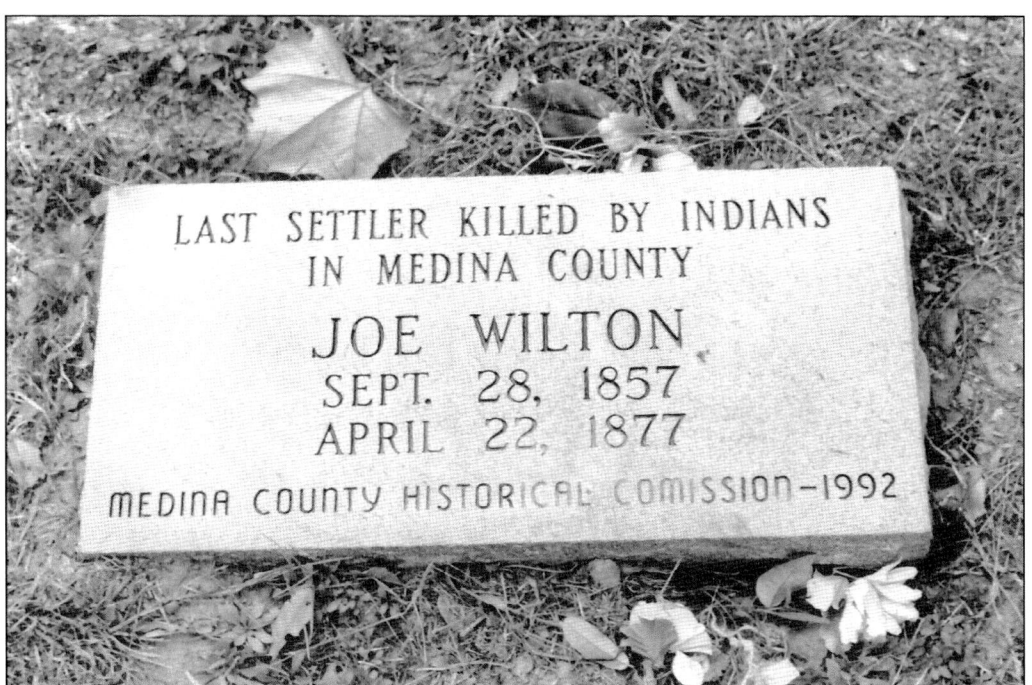

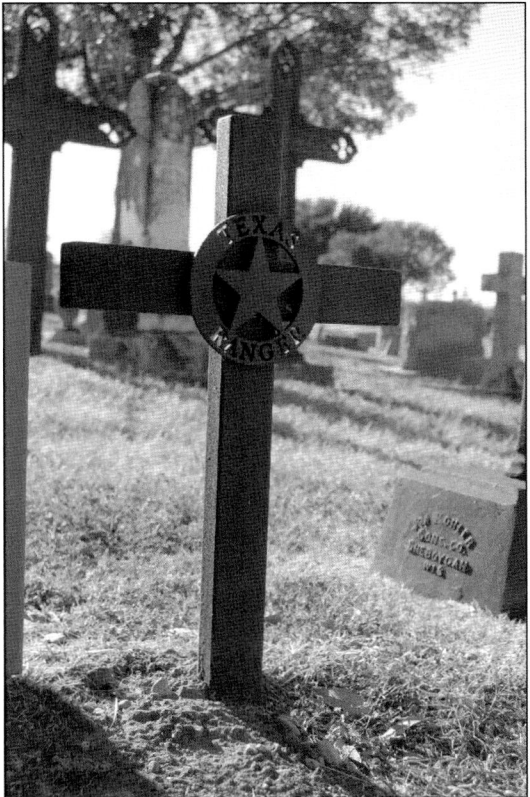

The "last settler killed by Indians in Medina County" was an 18-year-old man with a widowed mother. Joe Wilton left the ranch of Dan Patterson, outside of Devine, to go to the store in Hondo at the Eagle Pass crossing of the river. Indians who had stolen horses in the town of Devine attacked the young man, wounding him with arrows. They then stripped him and mutilated his body.

This cross was placed on the gravesite of Joseph Naegelin, a former Texas Ranger, in Castroville. Joseph was born in Hirtzfelden in Alsace-Lorraine, France, in 1841 and came to Texas as a child with his parents as Castro settlers in 1847. In 1860, he enlisted with the Texas Rangers and was stationed at Fort Inge, Uvalde County. His job was to protect settlers during the frequent Indian raids. When the Civil War broke out, he and his brothers enlisted with the Confederate forces. After the Civil War, he returned to the Texas Rangers Frontier Force. He later ranched and farmed on his land in Medina County and did so until his death. (Courtesy of the author.)

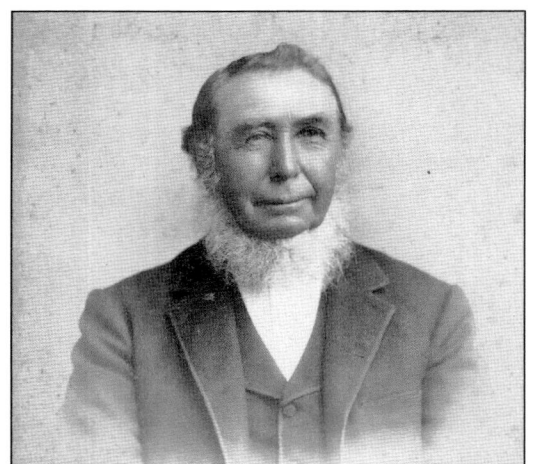

In April 1846, Gerhard Ihnken and his mother emigrated from Germany to Texas. He spoke six languages, was well educated, and became a merchant, rancher, farmer, and entrepreneur. He owned land in both Bexar and Medina Counties. An innovative man, he brought the first reaper, binder, and threshing machine to Medina County. He shipped cattle to New Orleans from Indianola and owned a cotton gin, a sawmill, and a steam engine. Ihnken was a magnanimous man and gave profusely to the church. (Courtesy of Bonnie and Lester Ludwig.)

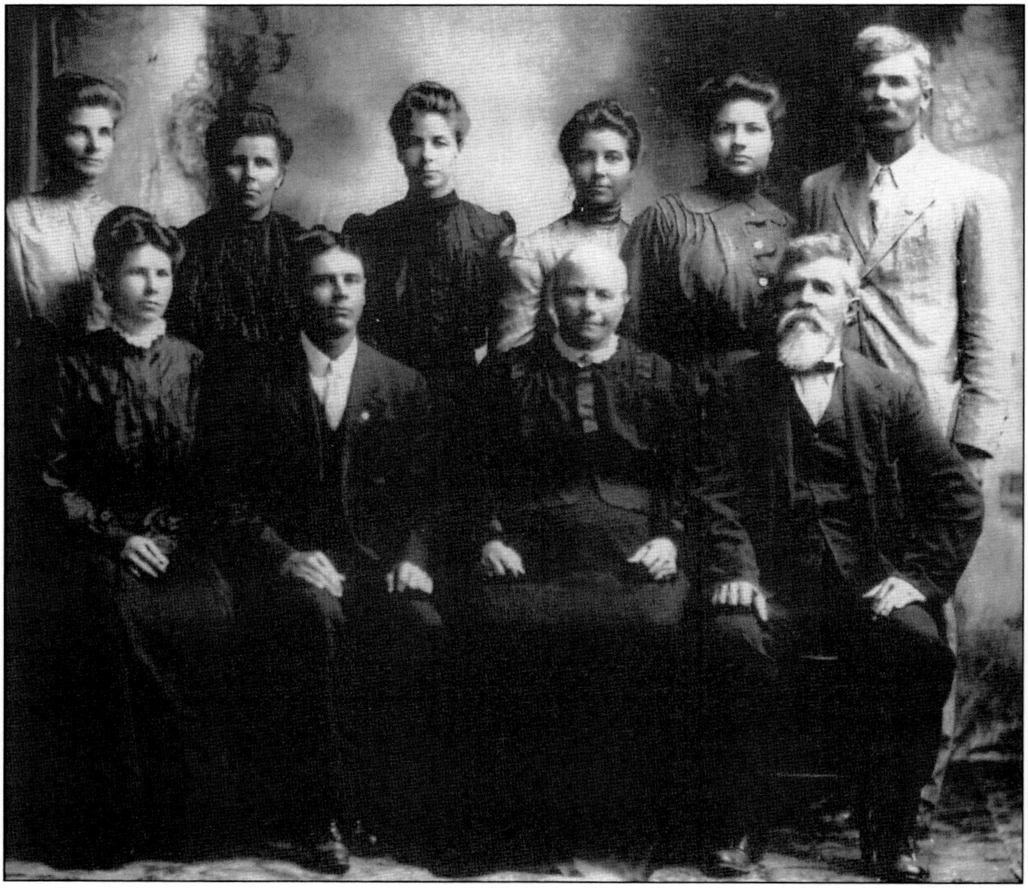

This is a family portrait of Andreas Brieden (right) and Josephina Ludwig Brieden (third from left). Josephina Ludwig came over from Europe as a four-month-old baby in 1847. She was the daughter of Franz Anton Ludwig and met Andreas Brieden Jr. when his family moved to D'Hanis. They married and reared their family on half of the land grant Josephine's father received from Henri Castro. (Courtesy of Bonnie and Lester Ludwig.)

The son of Adam and Catherin Droitcourt, farmer Fritz Droitcourt lived between LaCoste and Castroville. Adam was born in North Vernon, Indiana, and came to Texas in February 1877. Adam married his cousin Katherine Conrad and worked as a blacksmith, wheelwright, and farmer. (Courtesy of Bonnie and Lester Ludwig.)

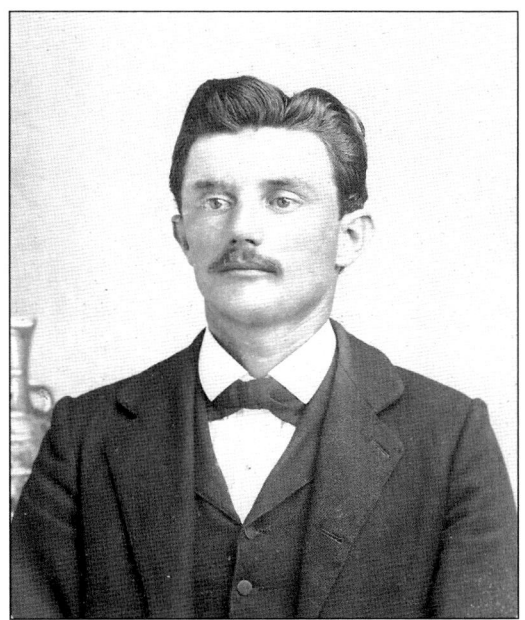

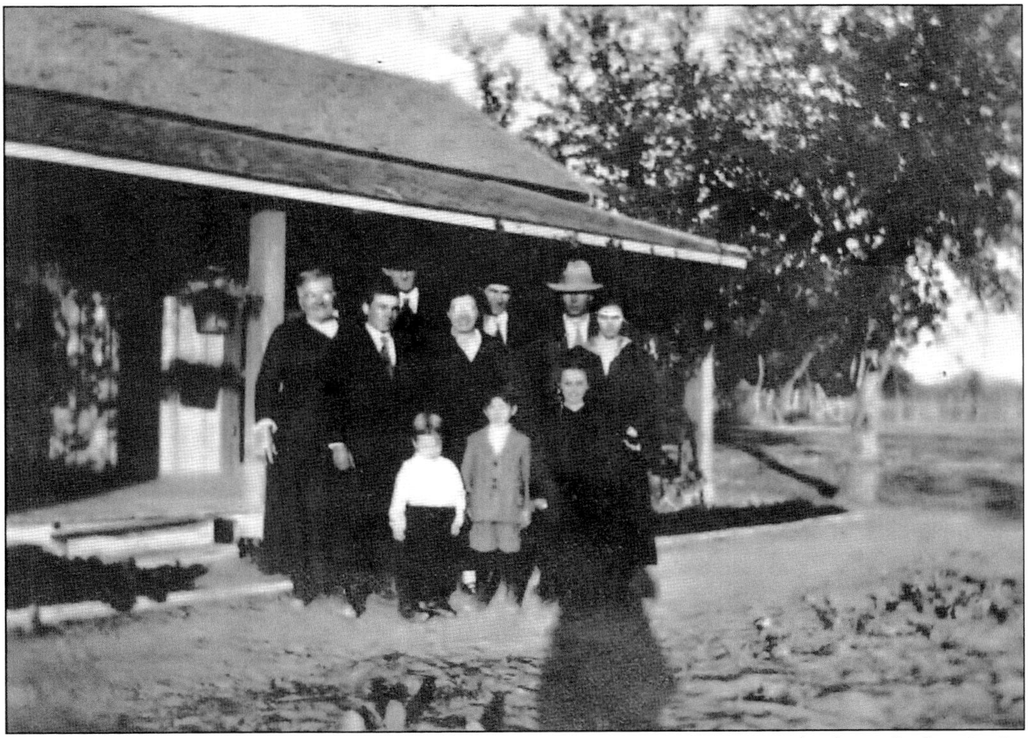

This is the home of Anna Walch Ludwig near Bear Creek and Devine. It was built on the headright land of Anton Ludwig. Shown standing are, from left to right, (first row) Beno, Hilmer, and Alice, all children of Charles Ludwig; (second row) Anna Elizabeth Walch Ludwig, Charles F. Haass, Charles Ludwig, Esmeralda Ludwig Haass, Lester Herman Ludwig, Charles W. Ludwig, and Ella Ludwig, second wife of Charles Ludwig. (Courtesy of Bonnie and Lester Ludwig.)

This is the George Heyen family of Hondo, shown in 1880. George Heyen was the son of Johann and Marie Losberg Heyen. Johann was born in Hanover, Germany, in 1831, and Marie was born in Hesse-Kassel, Germany, in 1834. His parents came to Texas with the Henri Castro Colony in the 1840s.

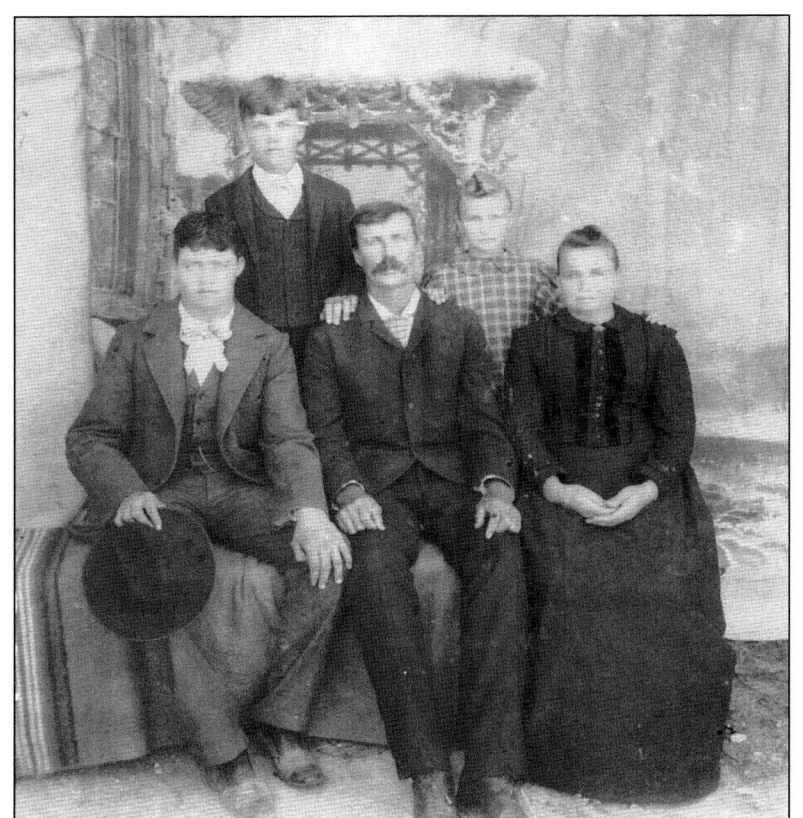

Valentine Nester was born on February 14, 1840, the first child born to Martin and Mary Nester, immigrant settlers of D'Hanis. Valentine married Regina Batot, daughter of D'Hanis pioneers John and Teresa Batot. The couple is pictured here in a formal photograph.

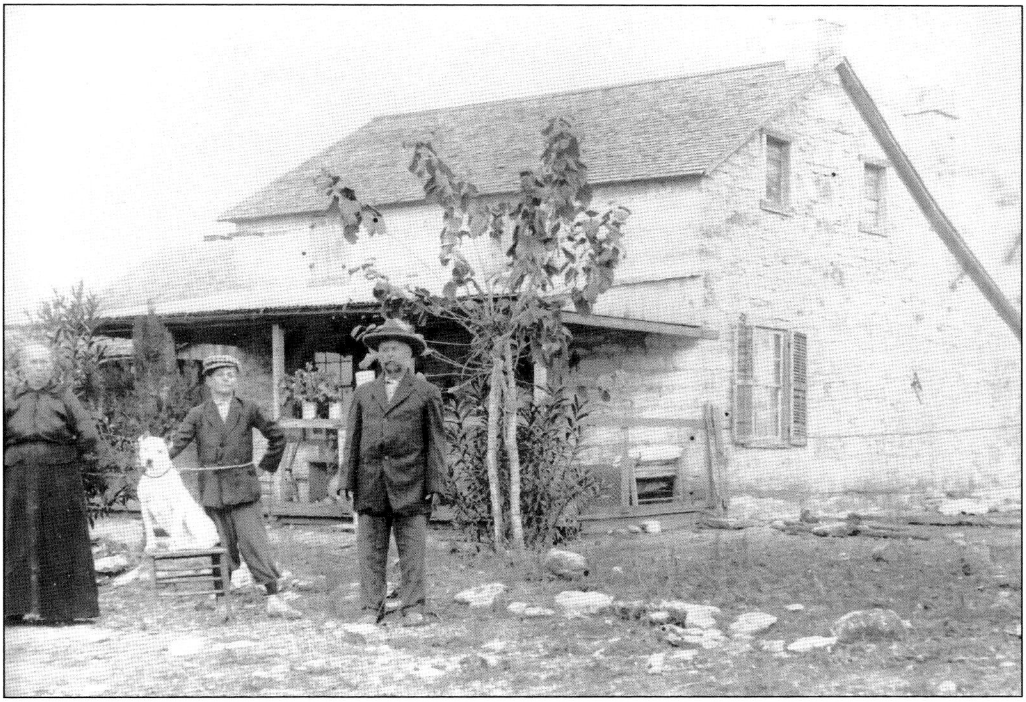

Pictured standing in front of their land-grant home are Jacob and Mary Anna Groff and their son Charles Groff, standing beside his dog.

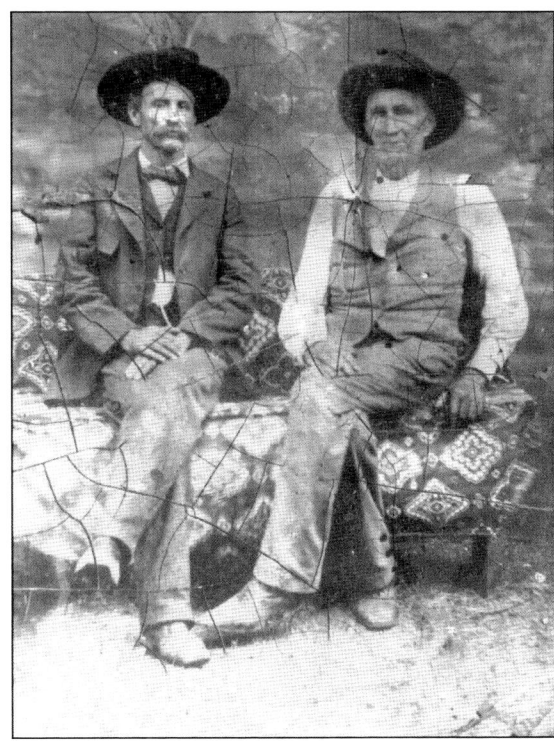

A.J. Sowell (left), author and Texas Ranger, poses with famous William "Big Foot" Wallace (Indian fighter and Texas Ranger) in 1895. Big Foot was part of the Mier Expedition into Mexico. He was captured but escaped to live an eventful life in untamed Medina County. (Courtesy of James Collins.)

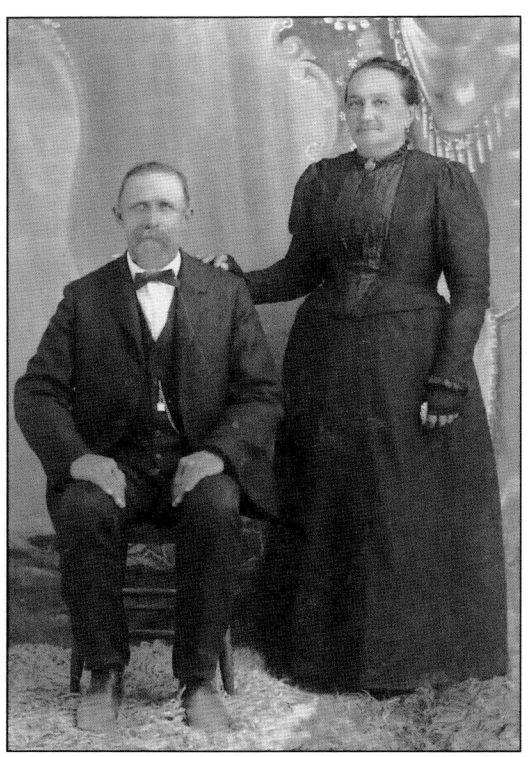

This is a photograph of Henry and Mary Anne Gross. Henry's father and brother were killed by Indians while cutting posts for a picket fence on Kauffman land. (Courtesy of Bonnie and Lester Ludwig.)

Pictured are Marie Jeanne Pichot and Gerhard Ihnken. Marie's father died after being bitten by a rattlesnake. Father Odin, a priest from San Antonio, said that Marie should either become a nun or return on the next ship to Europe. She and her siblings, younger sister Alexis and brother Nicolas, had come over from France. Both sisters resisted Odin's suggestions, marrying Castroville men in the first church west of San Antonio, St. Louis Catholic Church. (Courtesy of Bonnie and Lester Ludwig.)

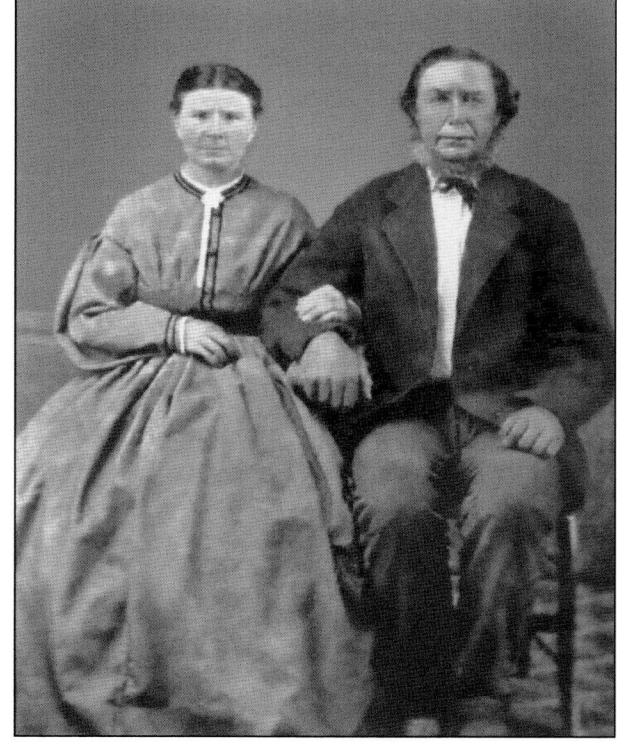

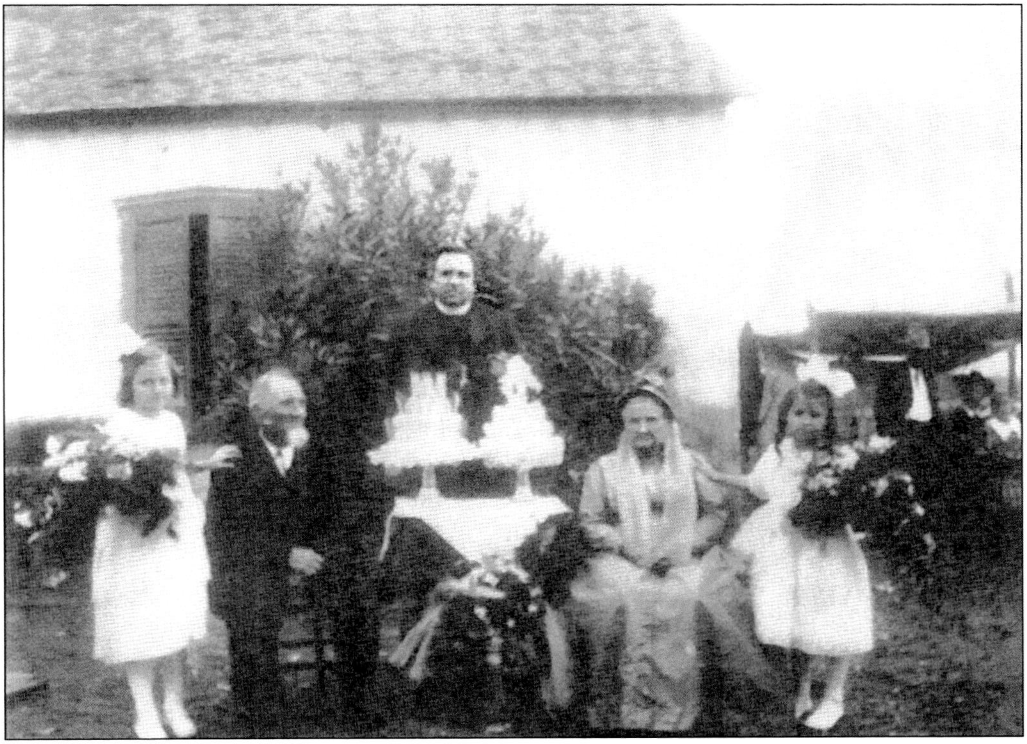

The wedding anniversary picture of Frank P. and Ida Seekatz was taken in front of their Alsatian-style home (rock and cypress covered in plaster made of lime and cactus juice, with a thatched roof). (Courtesy of Bonnie and Lester Ludwig.)

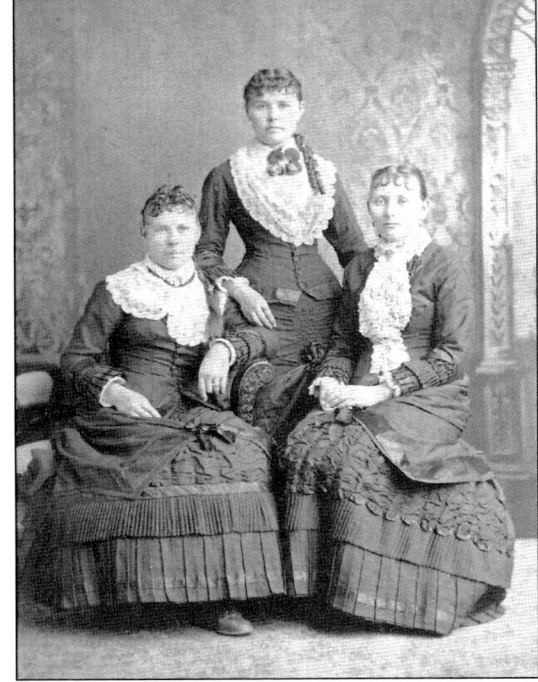

Daughters of Gerhard and Jeanne Marie Pichot Ihnken are pictured here. Seated on the left is Louisa, who would carry on the family business and never marry. Seated to her right is Mary. Standing is Annie, the youngest. She would eventually marry and move to Del Rio. (Courtesy of Bonnie and Lester Ludwig.)

Pictured are brothers Adolph (left) and Albert Ihnken, sons of John and Marguerite Droitcourt Ihnken. These second-generation Texans were very well educated. They are shown with their mother on the cover of this book, posed by an early automobile. (Courtesy of Bonnie and Lester Ludwig.)

This attractive girl, Adella Ihnken, was the seventh and last child born to John and Marguerite Droitcourt Ihnken. In 1906, she married Ed Seekatz in St. Louis Catholic Church in Castroville. (Courtesy of Bonnie and Lester Ludwig.)

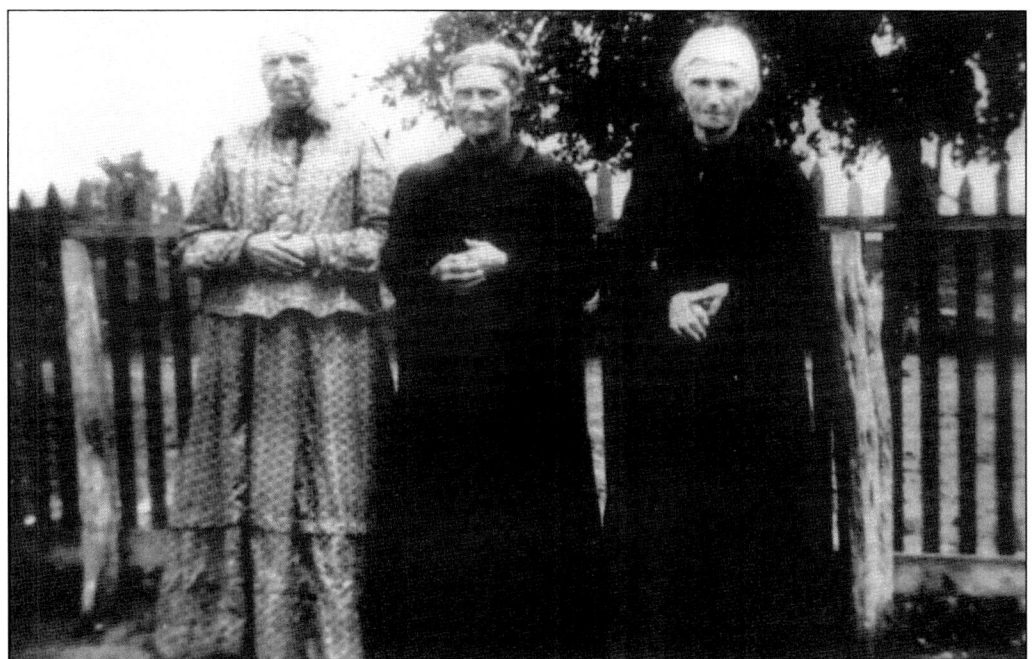

Shown are immigrant settlers of D'Hanis from Malmady, Germany. They are, from left to right, Catherine Fohn Karrer Rudinger, Elizabeth Fohn Enderle, and Margareta Fohn Koch, both cousins of Rudinger. The Fohn family came from what was then considered Rheinish Prussia. They all came to Texas as very young girls.

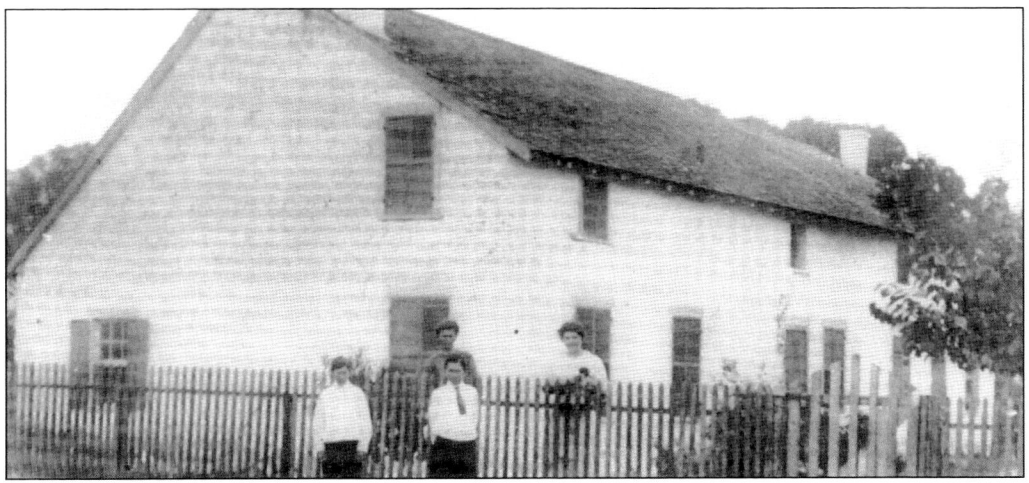

In Old D'Hanis, the Nicholaus Koch home was over 100 years old when this picture was taken in the late 1800s. The names of those pictured are not known.

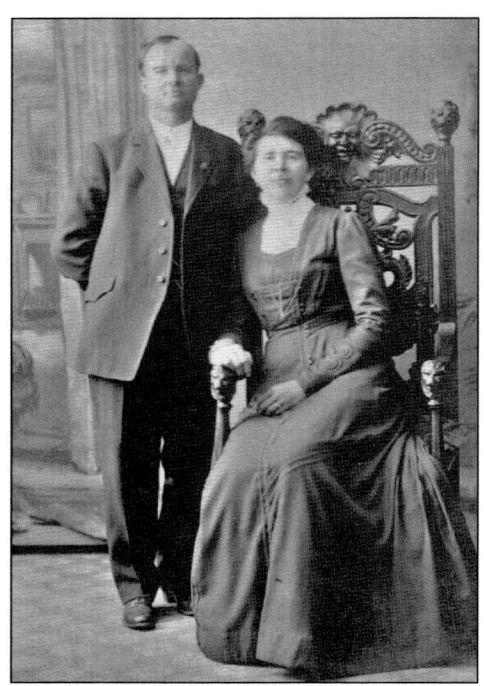

This picture, taken about 1928, is of Francis and Louise Ihnken Winans. Francis lost an arm to a gunshot from behind. A strong Catholic, he became a schoolteacher and was a first commissioner in Comal County. He became involved in agriculture on land in Medina County that Louise received from her parents as a wedding present. (Courtesy of Bonnie and Lester Ludwig.)

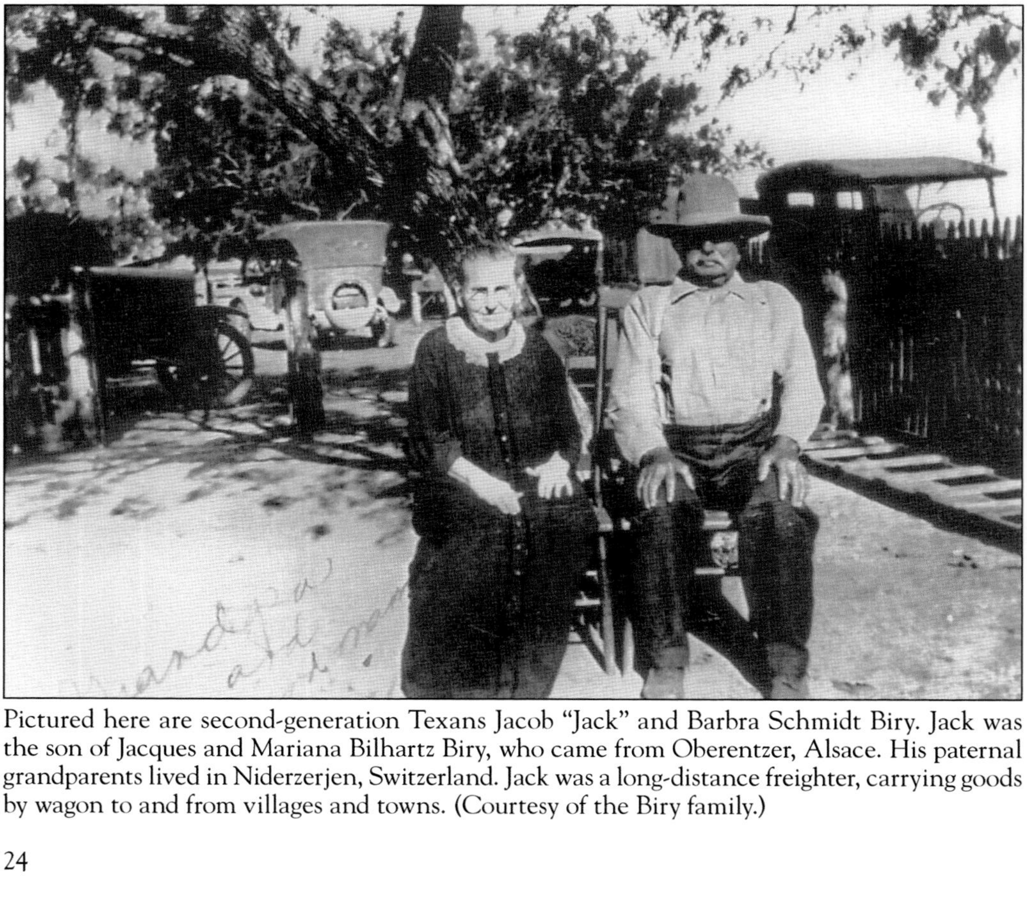

Pictured here are second-generation Texans Jacob "Jack" and Barbra Schmidt Biry. Jack was the son of Jacques and Mariana Bilhartz Biry, who came from Oberentzer, Alsace. His paternal grandparents lived in Niderzerjen, Switzerland. Jack was a long-distance freighter, carrying goods by wagon to and from villages and towns. (Courtesy of the Biry family.)

Posed for a formal picture, the daughters of John Ihnken are, from left to right, (seated) Mollie and Louise; (standing) Rose and Adela. Mollie, joined by one of her sisters, rode horseback three miles to the Haass School at Noonan from Francisco. When Mollie moved to Castroville to take care of her grandparents, she had to wade the Medina River to get to school each day. (Courtesy of Bonnie and Lester Ludwig.)

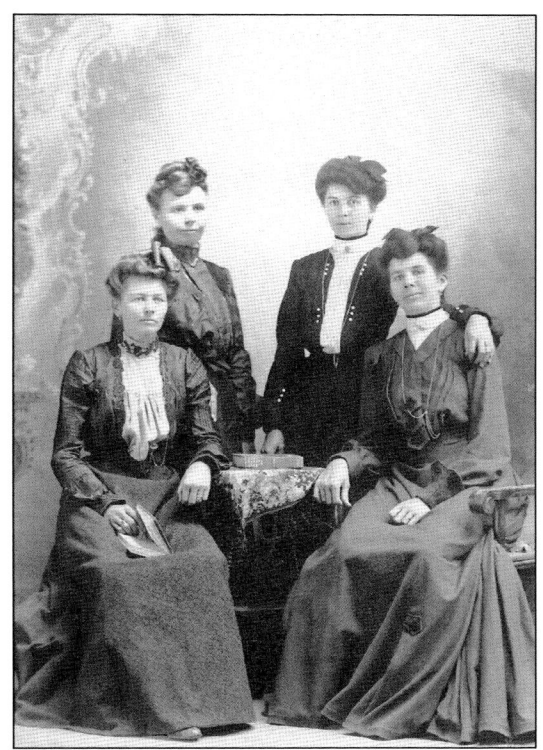

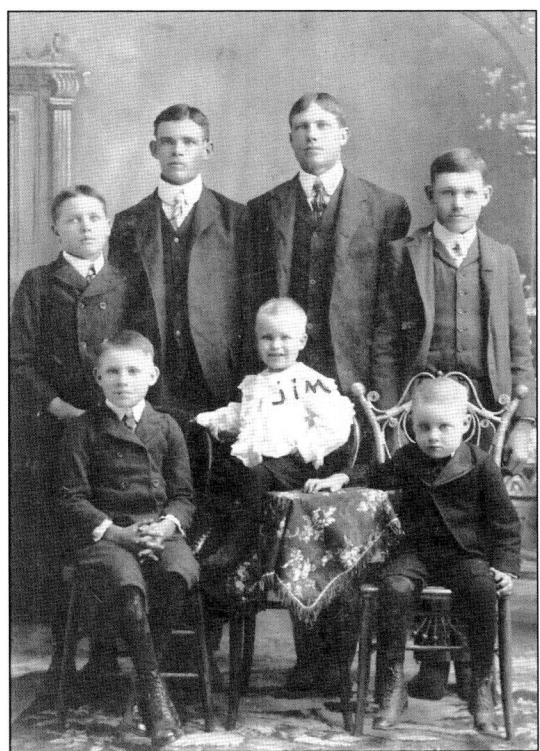

The Pichot boys, sons of Mary Dawson and Albert Adolph, are pictured about 1900. They are, from left to right, as follows: (seated) Leonard, Jim, and Willie; (back row) Joe, John, Adolph, and Louis. Another son, Earnest, was not born when this picture was taken. He would drown in the river at 14. (Courtesy of Bonnie and Lester Ludwig.)

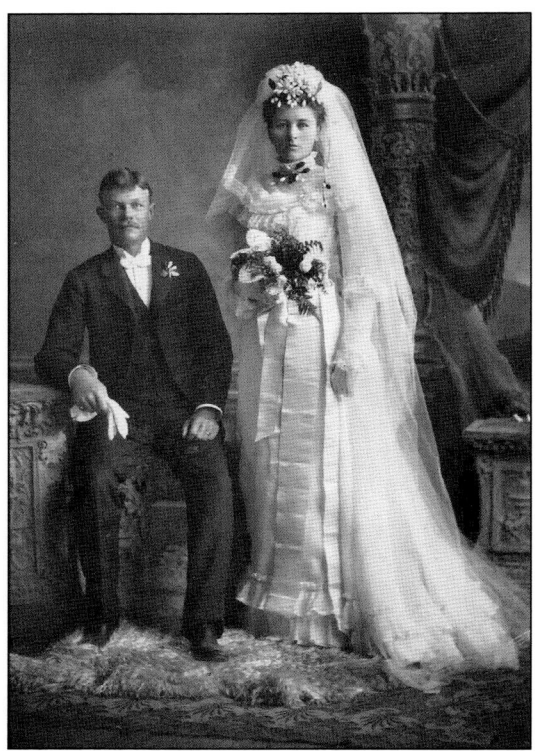

This is a wedding photograph of Henry and Mary (Mollie) Ihnken Kauffmann. As a child, Mollie picked cotton on the family farm until she moved to Castroville. Well educated, Mollie spoke four languages. Henry, a second-generation Texan, was a rising young stock farmer. The family's Sunday House is now part of the Landmark Inn in Castroville. (Courtesy of Bonnie and Lester Ludwig.)

This is a wedding photograph of farmer Jack Droitcourt and his bride, Adela Biediger Droitcourt. With only four or five years of formal education, Jack successfully depended on his mechanical aptitude to serve him throughout his life. He was elected Medina County treasurer, serving 16 years, and also deputy tax collector for Hondo, Texas. (Courtesy of Bonnie and Lester Ludwig.)

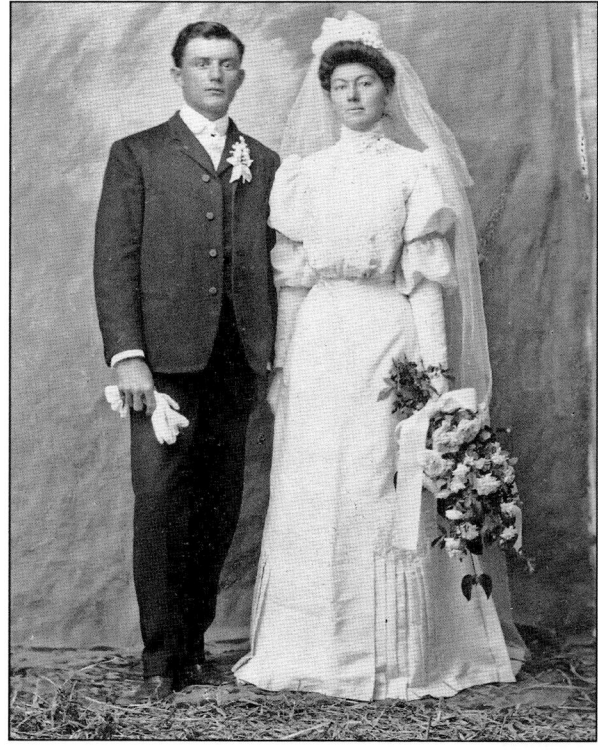

Hugo Randolph Ludwig was the son of Frank William and Anna Elizabeth Walch Ludwig. Hugo was born in Devine in 1898 and married Mary Annie Koehler. (Courtesy of Bonnie and Lester Ludwig.)

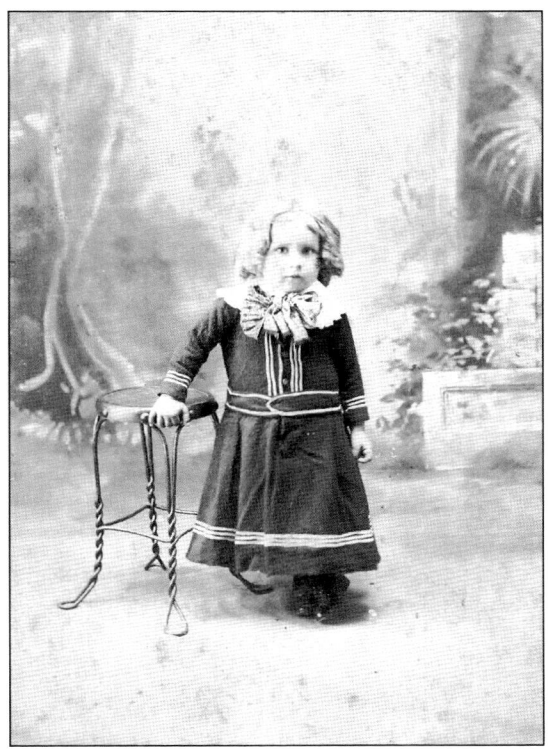

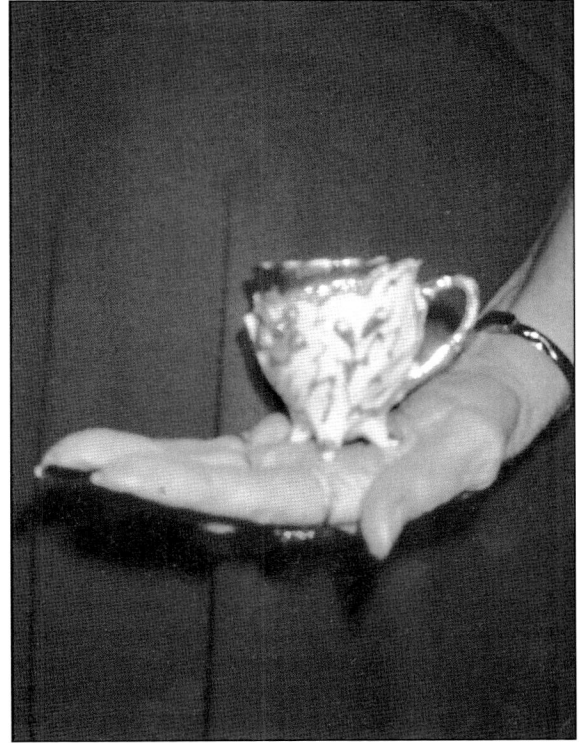

This teacup is part of a tea set given by the queen of France, Marie Antoinette, to Terese Antonie de Carpentier Pichot, mother of Jeanne Marie Pichot Ihnken, who in 1844 settled in Castroville. (Courtesy of Bonnie and Lester Ludwig.)

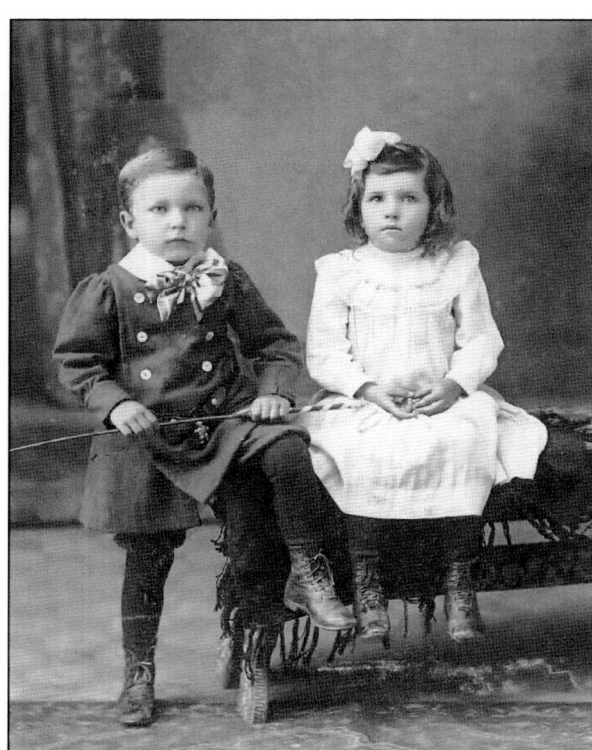

In 1910, a young Lester Ludwig Sr. poses with Mildred Bippert, daughter of Emilie Ludwig and Albert Bippert, in LaCoste. (Courtesy of Bonnie and Lester Ludwig.)

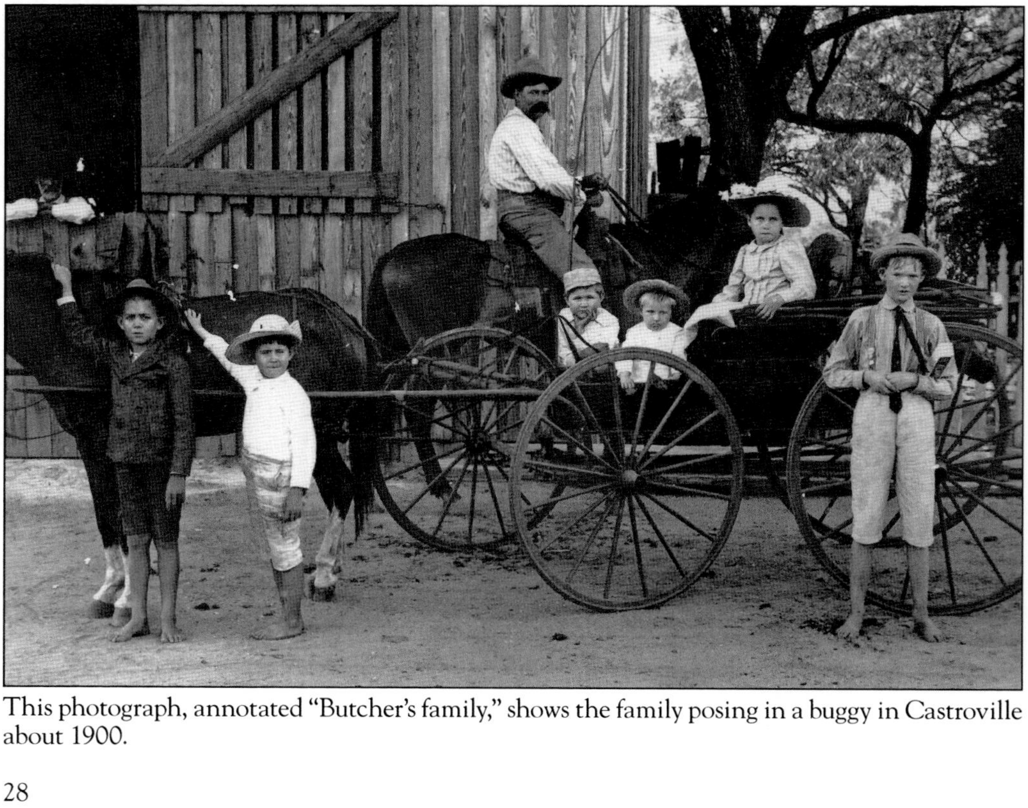

This photograph, annotated "Butcher's family," shows the family posing in a buggy in Castroville about 1900.

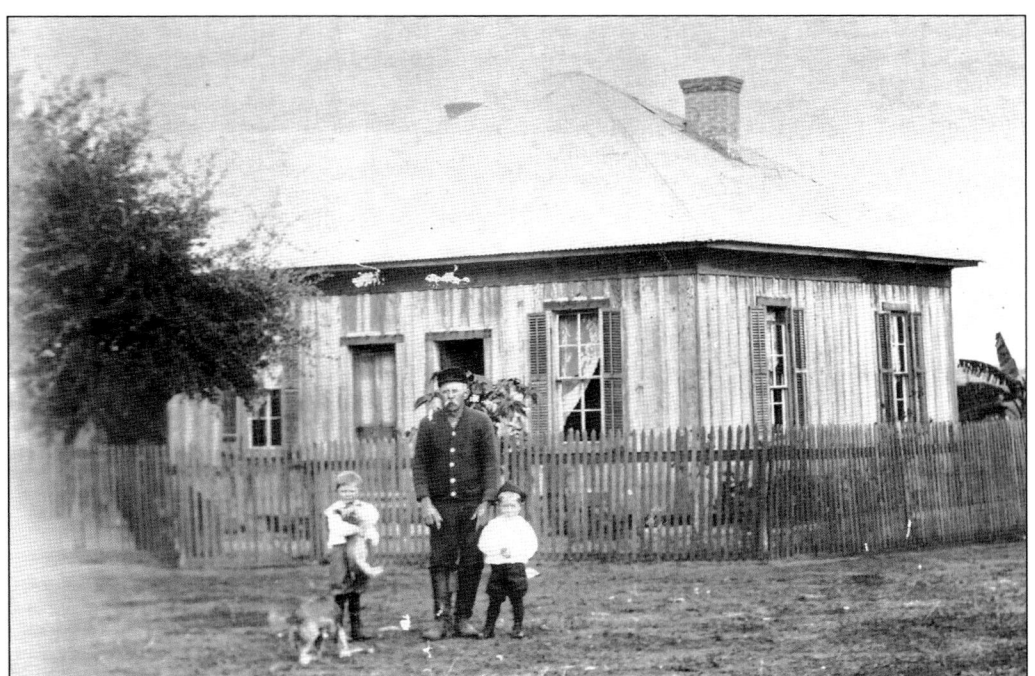

The gentleman pictured with two boys and two dogs in front of their home in Medina County is George Haass. The house is typical of the structures built by early settlers in Medina County. (Courtesy of Bonnie and Lester Ludwig.)

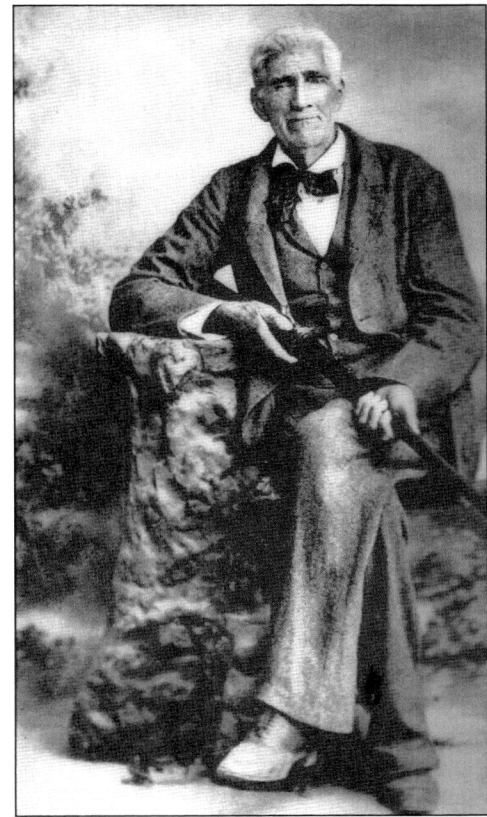

Painted late in the life of Big Foot Wallace, this oil painting by a lady from California was given to James Collins of Lytle and arrived in Medina County on Christmas Day, 2009. (Courtesy of James Collins.)

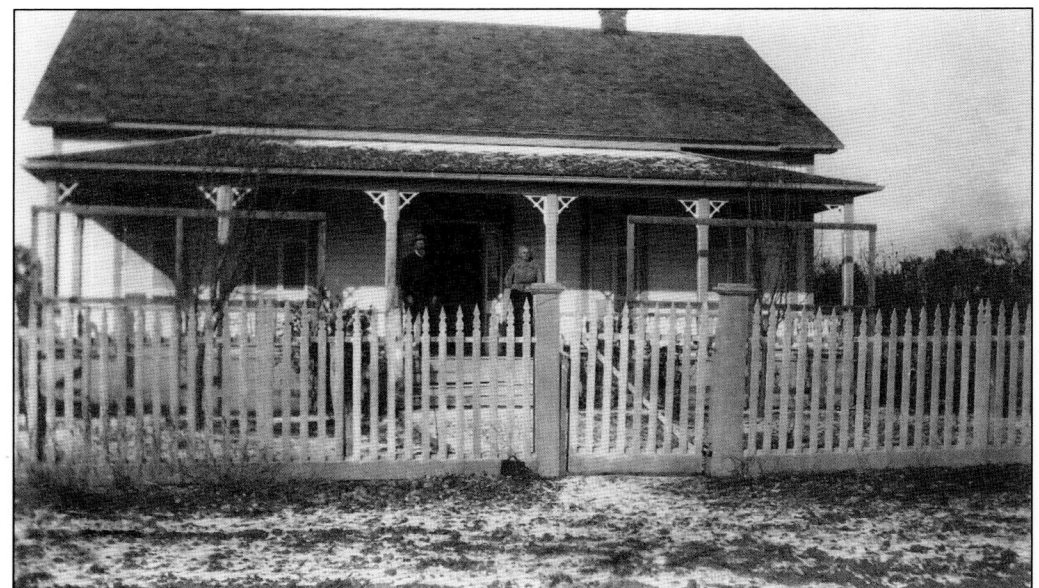

This was the ranch home of John and Marguerite Droitcourt, built in early 1900 on the property received in their land grant. According to a law passed by the Republic of Texas in 1840, every head of household received 640 acres and every single man 320 acres. (Courtesy of Bonnie and Lester Ludwig.)

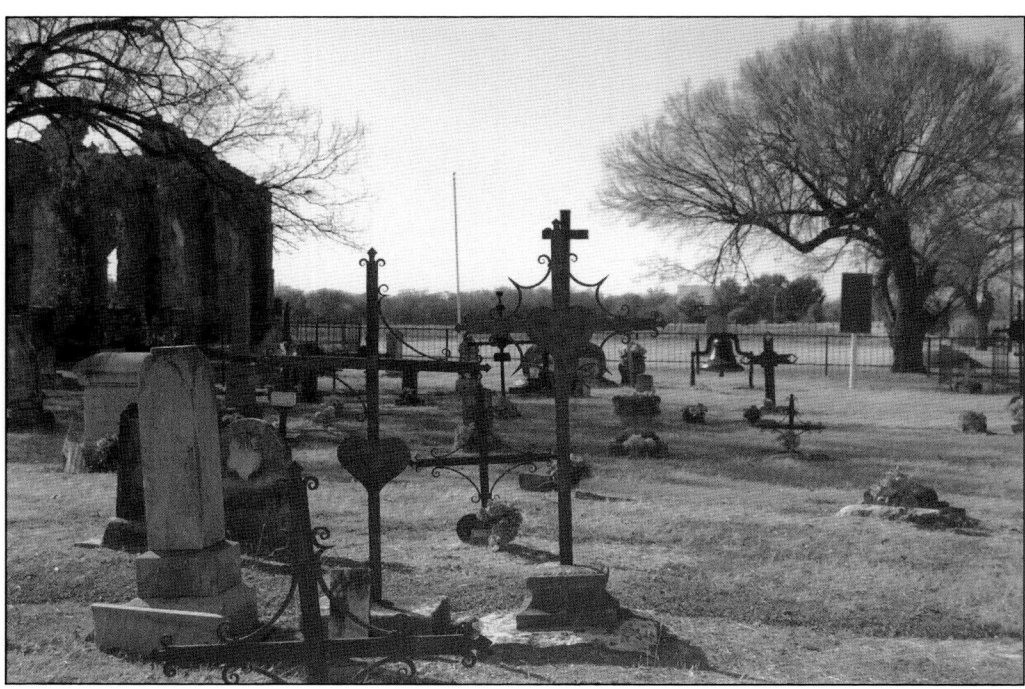

Pictured is old St. Dominic's Cemetery, which was first used in 1844 and continued in use through 1896. Shown are some of the beautiful wrought-iron crosses and hand-carved stones reminiscent of the European homes that the settlers left behind. (Courtesy of the author.)

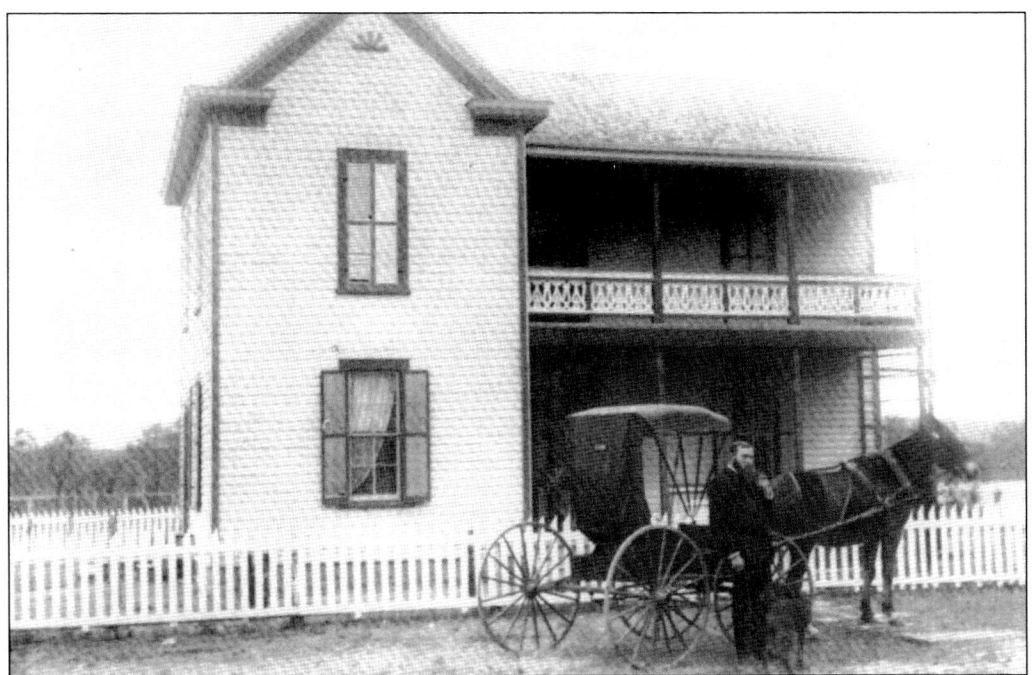

The Reverend H.M.J. Wirtz, pastor of St. Dominic's Catholic Church in D'Hanis, is shown with his carriage in front of the rectory in 1858. The rectory burned and was rebuilt.

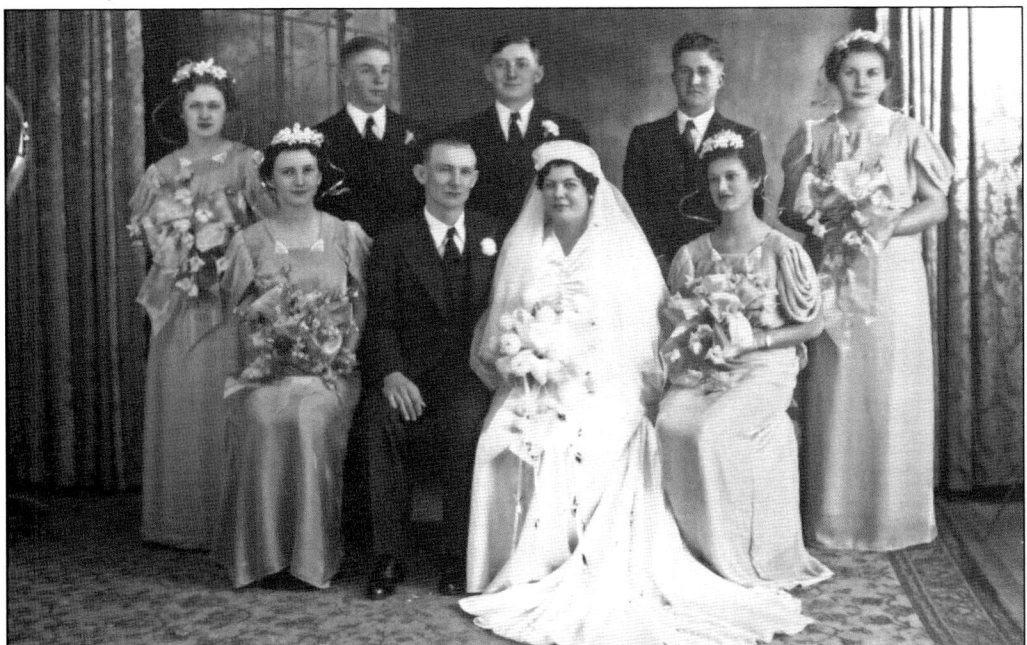

Pictured is the wedding party of Marguerite and Hugo Adam in November 1937 at Our Lady of Grace Church in LaCoste. The attendees are, from left to right, (first row) Mabel Tschirhardt, Hugo Adam, Marguerite Kauffmann (Adam), and Isabel Mangold; (second row) two unidentified, Herbert Adam, Mat Jungmann, and Patsy Zinsmeyer Fisher. (Courtesy of Bonnie and Lester Ludwig.)

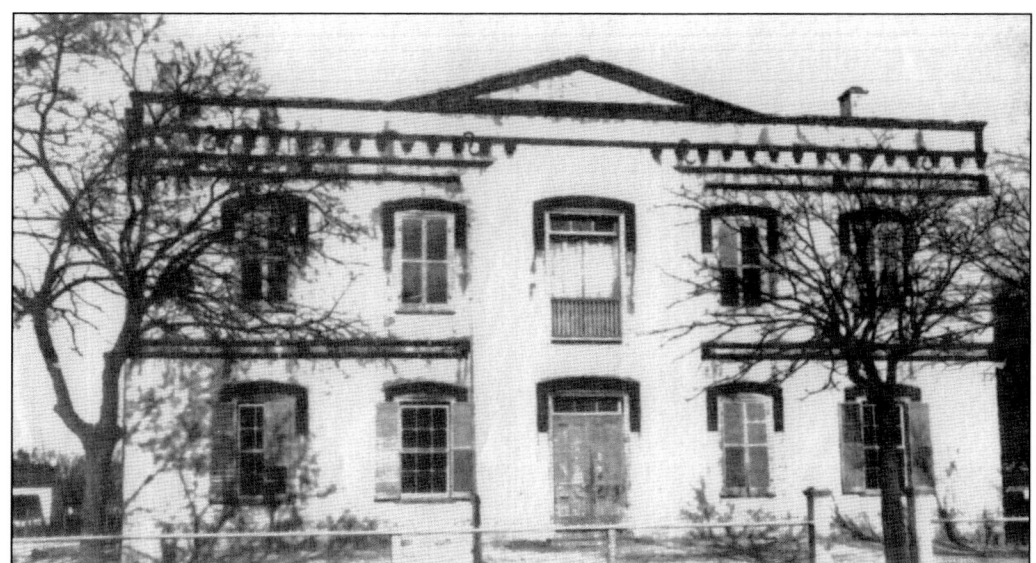

Medina County's first courthouse, established in 1848, was in Castroville, Texas. People in the county voted two times on the issue of moving the county seat; on the second vote, the move was approved, and the county seat moved to Hondo in 1892.

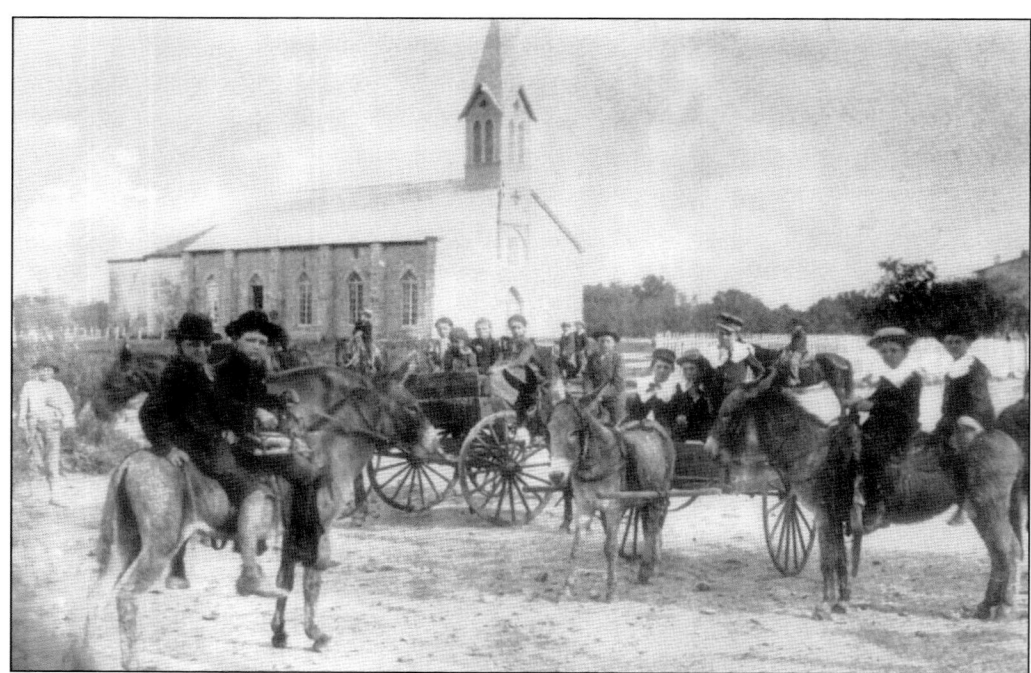

St. Dominic's Church was built in 1853 in Hondo and was abandoned when the railroad came to town. The portion at the rear of the church was an 1853 stone chapel that was incorporated into the 1868 structure. The large portion was added in 1868–1869 and contained five Gothic windows and wall buttresses; the wood steeple was added in 1890.

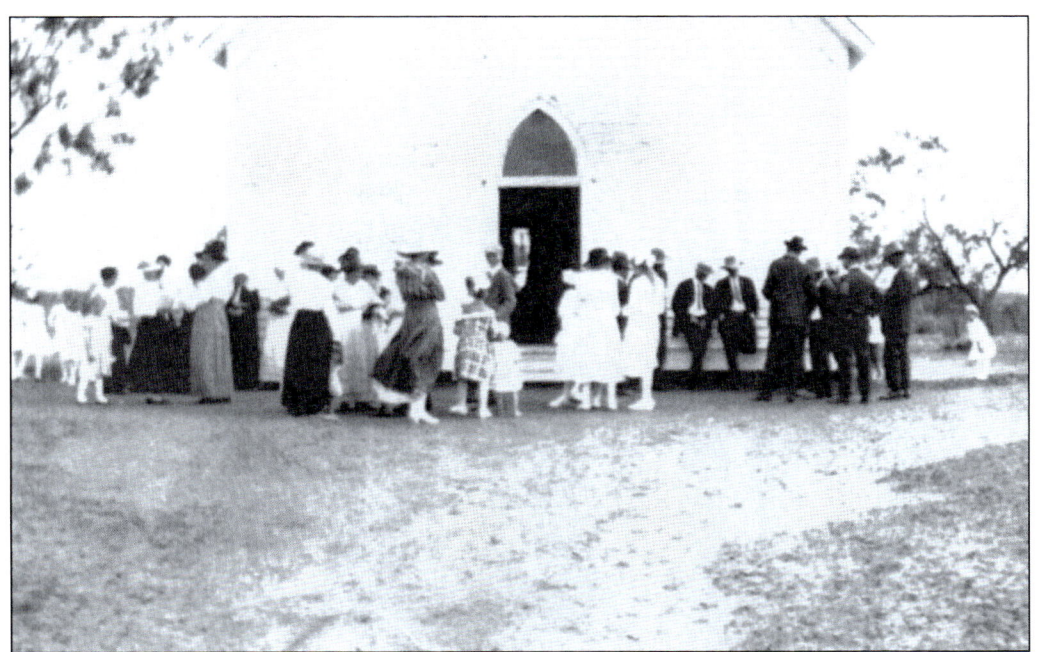

This is a picture of Yancey Ebenezer Methodist Church South, the local German-language church. The children in white communion dresses are celebrating becoming official members of the Methodist Church.

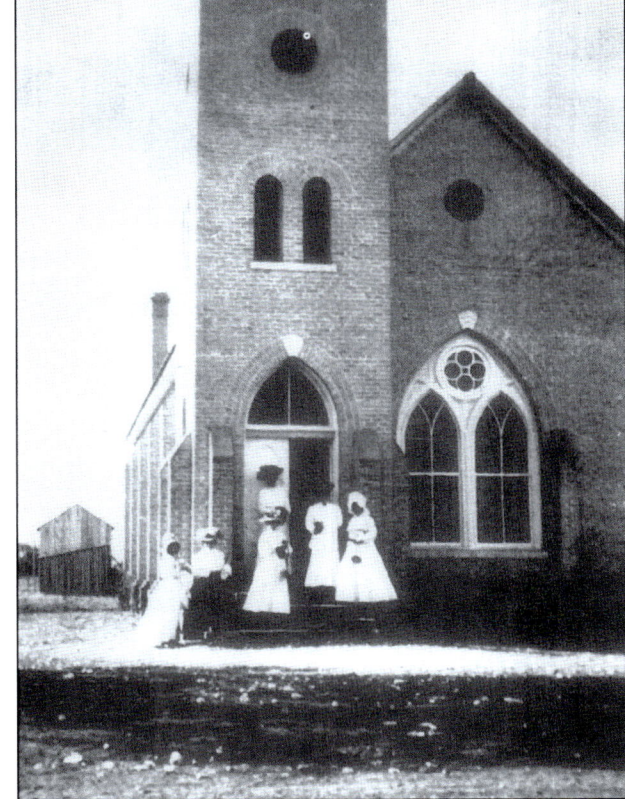

Pictured on the steps of the Hondo Methodist Church are, clockwise from the left, Mrs. Tom McClaugherty (holding her baby granddaughter, Leora Horger), Mrs. John A. Horger, Katie Laughinhouse, Mrs. I.H. King, Mrs. Tom McCall, and Mrs. W.P. Laughinhouse.

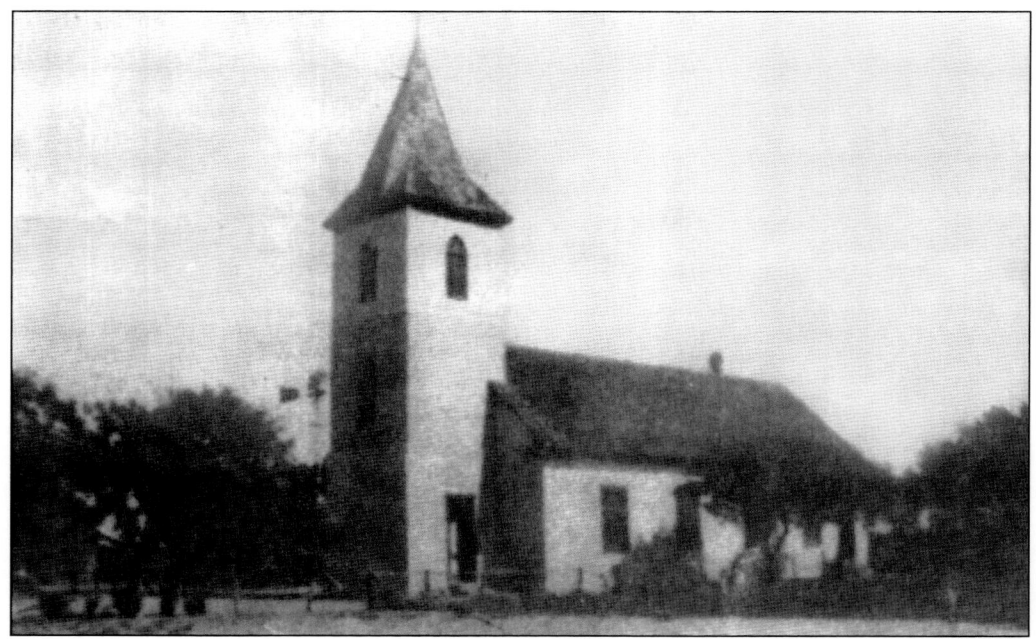

New Fountain United Methodist Church was organized in 1858, and the building was completed in 1872. This is the town that was created after Vandenberg ran out of water. Almost all of the people in Vandenberg moved to New Fountain. A historical marker stands on the grounds of this church. (Courtesy of Bonnie and Lester Ludwig.)

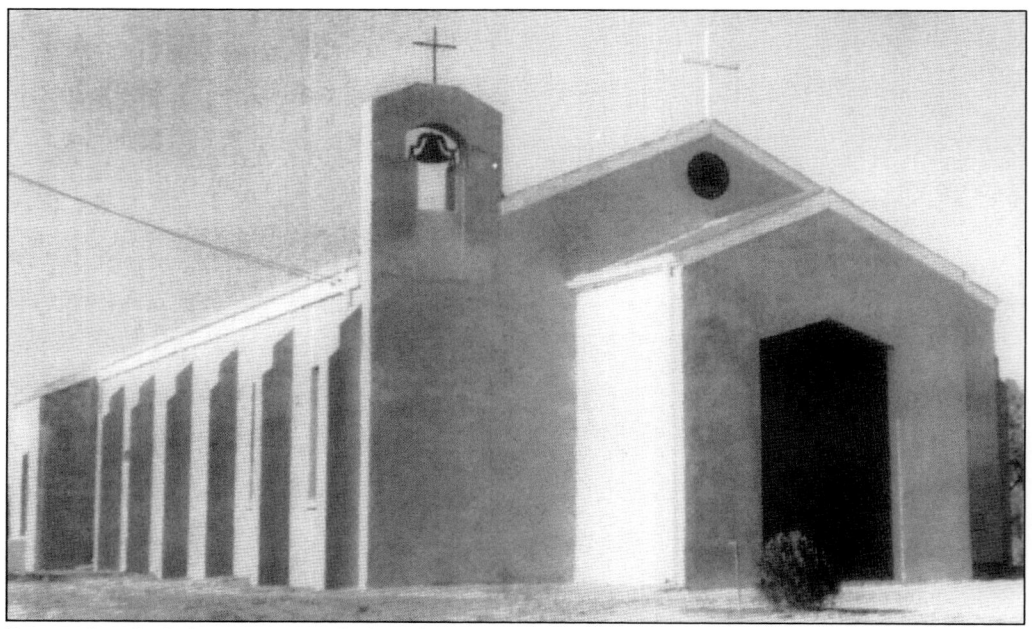

Pictured is St. John Bosco Catholic Church in Natalia, Texas, in 1949. The church has many faithful followers who support and attend services.

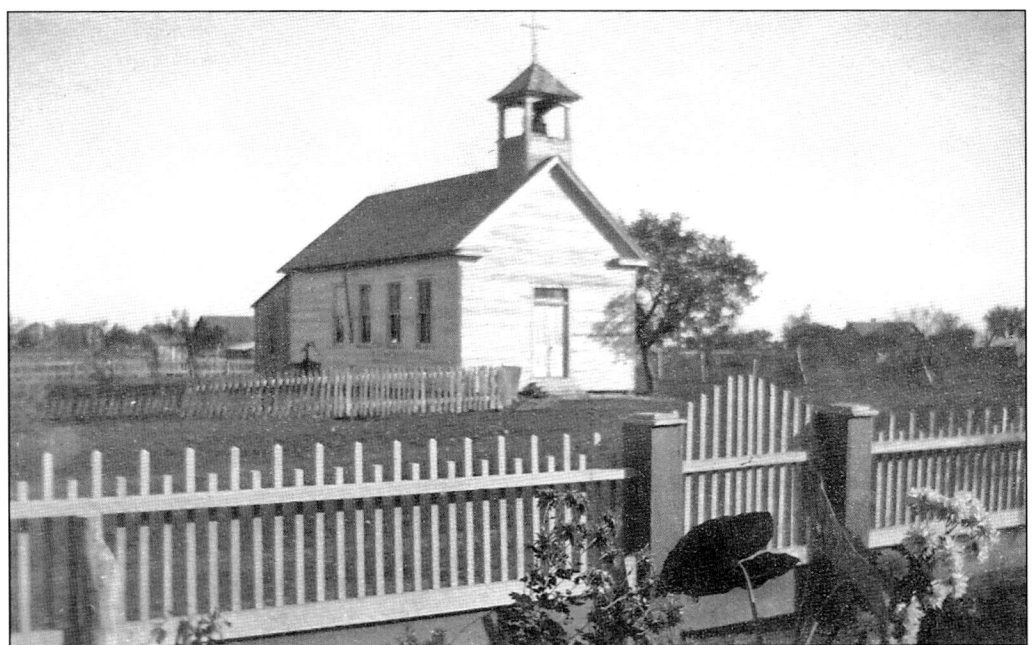

This was the Hondo Catholic church after the town moved closer to the railroad and deserted the large rock church. This Holy Cross Church was built on land donated by the railroad. The church burned down two times. Some people in Medina County still speak of the ill omen imparted by the desertion of the beautiful rock church.

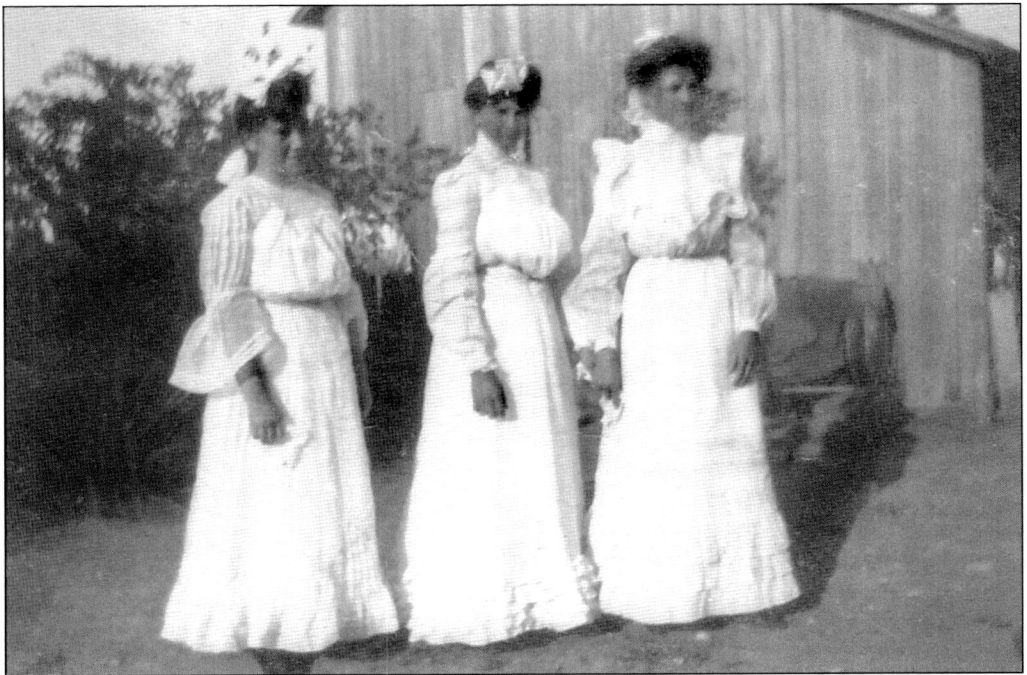

Three beautifully dressed ladies in Medina County are pictured wearing handmade dresses in front of a barn. None of the ladies is identified, but they are thought to be residents of Hondo.

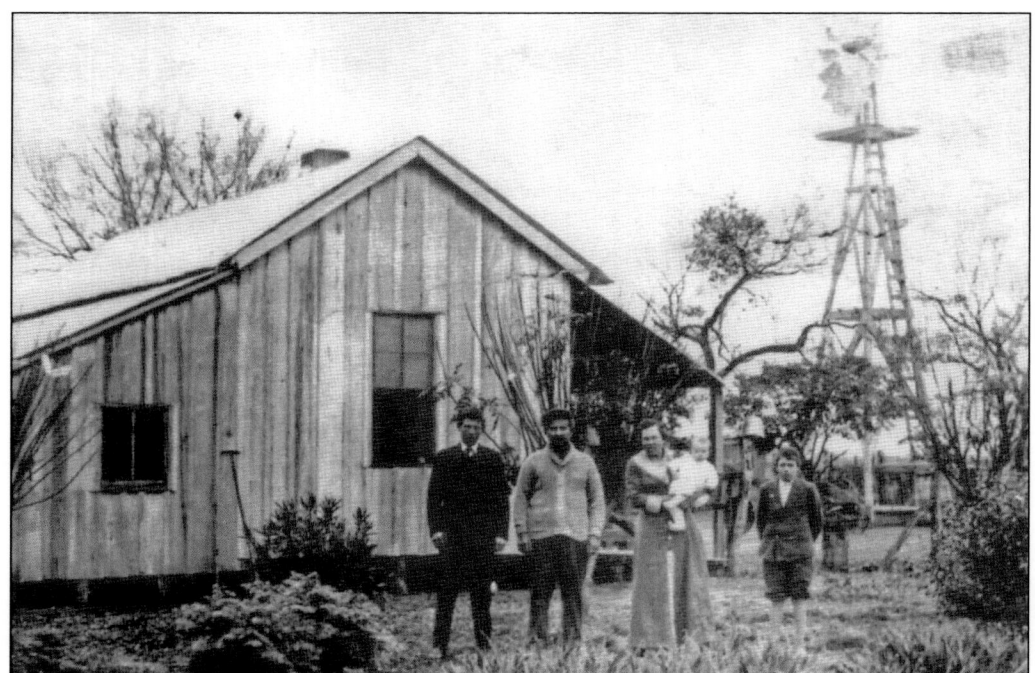

Located near Natalia was the early homestead of Max Ernest Koehler, shown in this image. Included in this photograph are, from left to right, Otto T. Koehler (son), Max E. Koehler, and Celeste Nixon Koehler (Koehler's third wife, holding a baby). The boy at right is unidentified. (Courtesy of Bonnie and Lester Ludwig.)

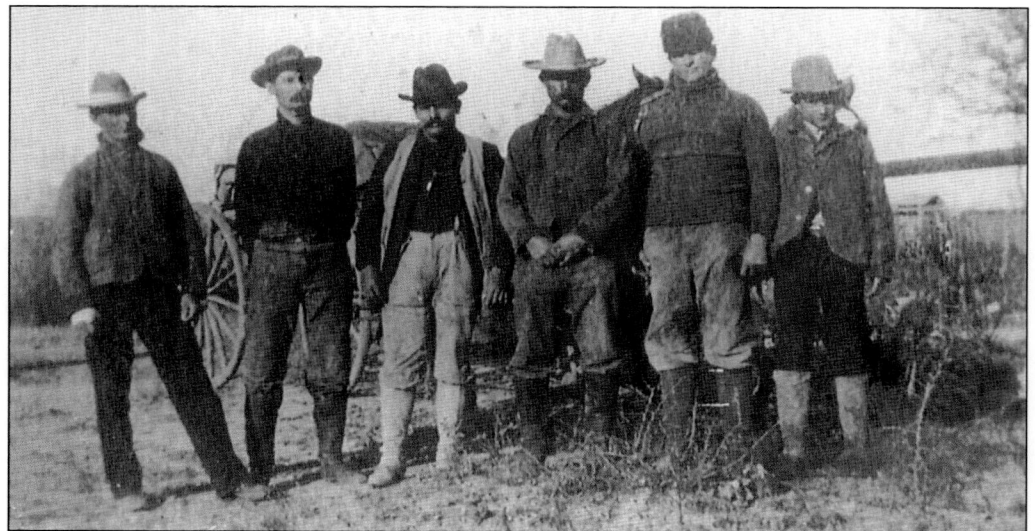

These men were the sons of Valentine Nester. Pictured are, from left to right, as follows: William J., Robert, Hugo, Alfred, Martin, and Emitt Nester. Their father, pioneer settler of D'Hanis Martin Nester, immigrated to Texas in 1846 from Anvers, France. His mother and father were born in Germany. His wife, Mary Ann Rapp, was eight months pregnant when they departed by ship. Somewhere in the Atlantic, a daughter, Catherine, was born. Upon reaching Galveston, the Nester family had to find their own way to San Antonio by ox cart. (Courtesy of Mary Ann Pringle.)

The man pictured is James Walton Heath, and his wife is Eliza Galbreath Heath, daughter of the famous Tom Galbreath, Texas Ranger and Indian fighter who ran with Big Foot Wallace. Tom Galbreath came to Medina County when it was part of the Republic of Texas. (Courtesy of Mary Ann Pringle.)

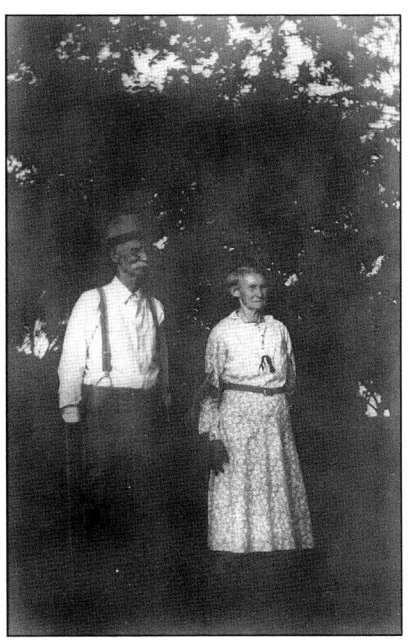

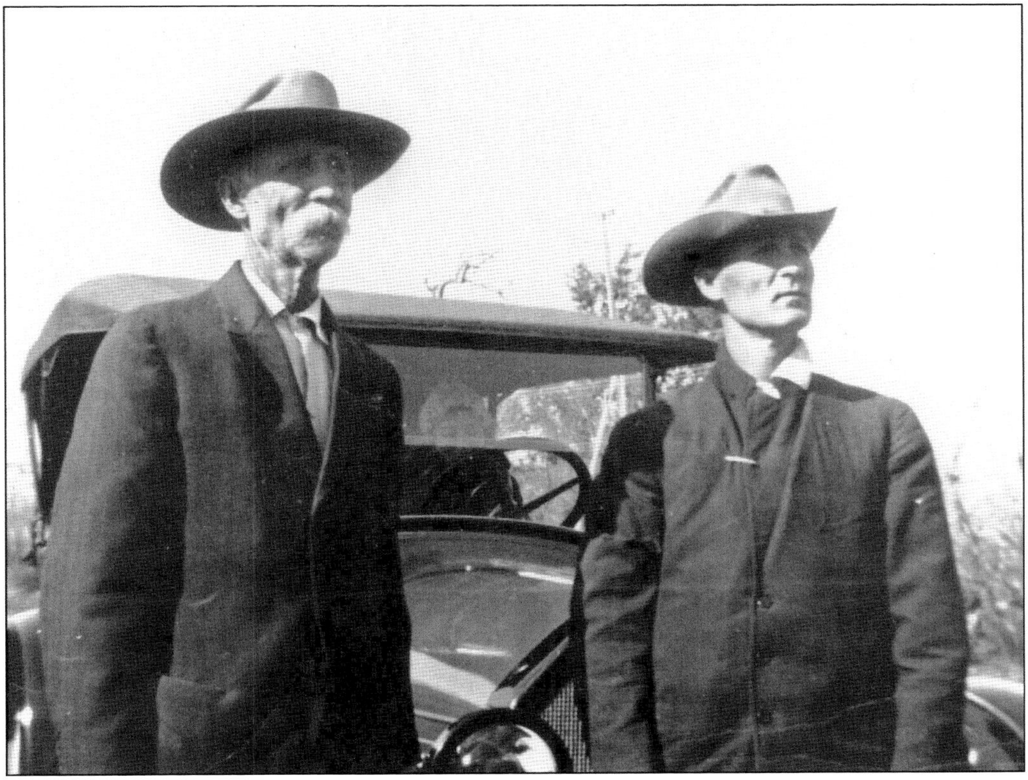

Shown are James Walton Heath and his son Benjamin Franklin Heath of Hondo some time around 1910. James Walton Heath's father started ranching on the Hondo River in 1855, when the people living in the county were particularly afraid of Indians. (Courtesy of Mary Ann Pringle.)

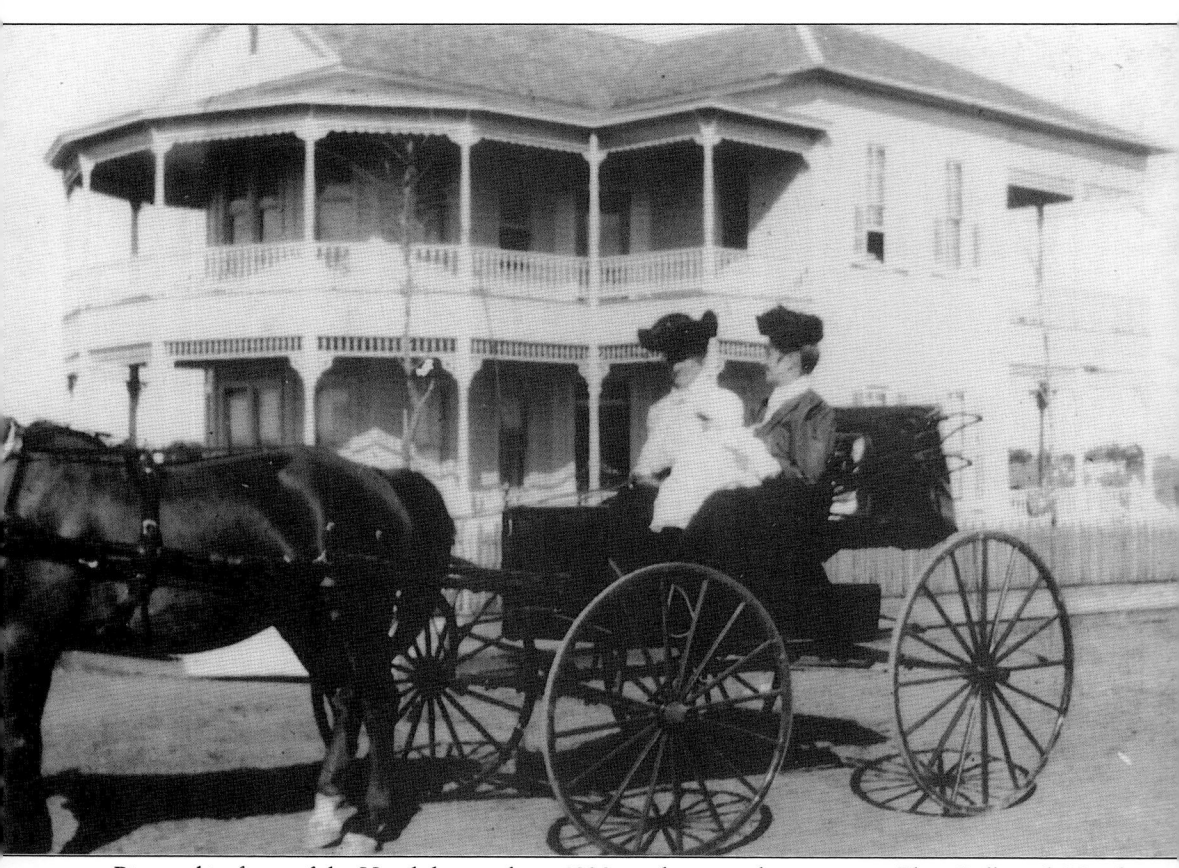

Pictured in front of the Heath home about 1890 in a horse and carriage are Eliza Galbreath Heath (left) and Nellie Thomas Heath, holding her baby, Gladys Heath. The home was a showplace in Hondo, Texas, but is not longer standing. (Courtesy of Mary Ann Pringle.)

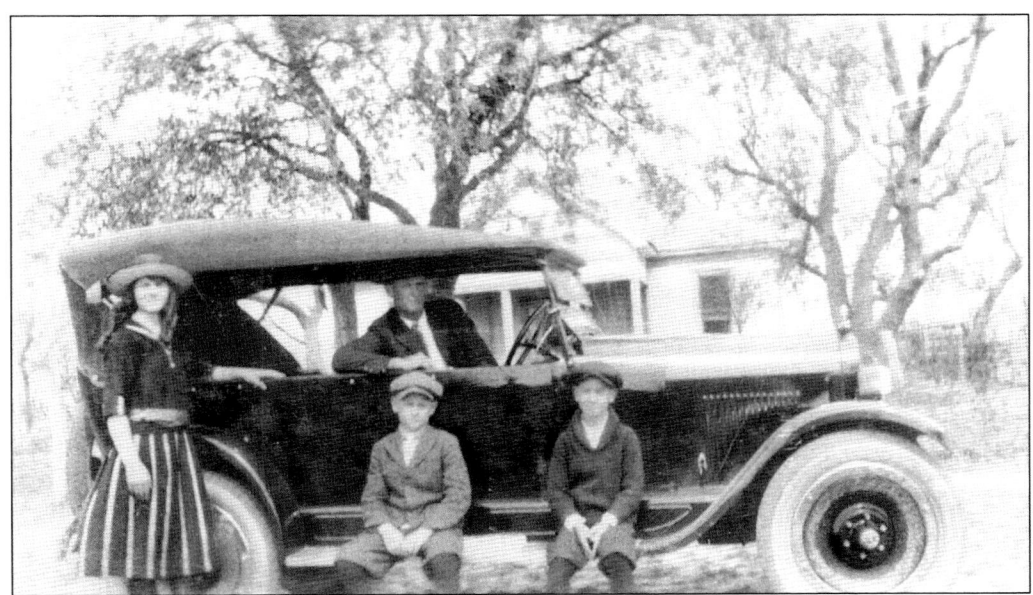

About 1920, Henry Raymond Bailey and family are seen posing for his wife, Nora Bailey. Henry is pictured leaning out of the window of his automobile. His children are, from left to right, Ramona, James W., and Bradley. (Courtesy of Mary Ann Pringle.)

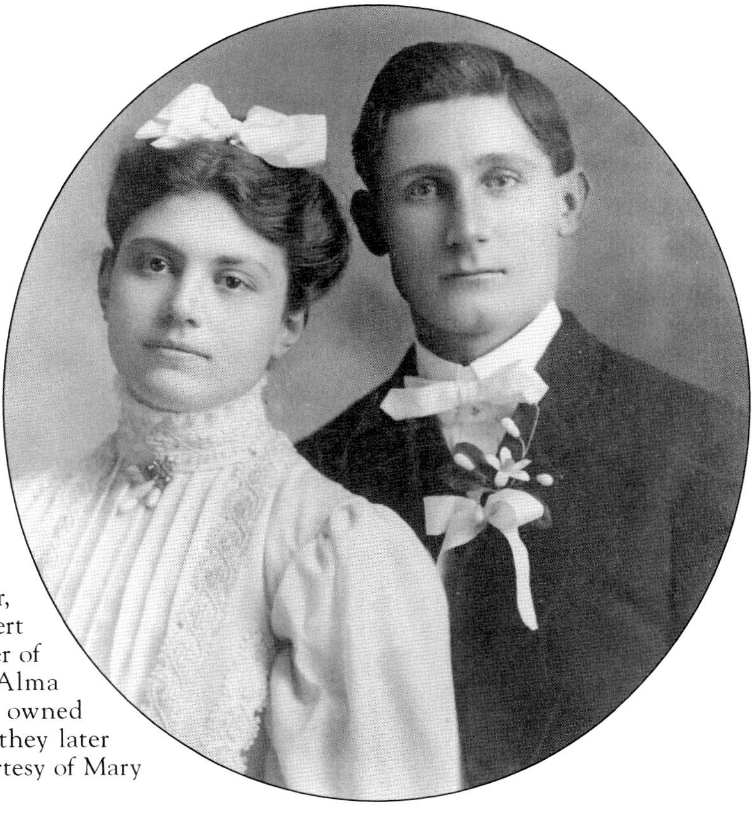

This is a wedding picture of William J. Nester and Alma Richter Nester taken in 1908. William was the son of Valentine Nester (who was the first baby born in D'Hanis to settlers from Germany). The bride, Alma Richter, was the daughter of Robert and Alice Reuter Richter of Hondo. William and Alma settled in Yancey and owned a meat market, which they later moved to Hondo. (Courtesy of Mary Ann Pringle.)

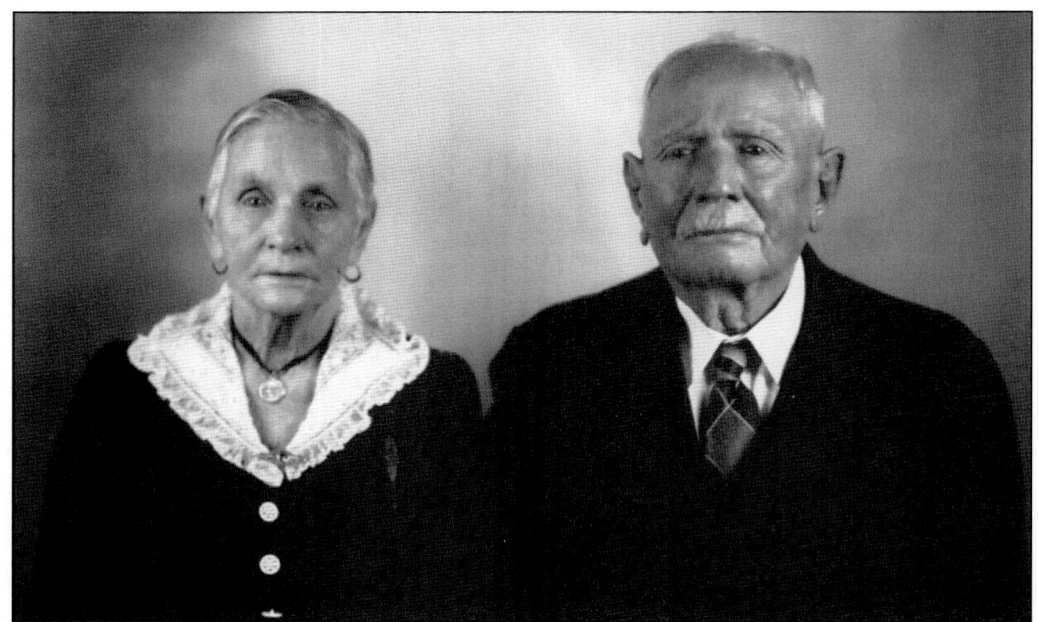

Pictured are Alice Reuter Richter and her husband, Robert Richter, in D'Hanis in 1930. Alice's father died, and she and her mother lived in a house on the Richter land. Alice married Robert, and they lived along Seco Creek. Later, they lived on a large ranch about six miles southwest of Hondo. (Courtesy of Mary Ann Pringle.)

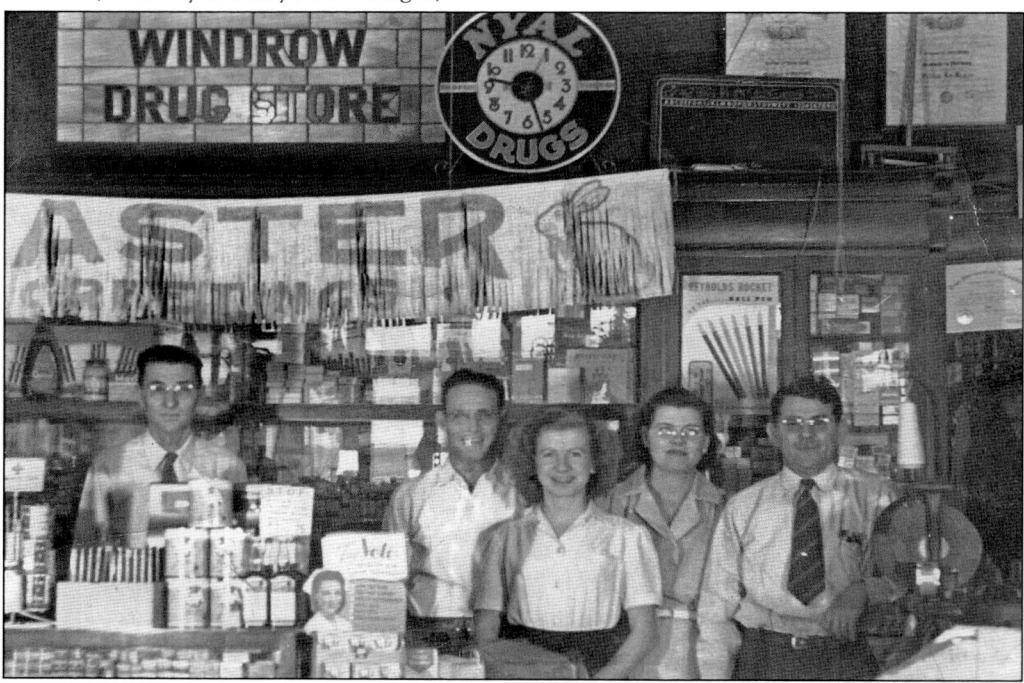

Included in this photograph taken in Hondo about 1947 are (left) Bill Windrow, pharmacist and co-owner of Windrow Drug Store, and (right) Henry Windrow. (Courtesy of Mary Ann Pringle.)

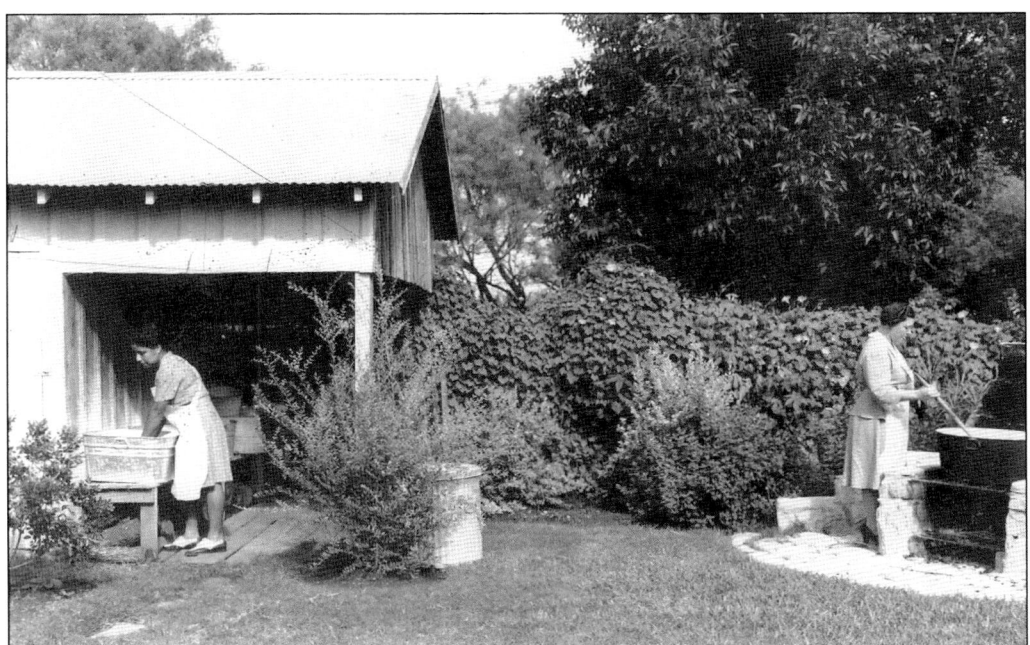

This picture depicts a typical backyard washing day at Laura and Henry Windrow's home in 1930, before modern equipment was available. Stained and soiled clothes required boiling to become clean. On the right, Laura Windrow oversees the boiling pot. (Courtesy of Mary Ann Pringle.)

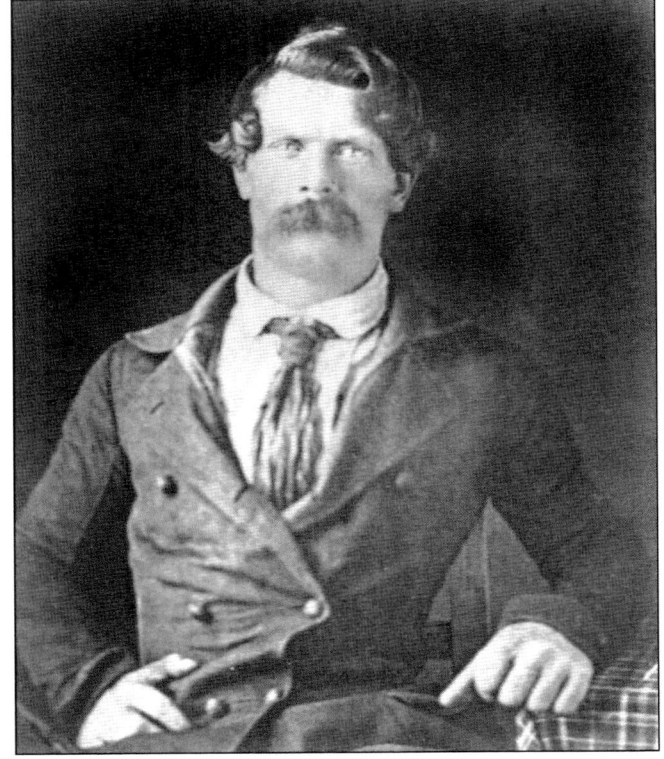

Wilhelm Reuter, father of Alice Reuter Richter and one of the first settlers during the days of the Republic of Texas, lived near the US Army post Fort Lincoln, which was established to protect the settlements from hostile Indians in the area. Fort Lincoln was closed at the onset of the Civil War. On October 6, 1863, Wilhelm was called to serve in the Confederate States provisional army. He died of a fever four days after being enrolled. (Courtesy of Mary Ann Pringle.)

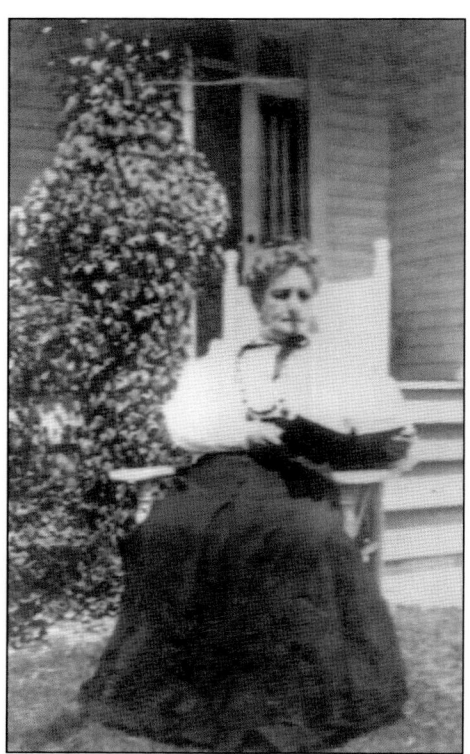

Emma Fisher Bailey, wife of pioneer William Wilson Bailey, who came to Medina County in early 1850 with his mother, Mary Elizabeth Bailey, is pictured here. Emma taught school in Castroville in the 1850s. (Courtesy of Mary Ann Pringle.)

Henry Raymond Bailey, a lifelong resident of Hondo, participated in the Jefferson Guard in the St. Louis World Fair in 1904. Henry was the son of William Wilson and Emma Fischer Bailey of Hondo, and he married Nora Heath in 1906. A rancher and farmer, Henry is shown on one of his horses at his ranch on Live Oak Creek Ranch about 1940. (Courtesy of Mary Ann Pringle.)

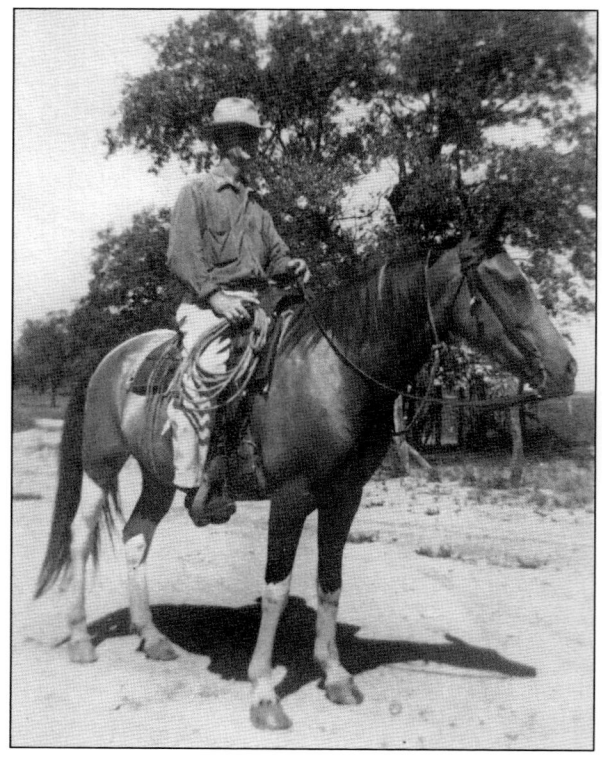

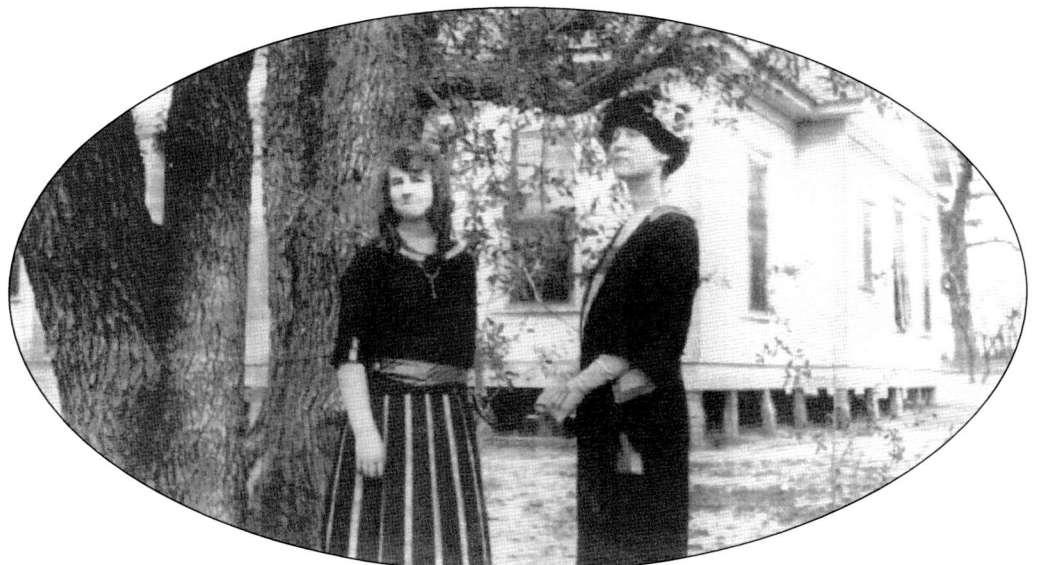

Nora Heath Bailey, wife of Henry Raymond Bailey, is shown with their daughter Ramona, who became a teacher. Their ranch home, built in 1914, is shown in the background. (Courtesy of Mary Ann Pringle.)

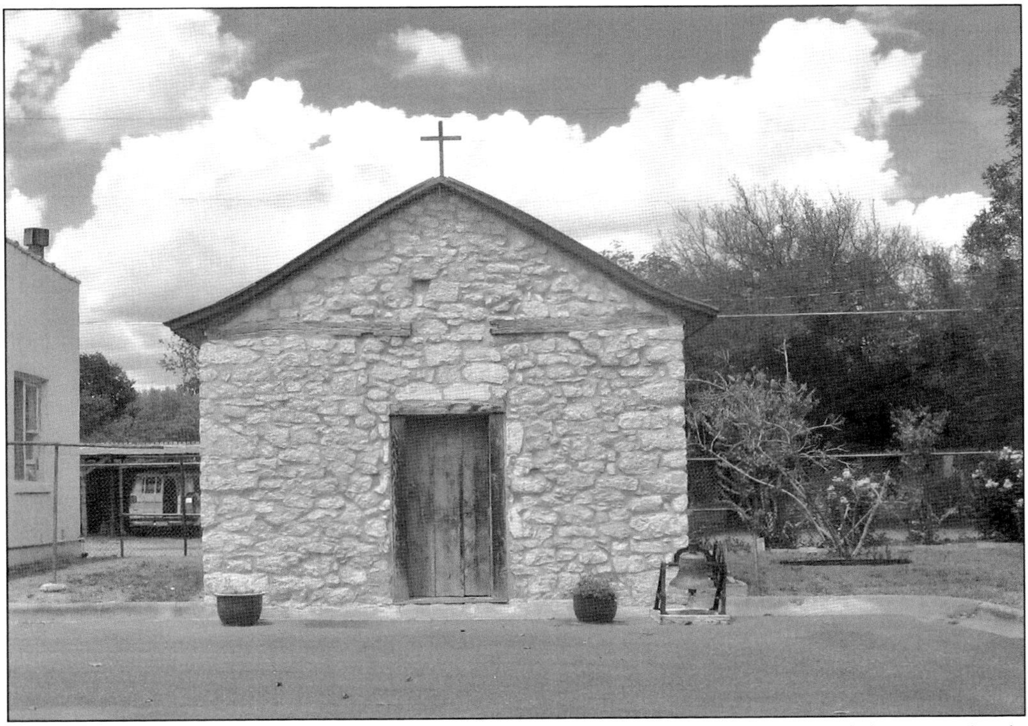

The tiny St. Louis Catholic Church, founded in 1844, is still standing today. Built by Rev. Claude Dubuis and Abbé Emmanuel Domenech with the help of a few local men, this church was the first Catholic church built in Medina County (and the first church west of San Antonio) and was formally organized as a parish in 1847. (Courtesy of the author.)

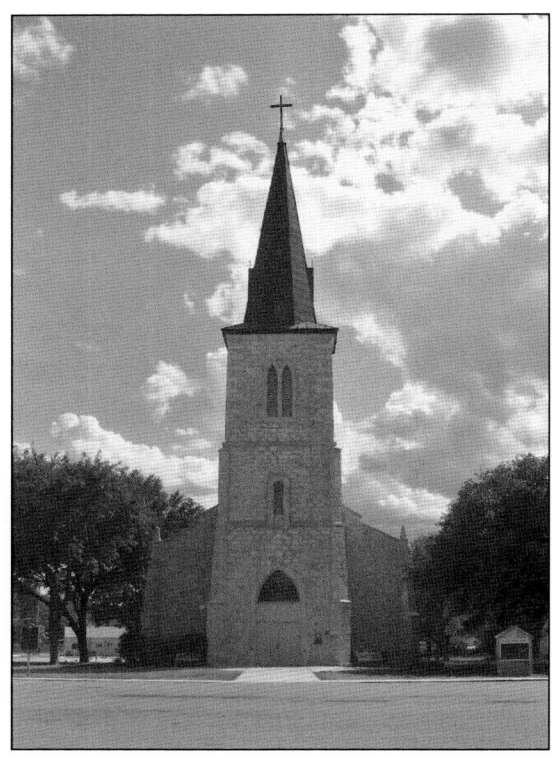

The newest St. Louis Catholic Church, built in 1887, is the third incarnation of the church. It is built on the same block of the street as the second church, built in 1850. This Gothic Revival building, made of native limestone and hand-hewn cypress, is 150 feet in length and 52 feet in width and was one of the largest churches built at that time in Texas. Most of the work was done by townspeople, and the church materials were donated by members of the church. St. Louis Church was named for the patron saint of the parish. The present hand-carved wooden Stations of the Cross were a gift from Alsace, France. The pews, wood altars, and statues are the originals. (Courtesy of the author.)

Many of the German settlers who arrived in the 1840s were Lutherans who kept their religious traditions by meeting for worship in homes. The Reverend Christian Oefinger sailed from Germany and helped organize Zion Evangelical Lutheran Church, which was chartered in 1852 with 12 members from Castroville and the surrounding communities. In 1853, construction began. Congregants provided the rock, sand, and timbers. A parsonage was erected next to the church using the remaining stone. Pictured is Bethlehem Lutheran Church in Quihi, which was also founded by Reverend Oefinger while he was pastor of Zion Lutheran Church in Castroville. (Courtesy of the author.)

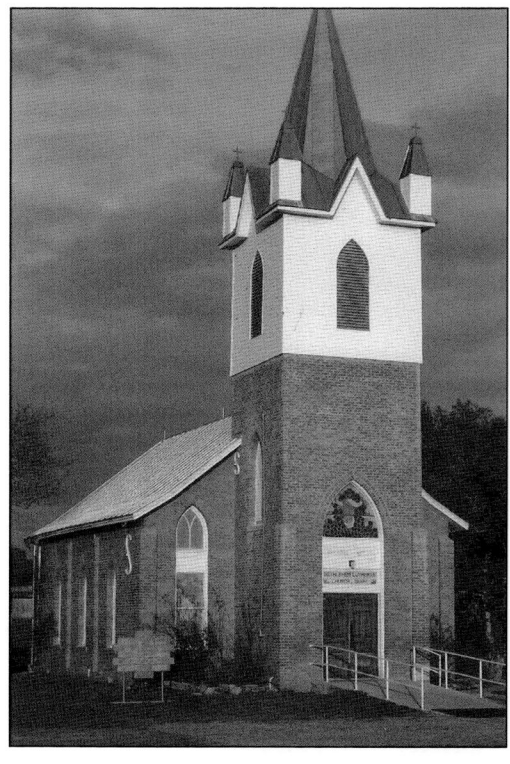

Dee Dee and Allie Laura Brown graduated from Our Lady of the Lake University in San Antonio in 1899. Dee Dee was the daughter of John (Jack) Kirby and Ida Brown, and Allie Laura was the daughter of Edward Cullen and Mary Kirby Brown. Allie married Edward Delbrail on December 25, 1900, and traveled to Mexico City, where Edward served as conductor for the Mexican Pacific Railway. Their little boy, who was born in Mexico, is shown in the picture below. (Courtesy of Laurel D'Orsogna.)

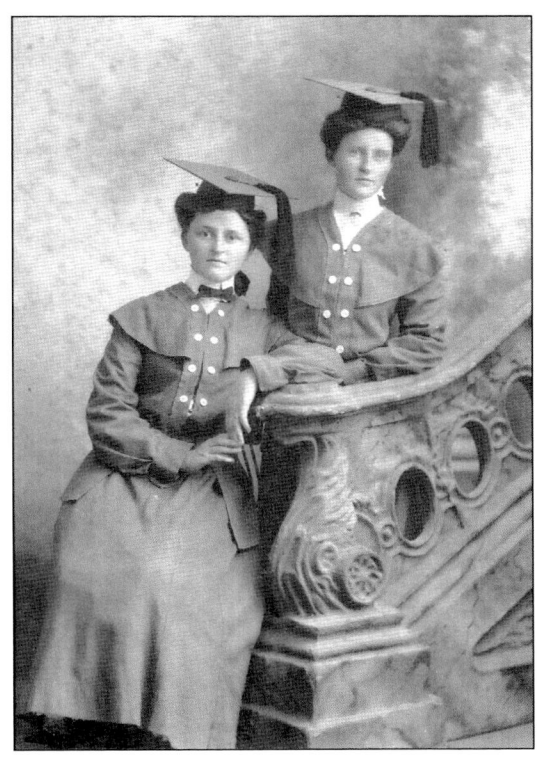

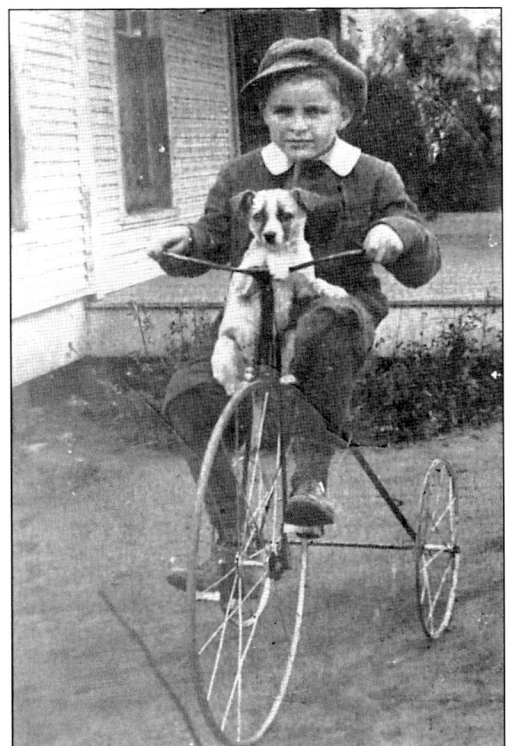

The little boy pictured on his tricycle (accompanied by his dog) is Lester Marshall Delbrail, the son of Allie Laura Brown. Lester's dog was named Tag. Lester loved his dog so much that all his friends nicknamed him "Tag." Lester was born in 1908 and died in 1987 in Devine, where he lived most of his life. (Courtesy of Laurel D'Orsogna.)

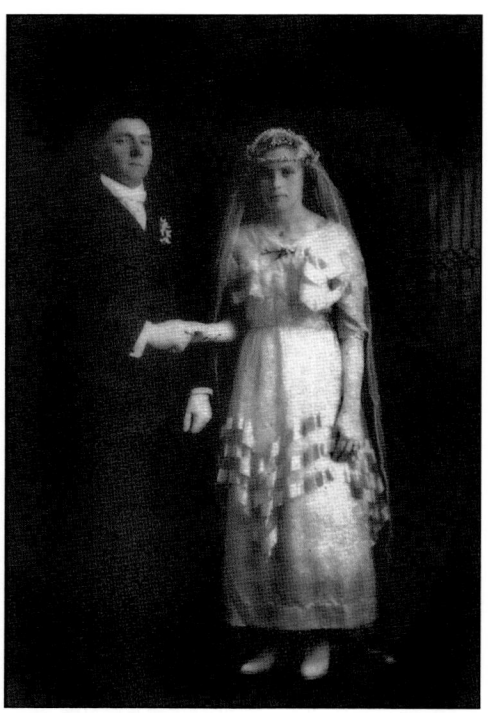

William (Willie) Joseph and Maude Newman Oppelt married in St. Louis Catholic Church on November 24, 1919. William was the younger of two sons born to Henry and Eugenia Sittre Oppelt. Both of his parents died by the time he was nine. He was reared by his mother's family, primarily by Jack Sitter. Maude was the only daughter of Harvey Newman and Laurie Ford Newman. Willie and Maude were married after Willie returned from serving in the Army during World War I. (Courtesy of Laurel D'Orsogna.)

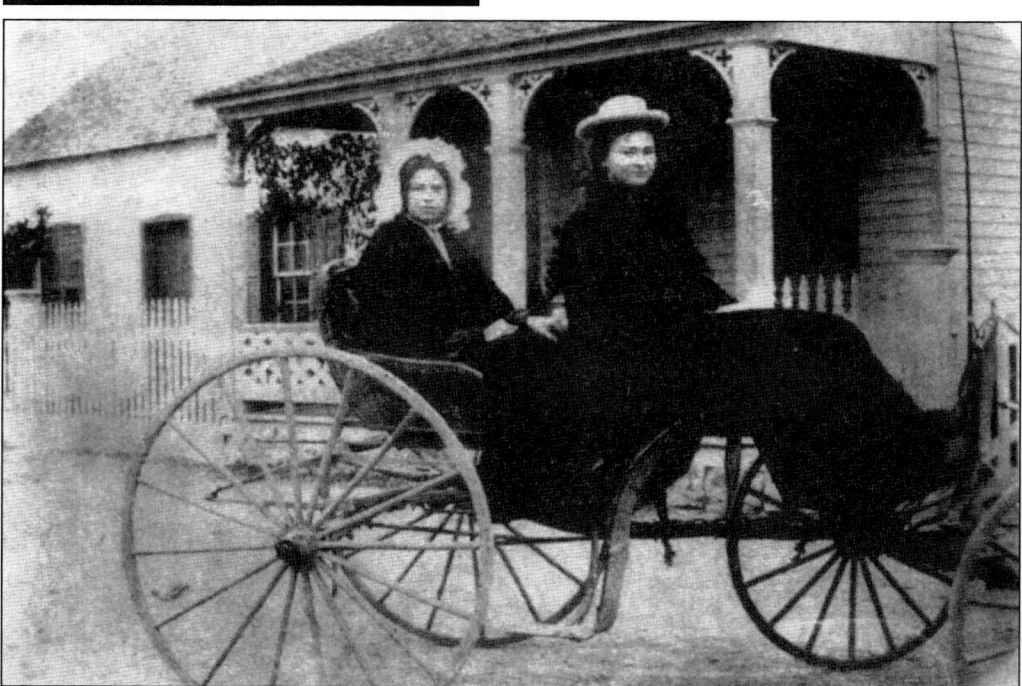

A Medina County trip to the Castroville Post Office in the early 1900s was a horse and buggy adventure over bumpy dirt roads. This photograph of Lucy Hopp (left), a schoolteacher, and her sister Roberta Hopp (right), who became a well-known lawyer and married Fletcher Davis, editor of the *Hondo Anvil*.

Pictured here is Fredrick Metzger of Hondo, who was elected to a very high position in the Masonic Lodge of Texas. Before the Battle of the Alamo, Santa Anna had ruled against Freemasonry in Texas. After his capture at the Battle of San Jacinto, however, Santa Anna was reputed to have used the Freemason distress signal and secret handshake while fearing for his life. After the Battle of San Jacinto, three Freemason lodges were chartered, and more would follow. Masons were some of the most vocal patriots of the Republic of Texas.

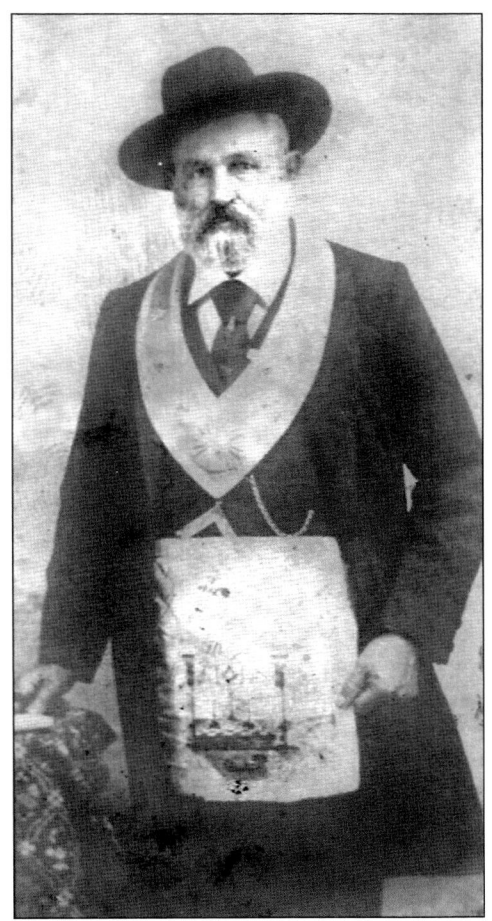

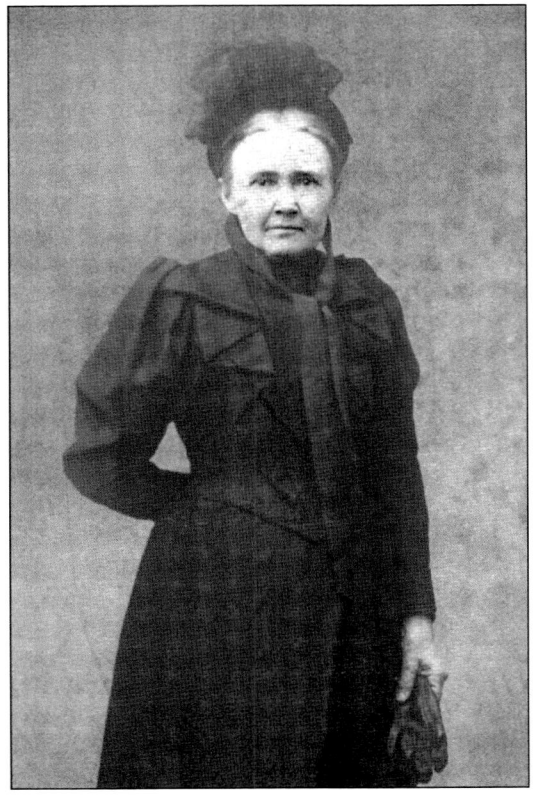

Louise Metzger, wife of Fredrick Metzger, is pictured here dressed in black. There was a very active Masonic lodge in Hondo during the formative years of the state.

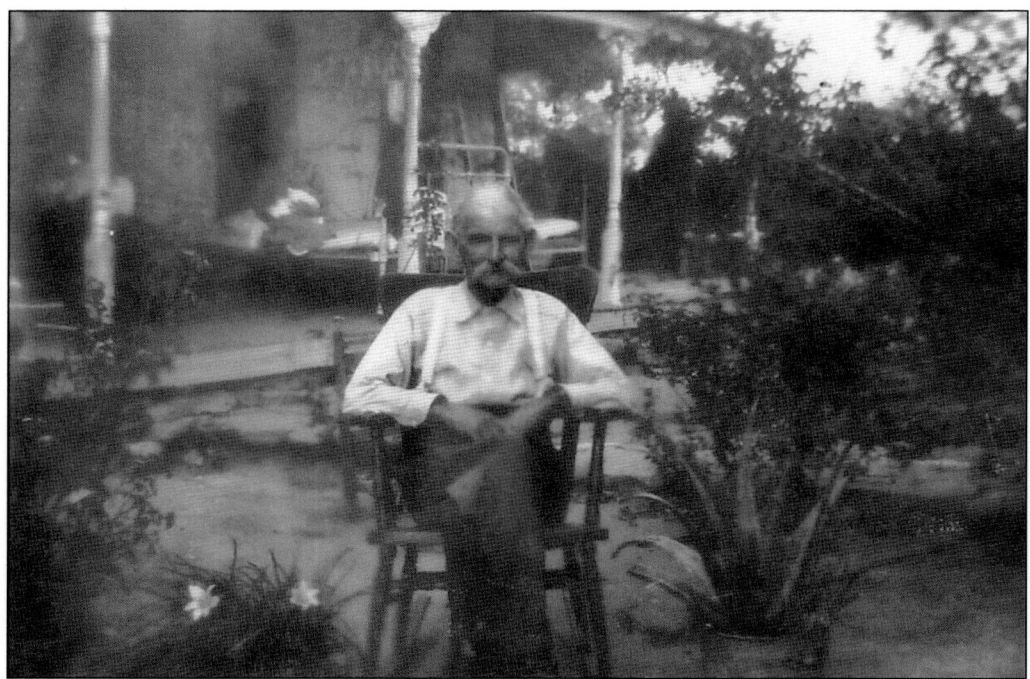

Edward Cullen Brown sits in the front yard of the home that he built on the Brown Ranch near Devine. Born in 1828 in Cincinnati, Ohio, Edward is descended from Chad Brown of Rhode Island, who came to America from England in 1632. Edward Cullen Brown traveled to San Antonio, Texas, in late 1840. He returned to Little Rock, Arkansas, and married Mary Elizabeth Kirby in 1849. After their last son was born in 1858, Edward convinced his father and mother, William and Deborah Kelly Brown, along with several uncles, to move to Texas. They arrived in Medina County around 1859 and settled along the Tehuacuana Creek near present-day Yancey. Edward served in the Union army. (Courtesy of Laurel D'Orsogna.)

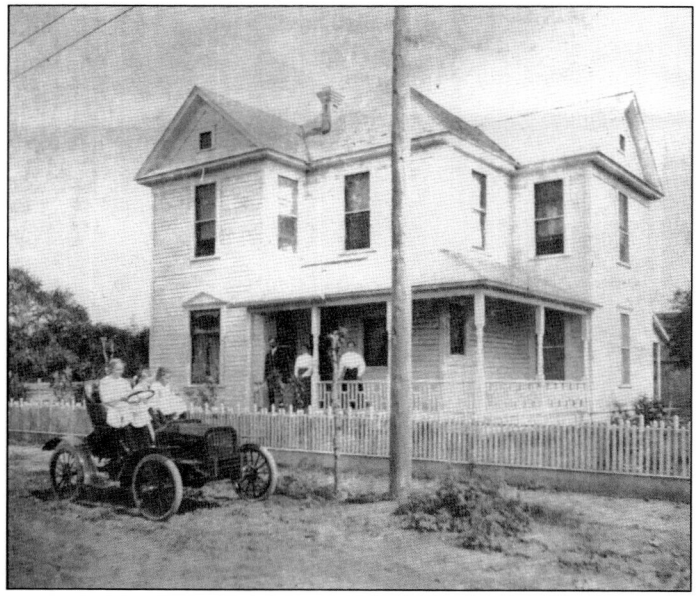

Pictured in front of the home of Dr. Beckmeyer, built in late 1890, this automobile is said to be one of the first automobiles in Medina County. The people in the picture are unidentified.

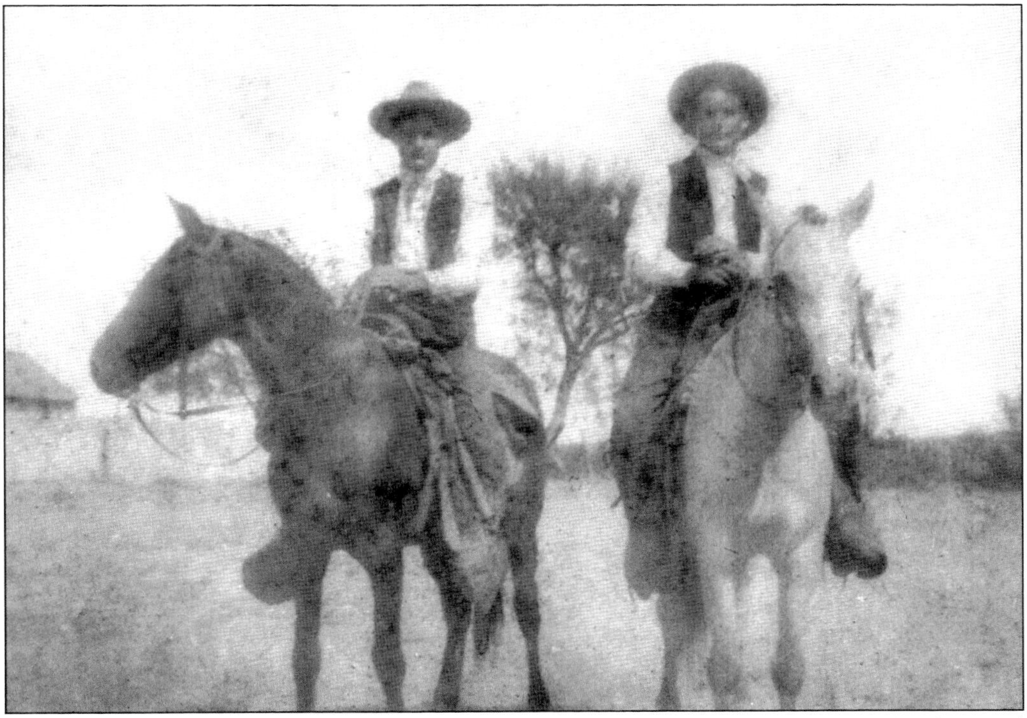

Pictured astride their horses are the two brothers from the Neiderhofer family. The family raised fine horses that were prized all over the county. The quarter horses trained and raised by this family were said to stop on a dime with the flick of the rider's crop.

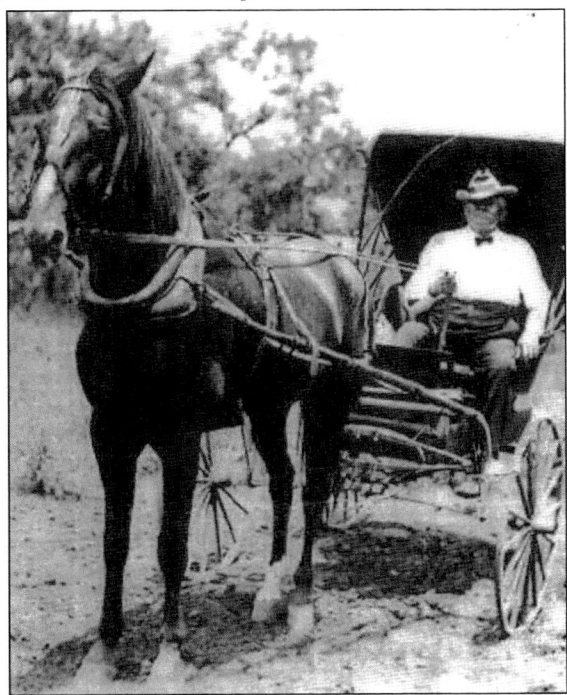

Seated in his horse-drawn buggy is an unidentified Medina County doctor. In the early days, doctors would travel to treat a patient in the country or in the villages. Many times they would take their pay in whatever produce the patient's family could provide.

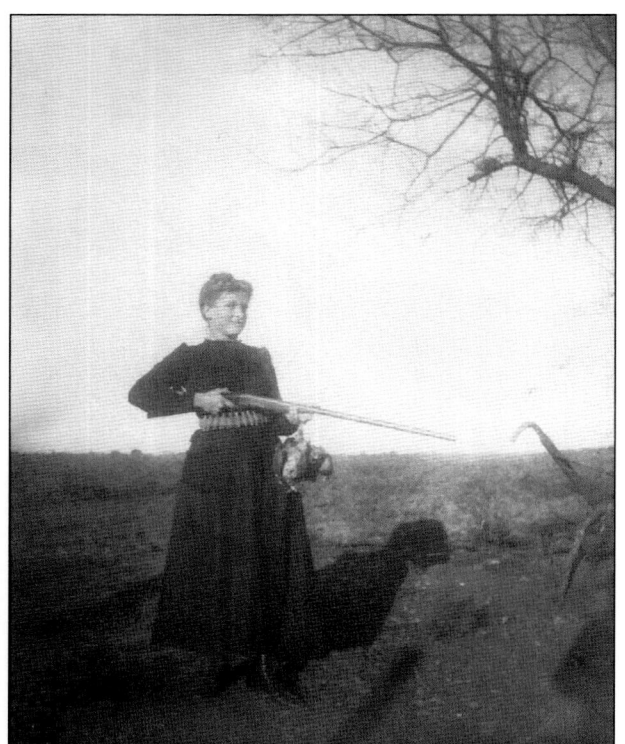

This picture of an unidentified woman holding a gun is from the Nutenhoefer estate. In the early years of Medina County, women were left alone when the men went to the fields to work, and many ladies could expertly shoot and hunt. At an early age, children were taught the rules of gun safety, so accidents were few and far between. Settlers knew that their lives might depend on knowing how and when to shoot.

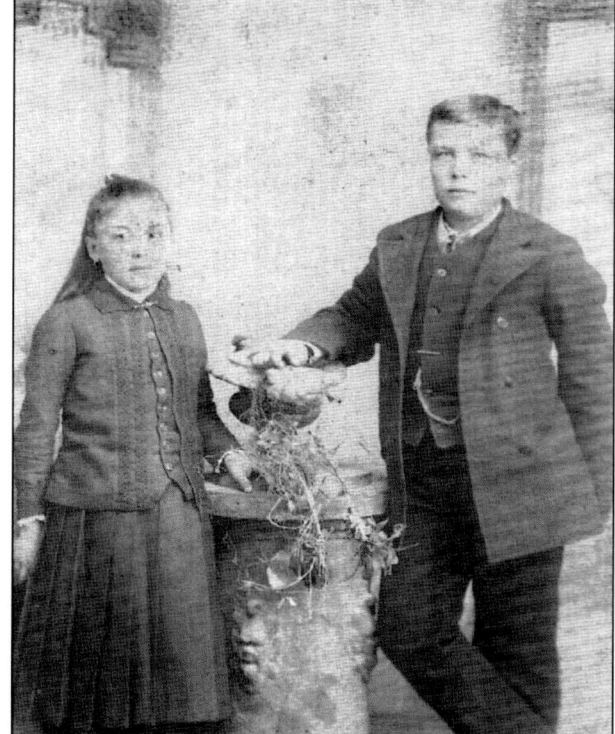

Emilia Ludwig and her brother Felix were the sixth and fifth children, respectively, of Joseph and Sophia Ludwig from LaCoste, Texas. Felix opened a butcher shop in San Antonio, not far from where the Alamo Dome is today. (Courtesy of Bonnie and Lester Ludwig.)

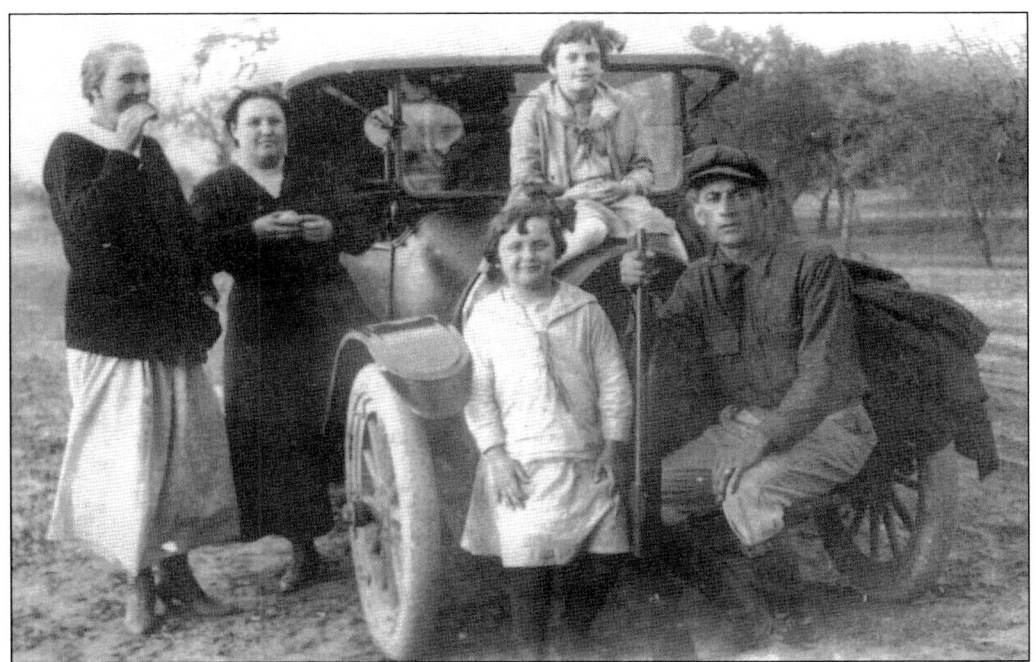

This photograph, taken in February 1919, shows a group posed on an automobile. From left to right are (in front of the car) Edwina Eifler and her father, Edward Eifler (a few days before his 35th birthday); (in back) Emilia Ludwig Bippert, Mary Estelle Foote Eifler, and Mary Elizabeth Eifler (the birthday girl, seated on the hood). (Courtesy of Bonnie and Lester Ludwig.)

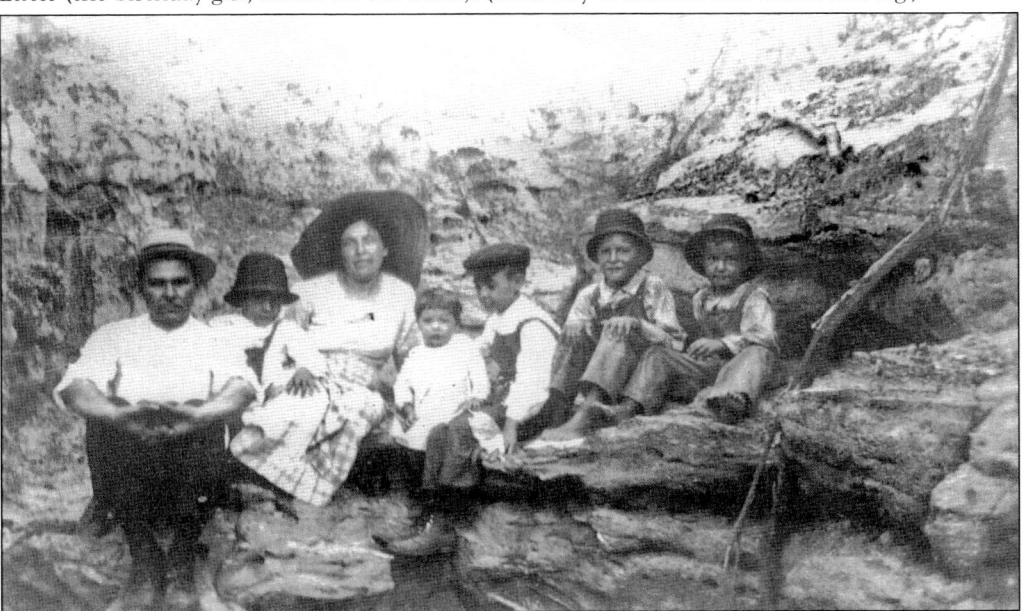

Having a picnic on their land grant outside of LaCoste in the early 1900s are, from left to right, the following: Ernest Feille, Gerald Feille, Edna Foote Feille, Edith Feille, Ludwig Bippert, Clarence Bippert, and Allen Bippert (the three boys of Emilia Bippert). (Courtesy of Bonnie and Lester Ludwig.)

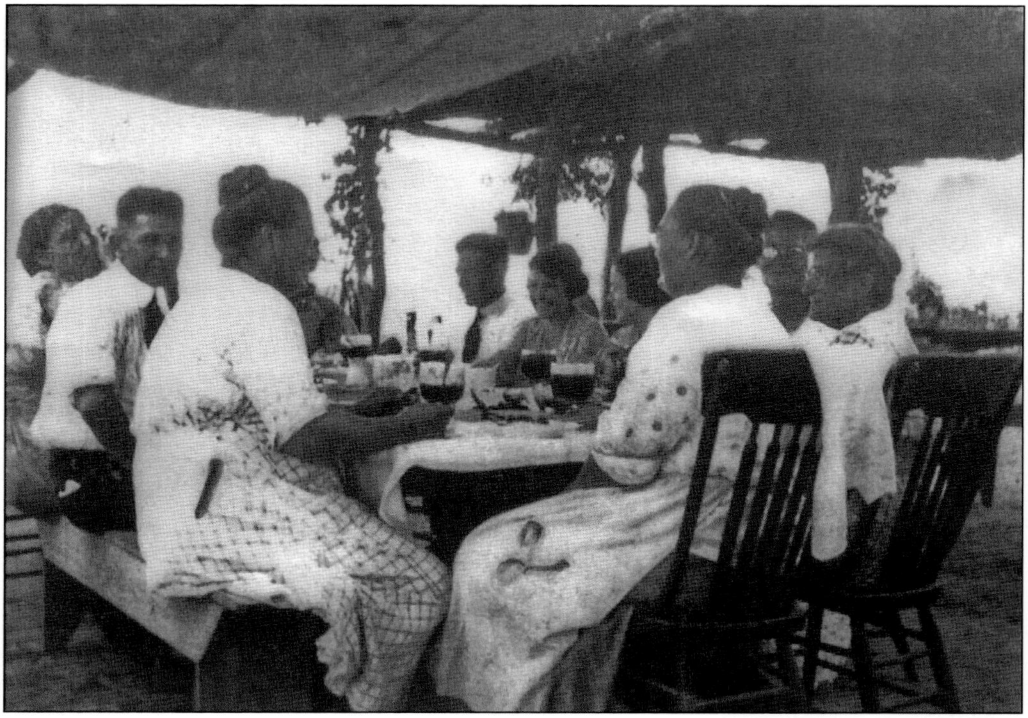

A lively dinner celebration takes place with several related families. Seated on the left is the Feille family, and on the right is the Bippert family, with Emilia Ludwig Bippert at the head of the table. Most of the settlers from Europe grew their own grapes and made their own wine. (Courtesy of Bonnie and Lester Ludwig.)

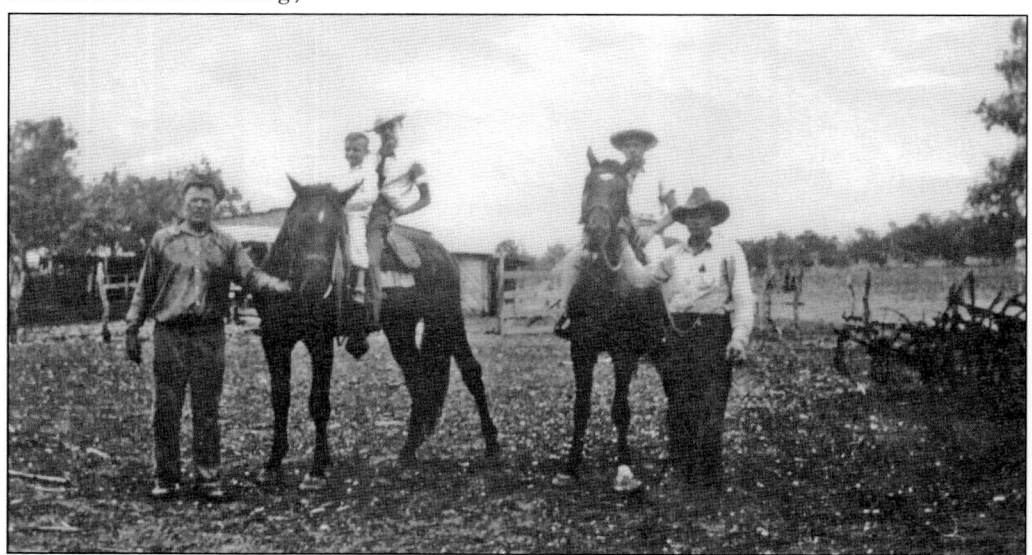

Medina County residents loved their fine horses. The boys shown are the grandchildren of Franz Joseph Ludwig, who came from Europe as one of Castro's settlers with his father, Franz Anton Ludwig, who settled, farmed, and ranched in D'Hanis. Becoming an expert rider was important to all who lived in Medina County. (Courtesy of Bonnie and Lester Ludwig.)

These two young ladies are Oma (left) and Lorine Kauffmann. They grew up in Medina County in the 1800s. Up until the third grade, they were taught at home out in the country by their mother, Mary Ihnken Kauffman, who spoke Alsatian, German, English, and Spanish. After the third grade, they moved into the town of LaCoste so that the girls could go to school. (Courtesy of Bonnie and Lester Ludwig.)

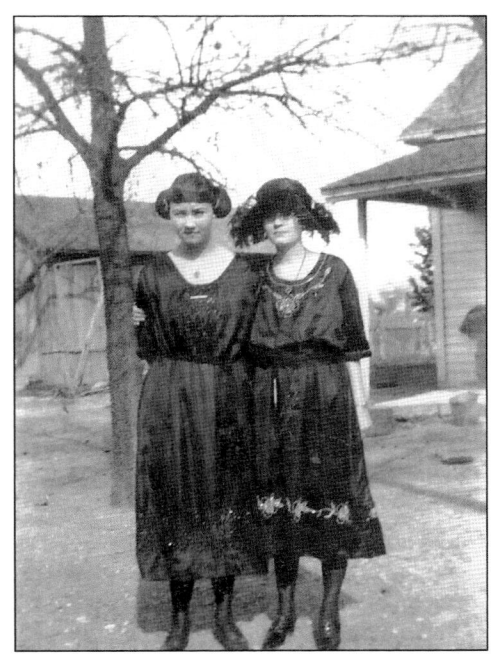

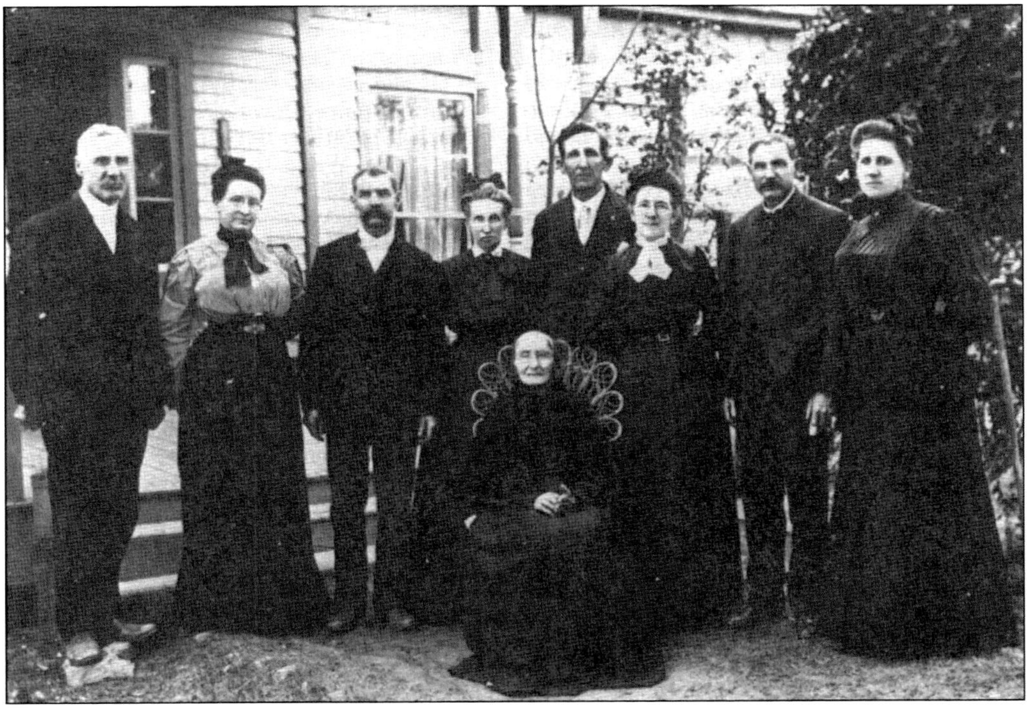

In 1883, the George T. Briscoe family came to Devine from Arkansas. Mary Gray Briscoe, wife of John Briscoe, is pictured seated before her family. Shown standing from left to right are George T. Briscoe Sr., Susie Robinson Briscoe, John Franklin Briscoe, Molly Robinson Briscoe, John A. Whitfield, Lena Briscoe Whitfield, Nottley Briscoe, and Mary Briscoe. The Briscoe family remains today an important part of the county. (Courtesy of the Mary and Henry Briscoe family.)

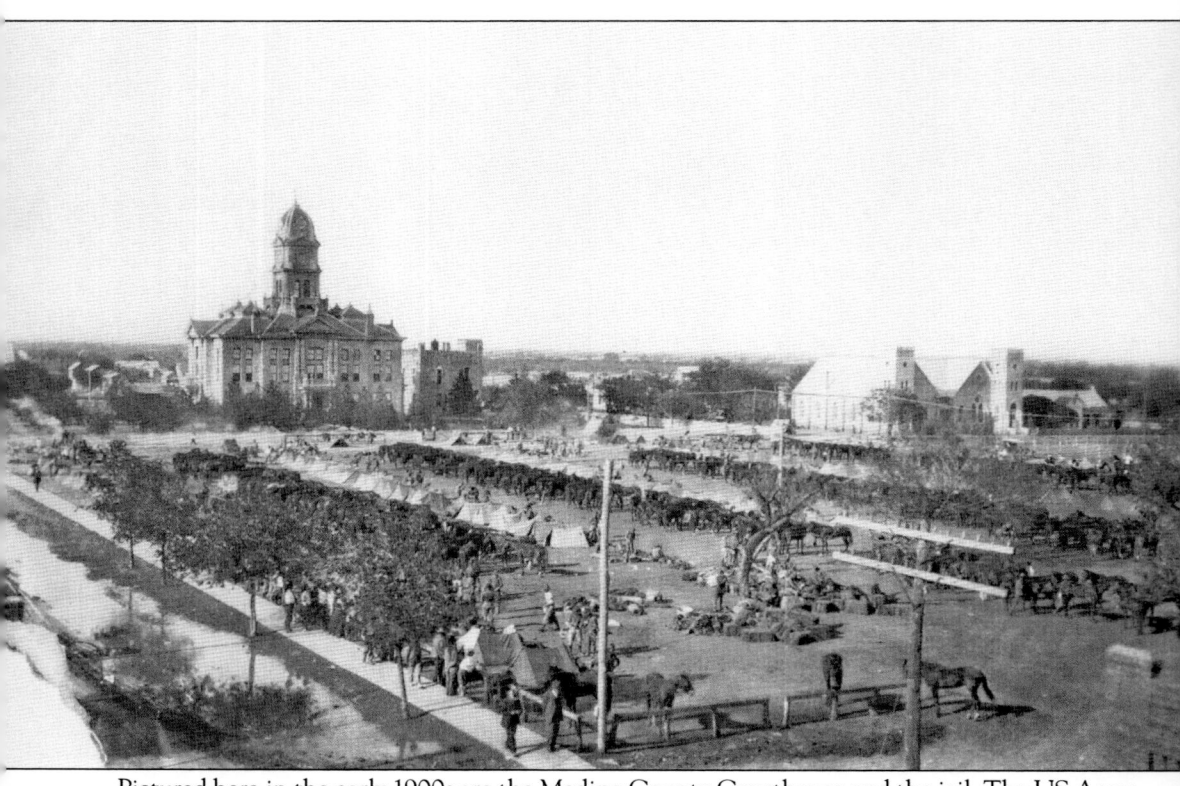

Pictured here in the early 1900s are the Medina County Courthouse and the jail. The US Army is camped with their tents, horses, and mule teams in the square in front of the courthouse. To the right can be seen the large Hondo Methodist Church.

Two
Towns, Railroads, and Schools

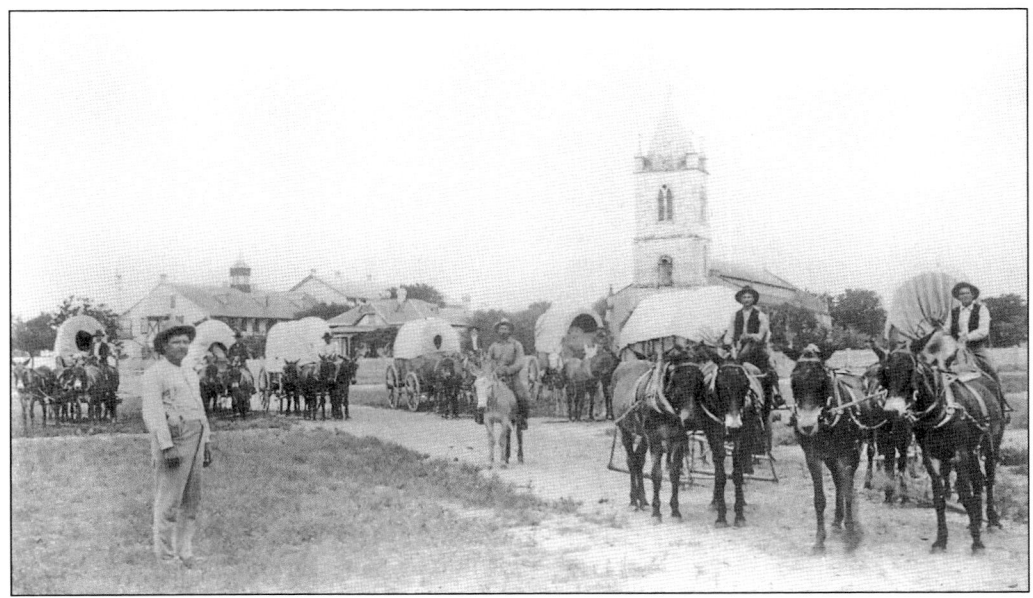

This image captures a wagon train ready to leave Castroville for Carrizo Springs in late 1800. Pictured standing to the left is Joe Baden. The St. Louis Church steeple can be seen in the background. Most of the wagons were pulled by mule teams. A man astride a donkey can be seen in the center of the picture.

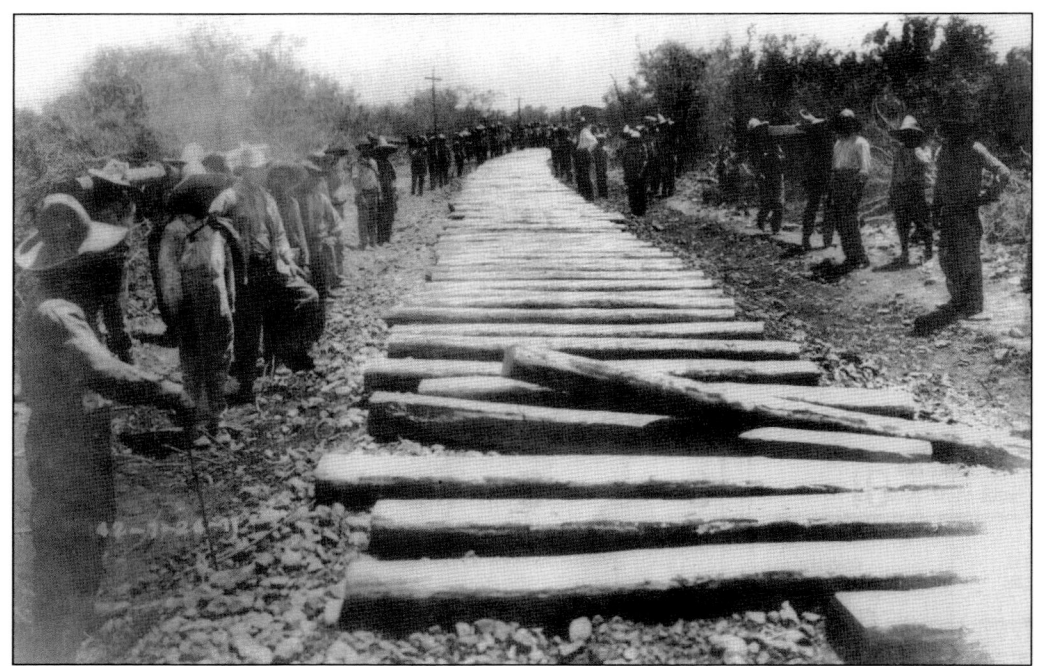

By the 1880s, the need to move goods and people faster than horse- or mule-drawn wagons could was keenly felt. The railroad fulfilled this great need. The cost of the construction of the railroad was paid largely by land grants from the State of Texas—16 to 20 sections of land for every mile of rail construction. Pictured here are workers building the railroad line from the Southern Pacific tracks at Dunlay to Medina Dam, which was 19 miles northward.

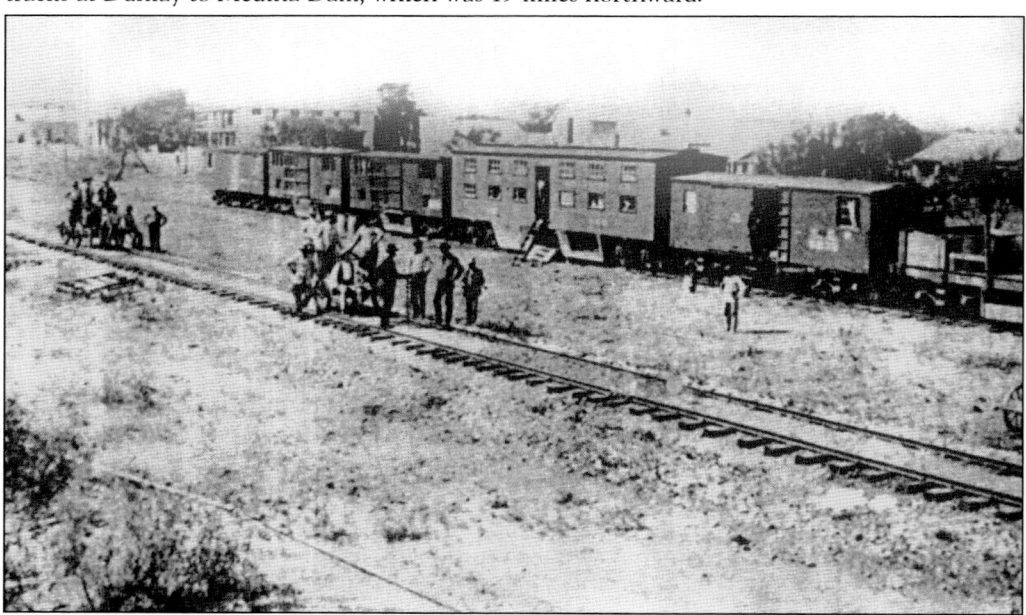

Old railroad cars were brought in to serve as living quarters for the workers. This solved the problem of housing, as the railcars could easily be moved along as the track progressed. This picture was taken on the outskirts of Hondo, Texas.

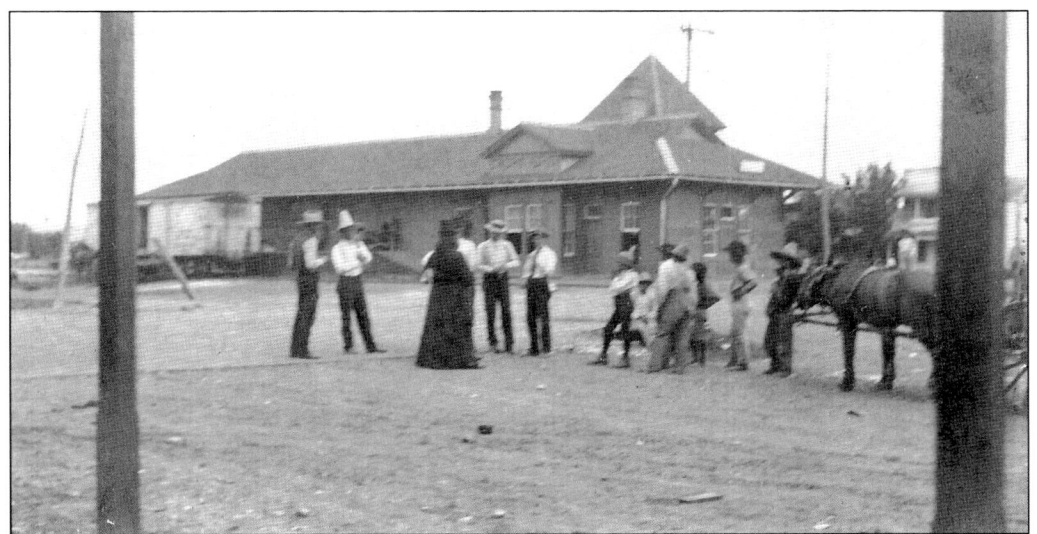

This 1888 picture is of the railroad station built in town along the tracks of Hondo. A lady wearing black lace appears to be talking to a group of men and boys while waiting for the train. This railroad station would later be moved and house the Medina County Museum on the west side of the town.

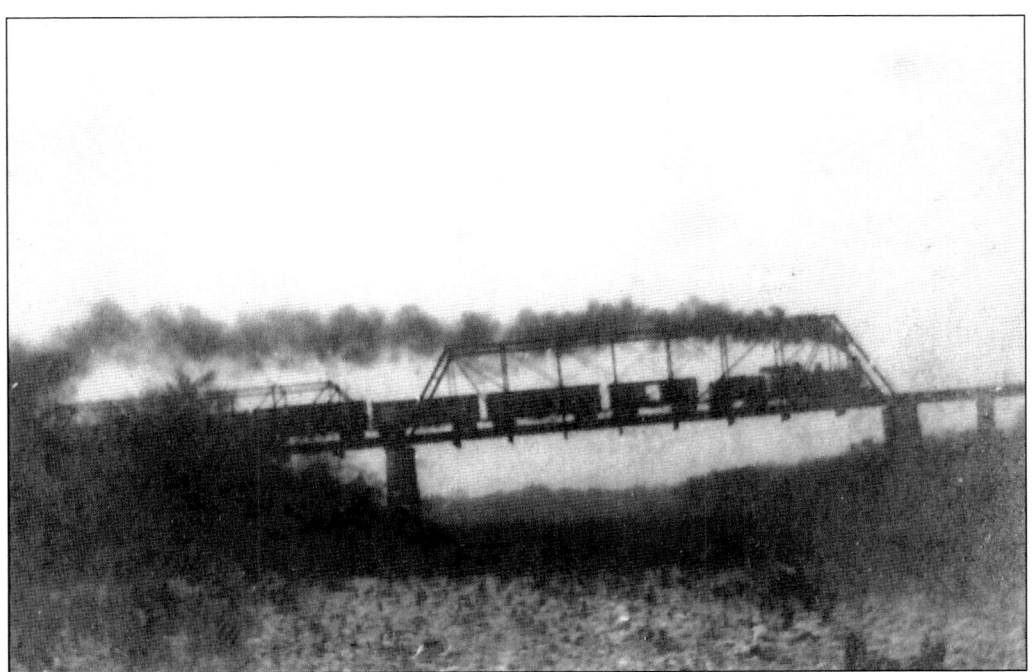

This train is steaming out of Hondo City, across Hondo Creek and eastwards toward San Antonio in the late 1800s. The same route is used today. Both the town and the creek got their name from the Spanish word *hondo*, meaning "deep."

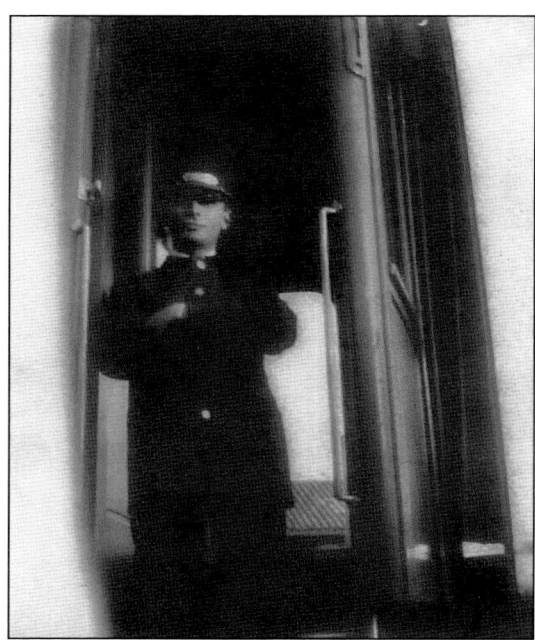

Edward Delbrail was a conductor for the railroad and eventually was on the Texas-to-Monterrey, Mexico route. The Delbrail family would make their home in Mexico for several years but returned to Medina County to reside. (Courtesy of Laurel D'Osogna.)

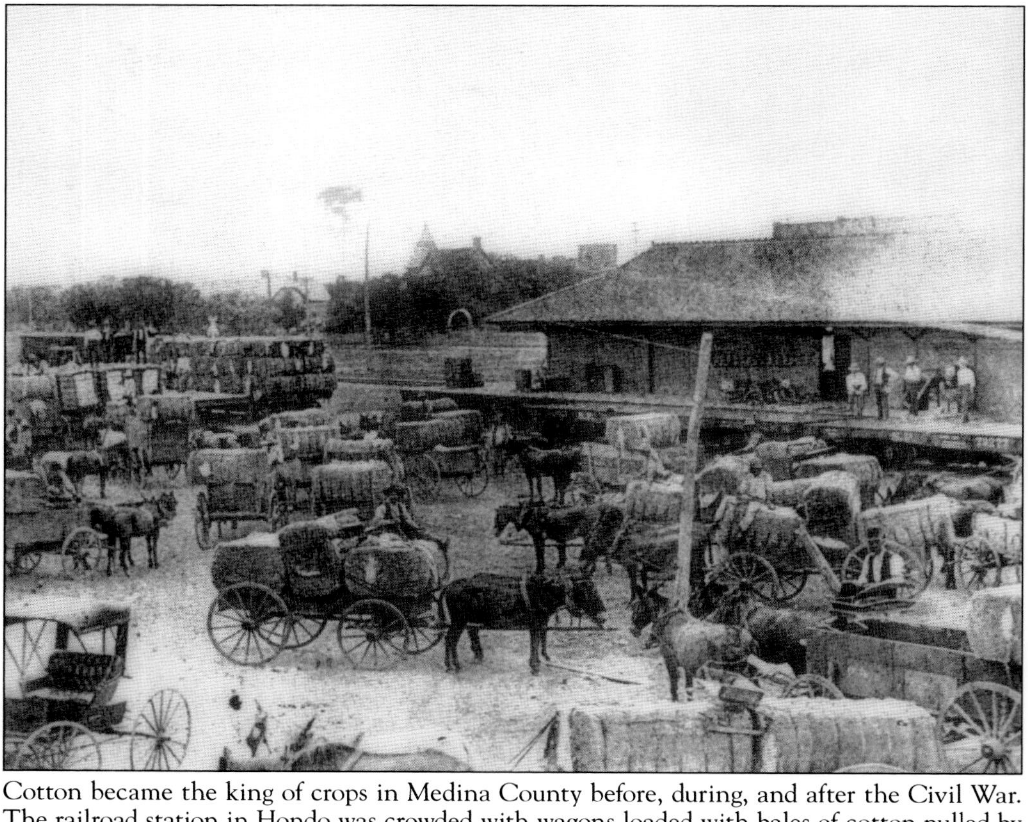

Cotton became the king of crops in Medina County before, during, and after the Civil War. The railroad station in Hondo was crowded with wagons loaded with bales of cotton pulled by mule teams.

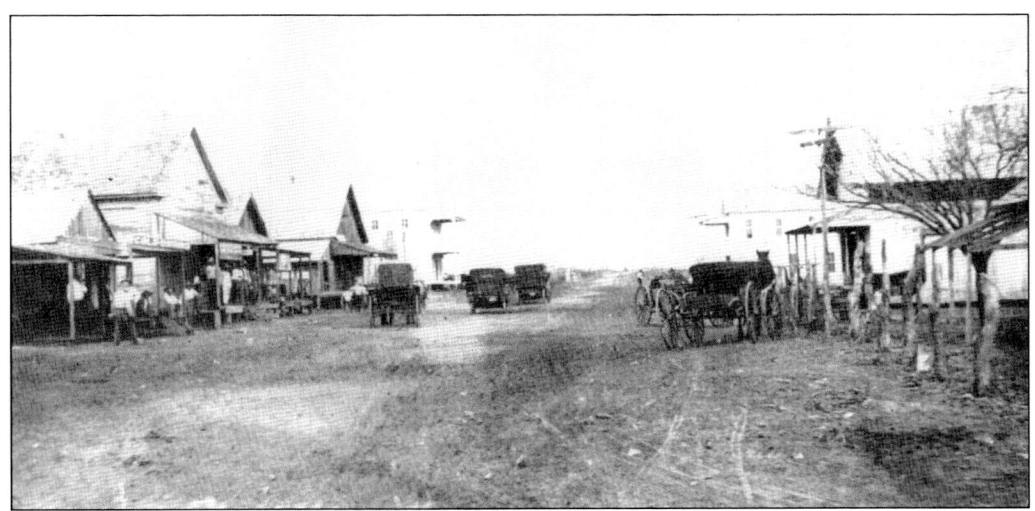

Downtown Yancey is pictured here in 1914. On the left side of the street are John Kennedy's Ice Cream Parlor and Confectionary, Henry Burgin's Store, the post office, a warehouse, Yancey Mercantile Company (owned by Sim Ward, Henry Koeck, and Tom Coopwood), and Dr. W.T. Lytle's Drug Store and office (the town of Lytle in Medina County is named for his family). On the right side of the street are John L. Oefinger's drugstore, Bill Nester's Meat Market, and the front of Henry Kueck's Cotton Gin. Part of this area became McCrea's Tehuacana Farms and the pecan shelling plant. Above Dr. Lytle's office, there was a meeting hall for Woodmen of the World that became a Masonic hall.

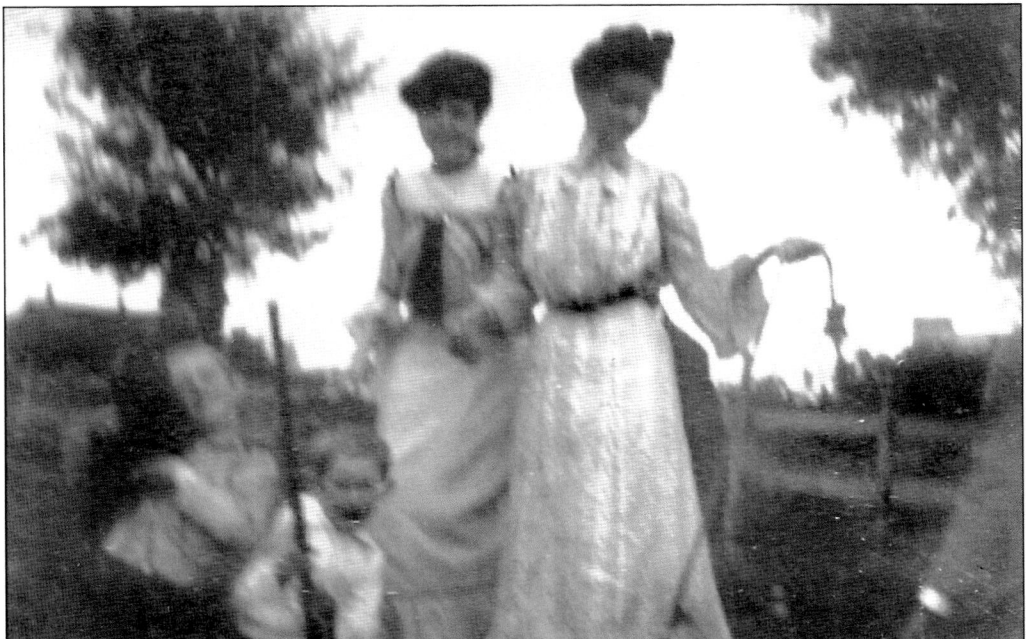

Edith De Montel Behan (standing left) and Mollie De Montel Haass are pictured with Pauline De Montel Taylor's sons, O.B. (left) and Monroe Taylor (holding the gun) in Hondo in 1800. The De Montel family was one of the first families of Medina County. Many people claim relationship to this line, although the family surname has disappeared from the rosters of Medina County.

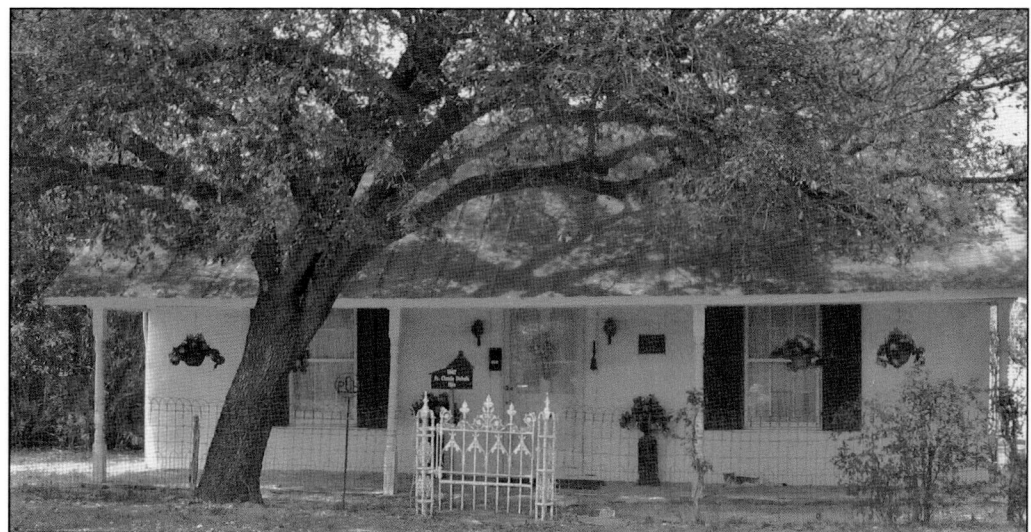

The Claude Dubuis house was built in 1847 in Castroville (the first settlement west of the village of San Antonio). It was the first rock home built in Castroville and is still standing today. The front two rooms were built by Father Dubuis, first priest to the settlement, and his assistant, Fr. Matthew Chazelle. Father Dubuis, a native of France, was educated in French seminaries and ordained in France in 1844. Both priests contracted typhus in the new settlement, and Father Chazelle succumbed in 1847. Father Dubuis taught himself the Alsatian language after arriving in the Castro settlement, and through his recruiting efforts, the first school west of San Antonio was opened by the Sisters of Divine Providence of France. Captured by Indians many times as he traveled to Fredericksburg, Quihi, D'Hanis, Vandenburg, and San Antonio, Father Dubuis was always released unharmed. (Courtesy of the author.)

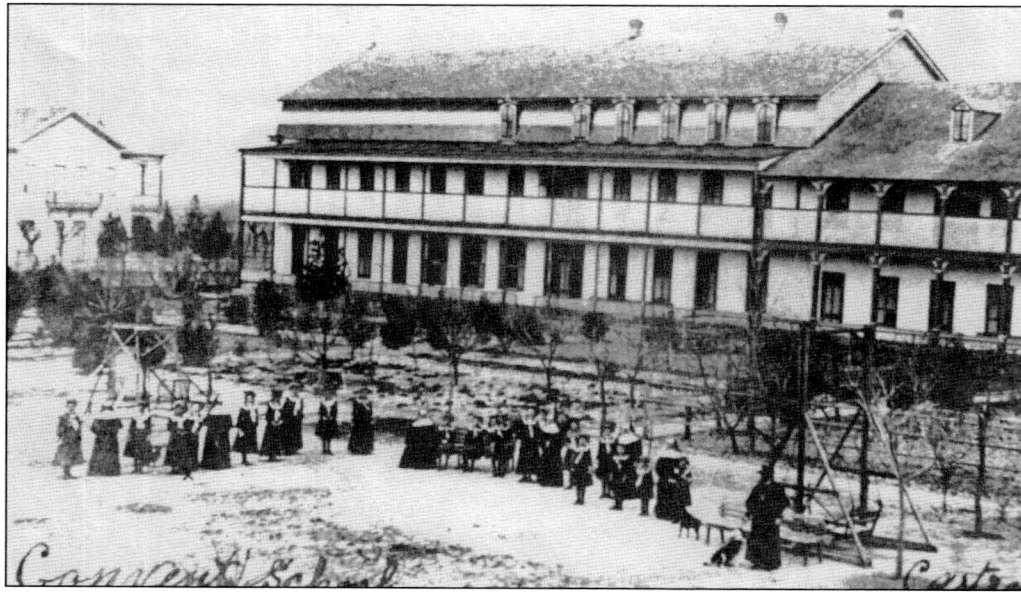

This is an exterior view of Moye Convent and Boarding School in Castroville in 1890. The Sisters of Divine Providence, brought from France by Father Dubuis to teach in the wilds of Texas, were dressed in the black habit of their order. The school was founded by the sisters in 1868.

This is a close-up portrait of some of the music students of St. Louis Convent. As their families lived at a distance, many children were sent to board with the sisters. Music was considered an important part of education, and almost every student excelled in some form of music.

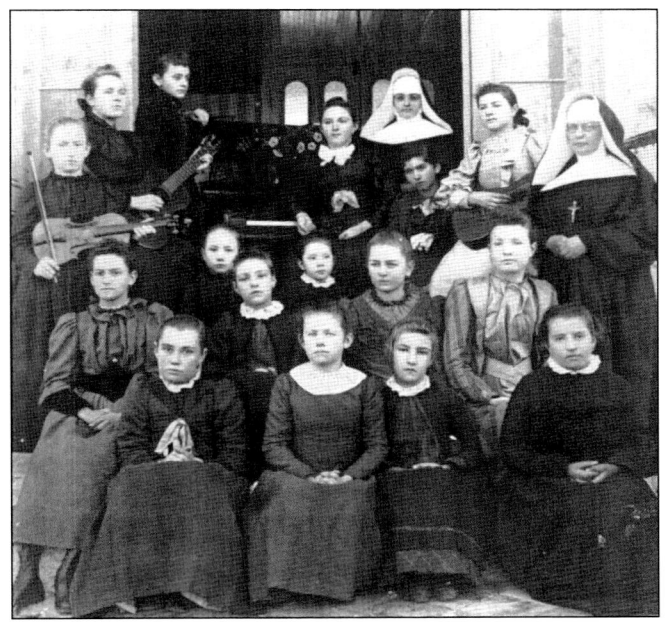

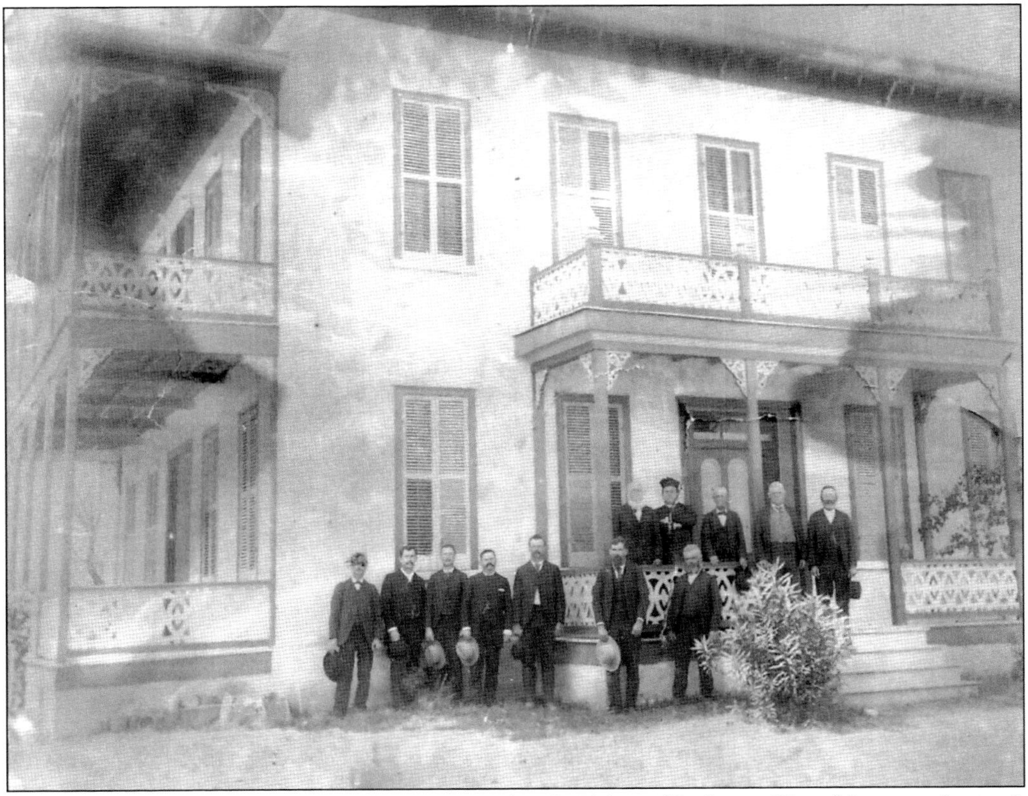

This photograph, taken some time between 1885 and 1890, is of St. Louis Church's original priest's residence in Castroville. It burned down in 1890 and was rebuilt as a modern brick structure that serves the priests today.

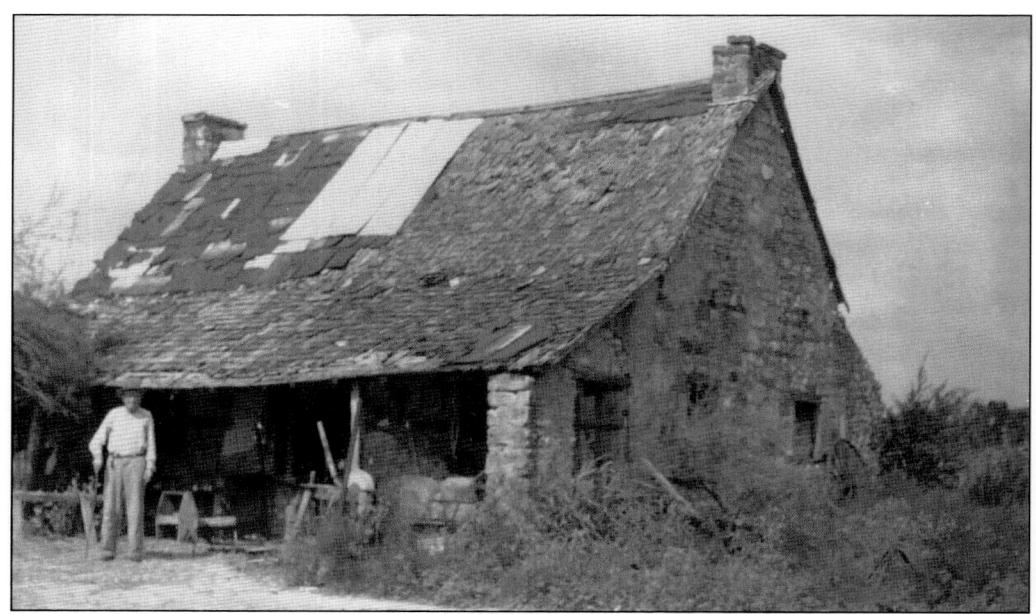

Louis Naeglin, a well-known stonemason, is shown standing in front of the old Richard Mechler house in 1912. Replacing sod roofs were roofs made of cypress that was cut to make shingles. Cypress is a strong wood that is it still used today and was prevalent in the early Alsatian and German homes of Medina County. Most of the stonemasons who were so necessary in former times have faded from memory, but many of the old homes they built remain and have been renovated by area residents. (Courtesy of Bonnie and Lester Ludwig.)

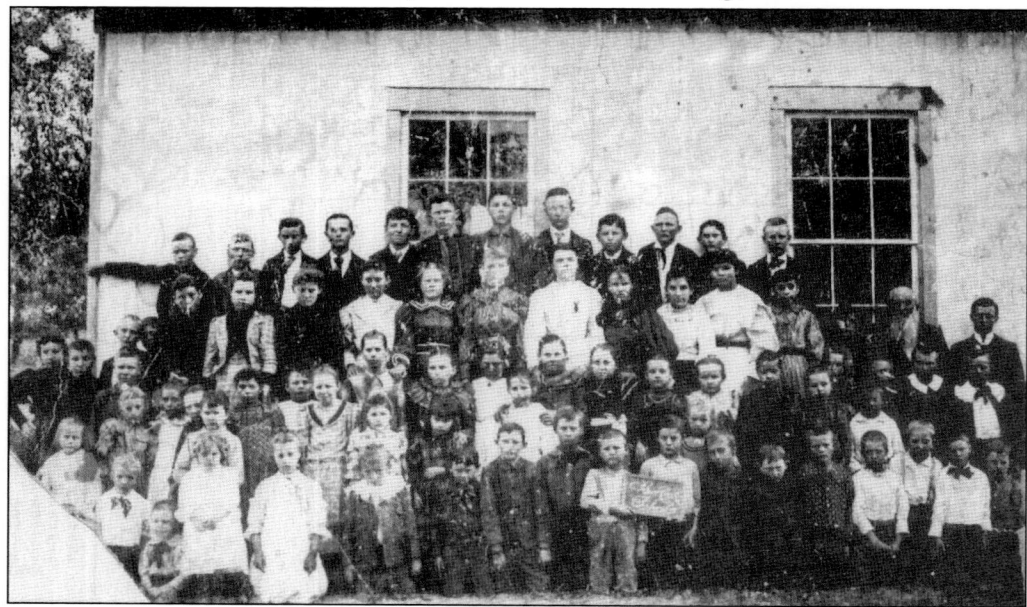

The Bear Creek School in Medina County is shown in the early 1900s. Most schools were one-room schoolhouses, and the teachers had to teach many different grades at once. In front, the youngest student holds the Bear Creek school sign, and the other children appear to be dressed in their Sunday best for the event.

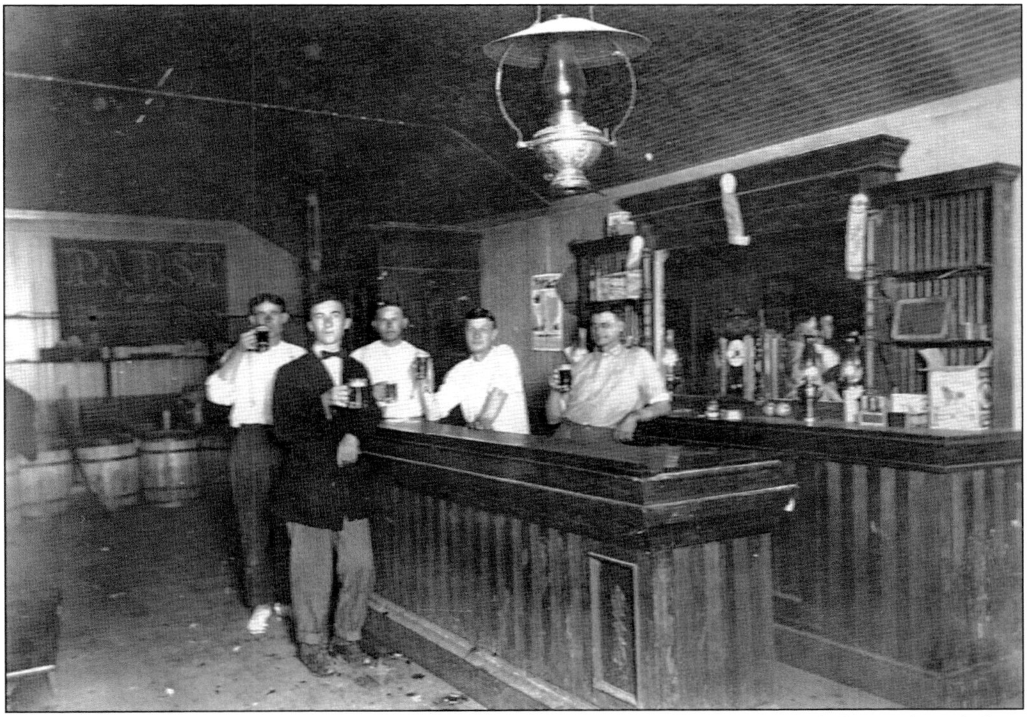

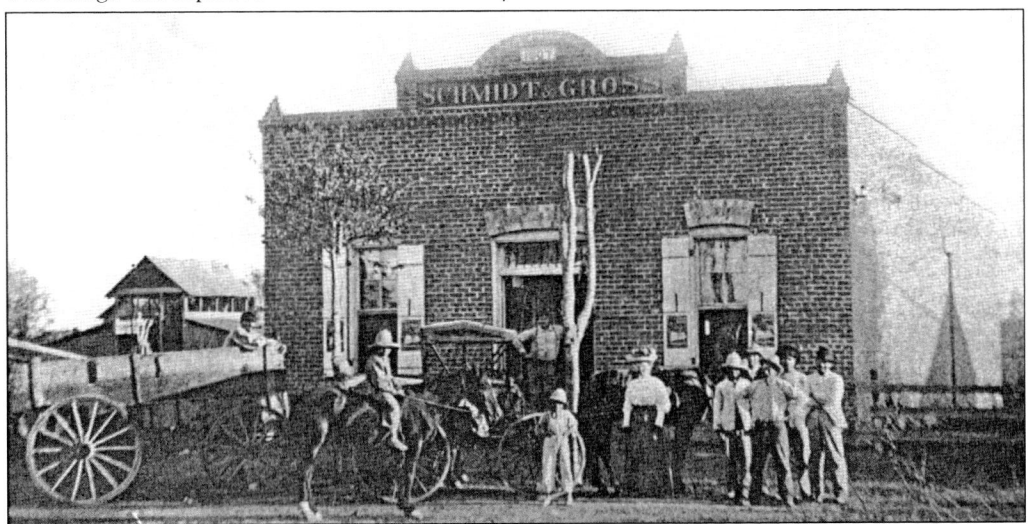

Every town had a saloon, and the town of LaCoste was no different. Pictured above, from left to right, are Gus Keller, John Hassler, William Luckenbach, Henry Kauffman, and Paul Jungman. The image was captured some time in the early 1900s.

The Schmidt & Gross Store in LaCoste was a very popular and busy place. Ed Schmidt stands in the door of the store, while a barefoot boy stands in front of a surrey. Edward Schmidt was the son of Louis and Amelia Zimmerman Schmidt. Edward Schmidt built this store as well as an icehouse, both with the help of Henry Groos. The ice was shipped from San Antonio by train. Edward married Carolina Monier of San Antonio and had two daughters, Alice Schmidt Batto and Irene Schmidt Zinsmeyer.

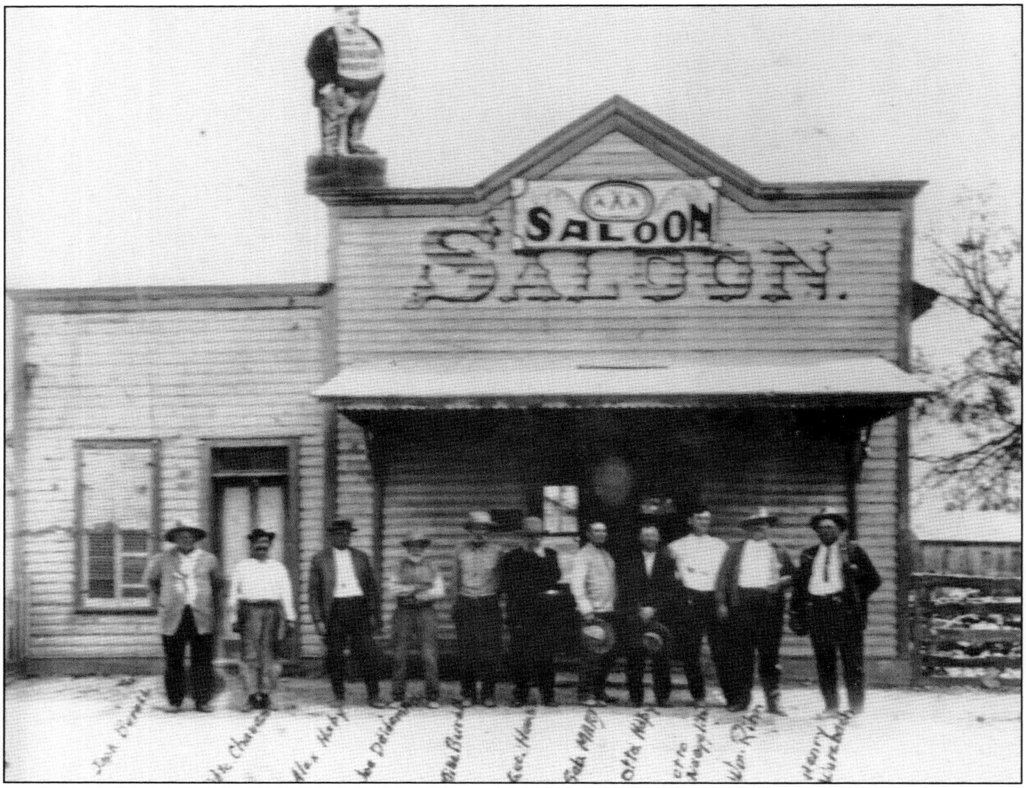

In 1913, Castroville Saloon was very successful. Pictured in front of the saloon are, from left to right, Jack Burell, Pete Chaves, Alex Haby, Joe Deidemann, Mike Burell, George Hauss, Sebastian Marty, Otto Haby, Otto Naegelin, William Rihn, and Henry Wurzbach.

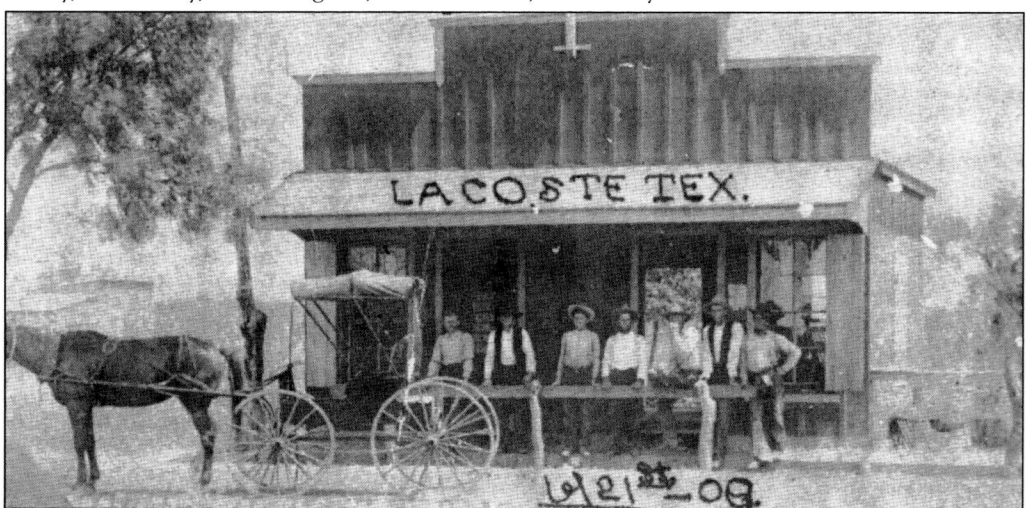

This photograph of the LaCoste Post Office was on a postcard from 1908. The railroad came to LaCoste in 1888 and is the reason that the town was born. Had the railroad gone to Castroville, history in the area would have been different. Many people chose to move from Castroville to LaCoste to be near the railroad.

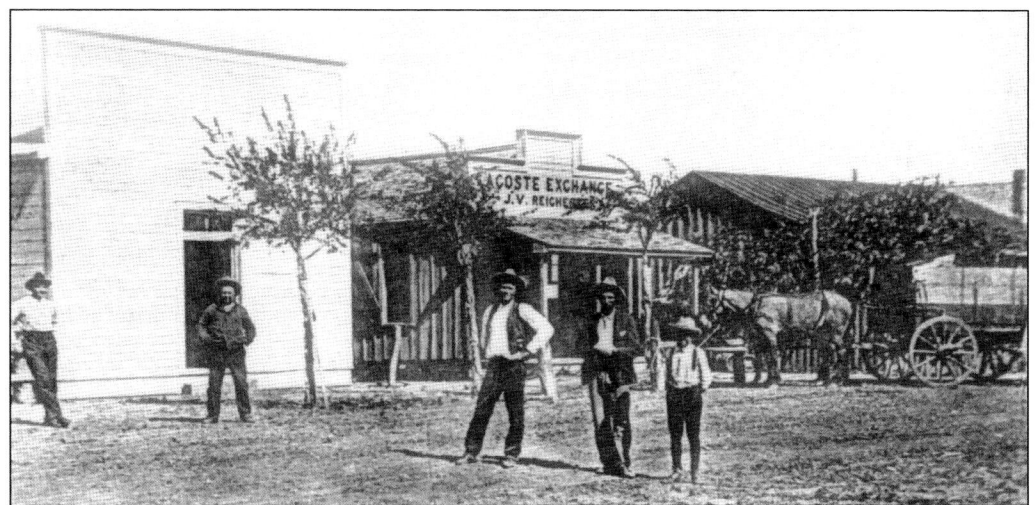

Four men stand abreast in the muddy main street of LaCoste in front of the LaCoste Exchange while a two-horse wagon awaits its driver. The men standing in the street are dressed in clothing typical of the day and area—boots and hats—and await the start of another Texas day, ready to hop on a horse, mule, or even a coyote if one were to amble by.

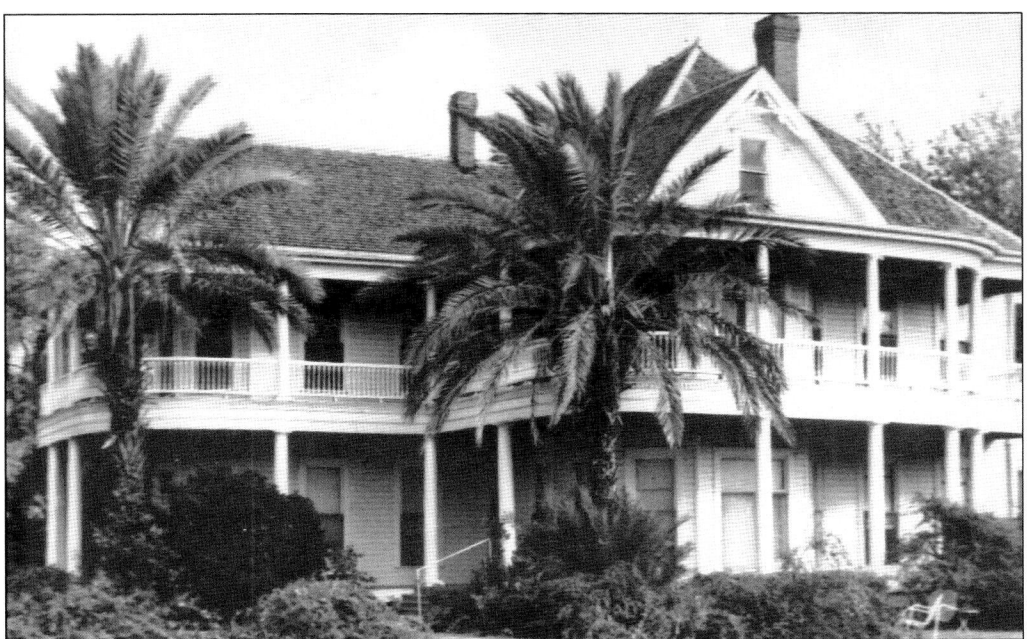

Built in 1906 by farmer and rancher George T. Briscoe, this Victorian home had large galleries on three sides. Briscoe owned the Devine Lumber Company and built many homes in Medina County. George T. Jr. was involved in agriculture as a farmer and rancher.

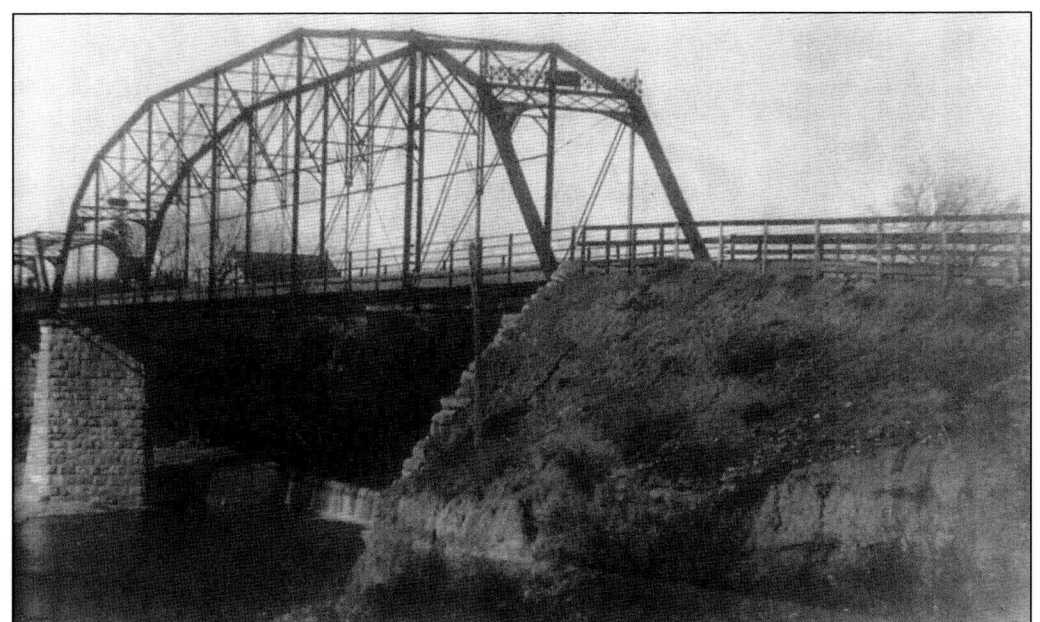

Construction of this bridge over Medina River in Castroville began in 1903 and was completed in 1904, but it has since been replaced by a modern bridge. Many residents bemoan the loss of the statuesque old bridge. (Courtesy of Bonnie and Lester Ludwig.)

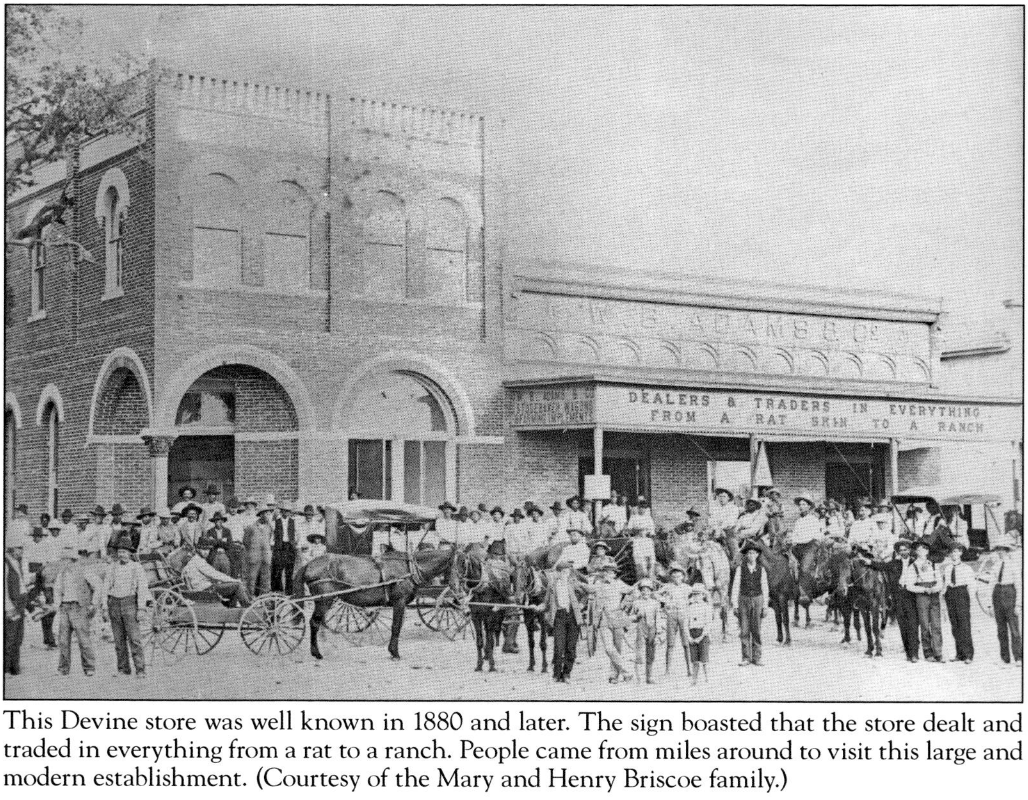

This Devine store was well known in 1880 and later. The sign boasted that the store dealt and traded in everything from a rat to a ranch. People came from miles around to visit this large and modern establishment. (Courtesy of the Mary and Henry Briscoe family.)

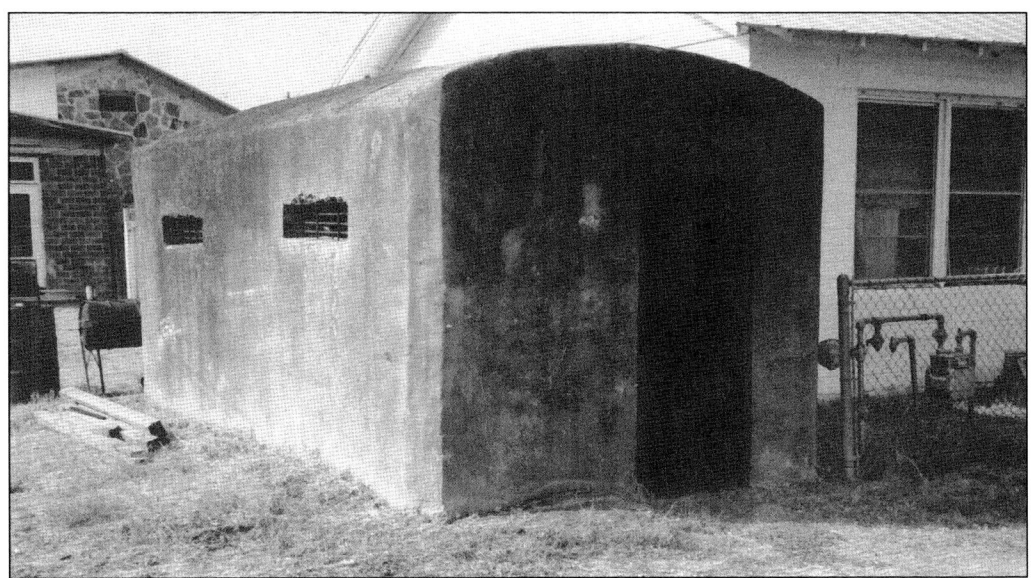

The old LaCoste Jail, built in 1880, still stands today. Made of mortar and steel, the jail was built to hold wrongdoers and to afford no prospect of escape. The structure was said to be cool during the summer months but unfortunately retained little heat in winter. (Courtesy of Bonnie and Lester Ludwig.)

Wild pigs roam Eighteenth Street freely in this shot, taken facing southeast in Hondo in the early 1800s. These particular pigs look to be of the native javelina Texas-Mexican breed, which is most prolific in the south and west of Texas and is hunted by sportsmen today.

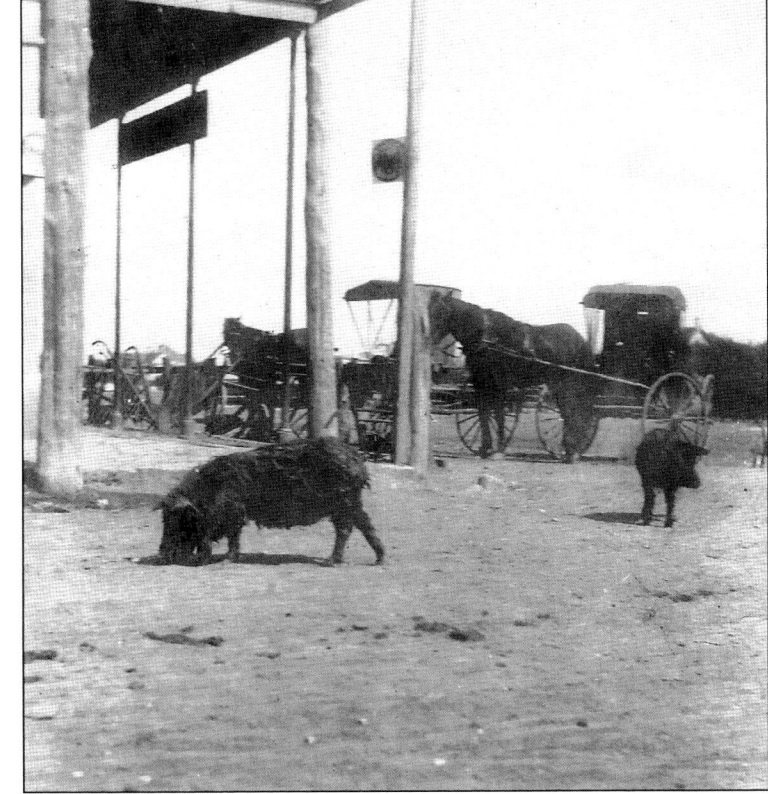

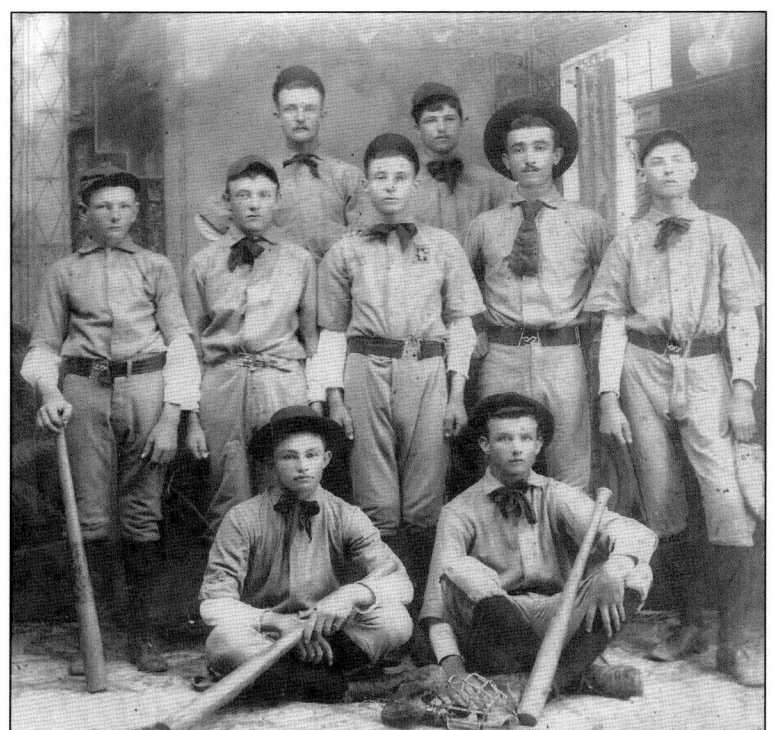

Pictured in 1910 is a group of young baseball players in D'Hanis. Baseball was a sport that every Texan knew and loved, and each town had a team cheered on by enthusiastic fans.

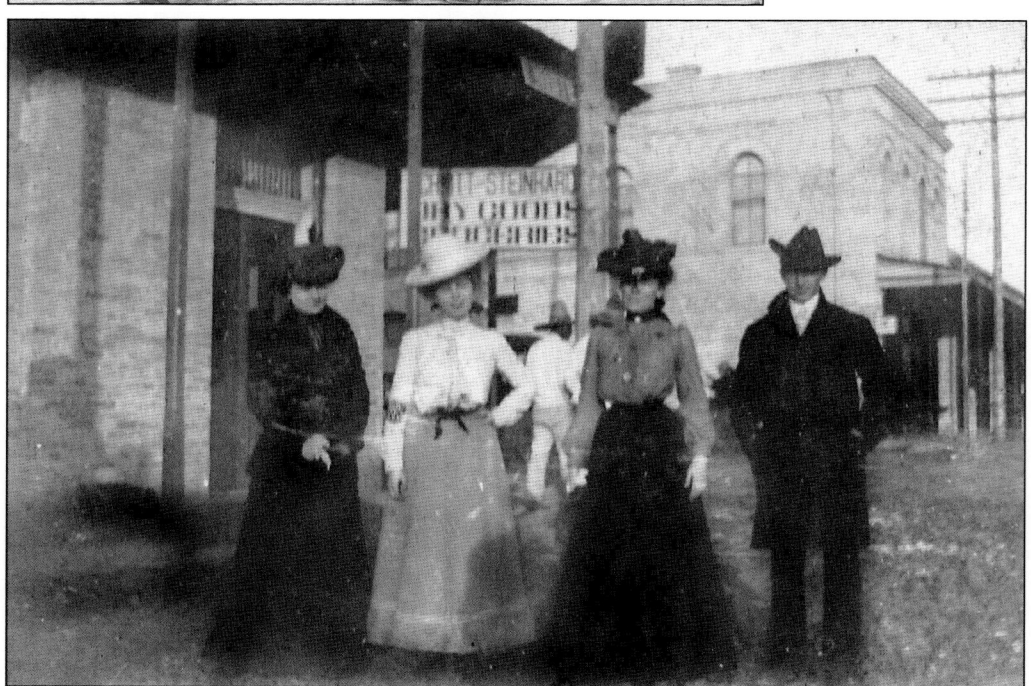

Standing in front of the old Schmitt and Steinhart Store in Hondo are three finely dressed ladies escorted by a gentleman in overcoat and hat. All of the people pictured are unidentified but agreed to stop to have their photograph taken.

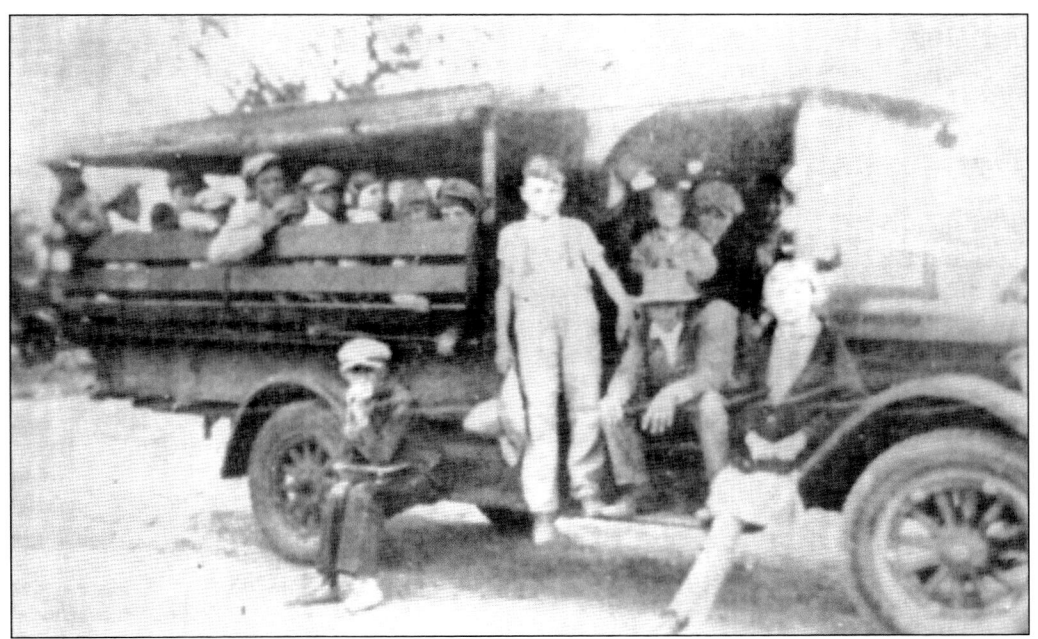

The Natalia school bus is pictured above. Natalia is in the extreme southeastern part of Medina County, and this bus provided transportation for the many children scattered over the district.

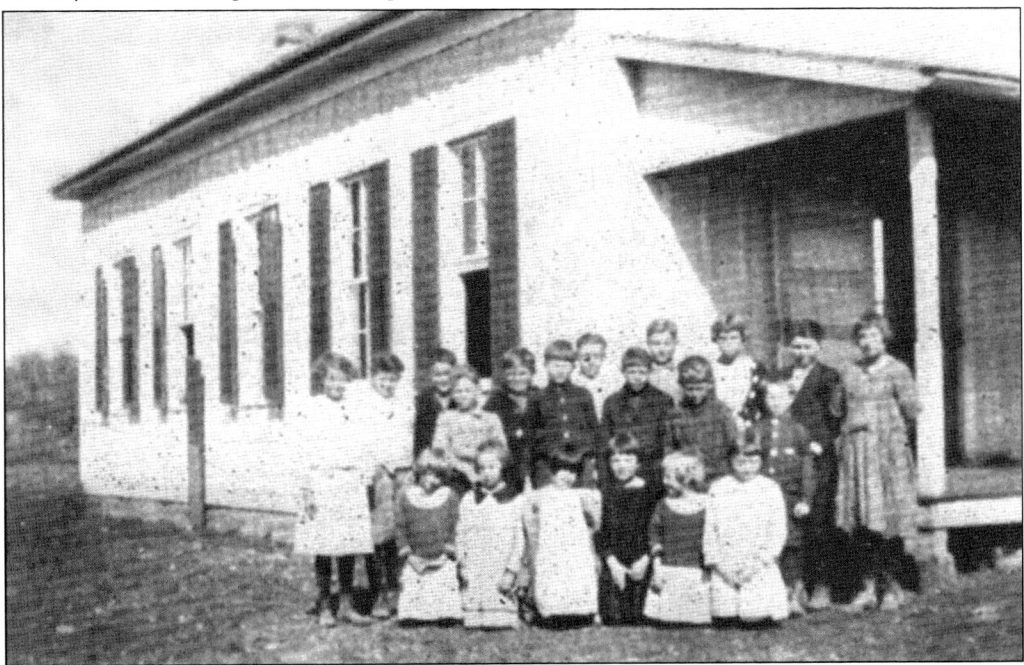

The Old Spanish Trail passes through Dunlay School District from east to west. Originally, the school was situated in the little village of Dunlay, but due to the number of families living in the northern part of the district, the school building was moved to the highway, one mile away, to accommodate the rural people. It was a one-room building, but the space was ample for a school with only one teacher. The district had no local tax.

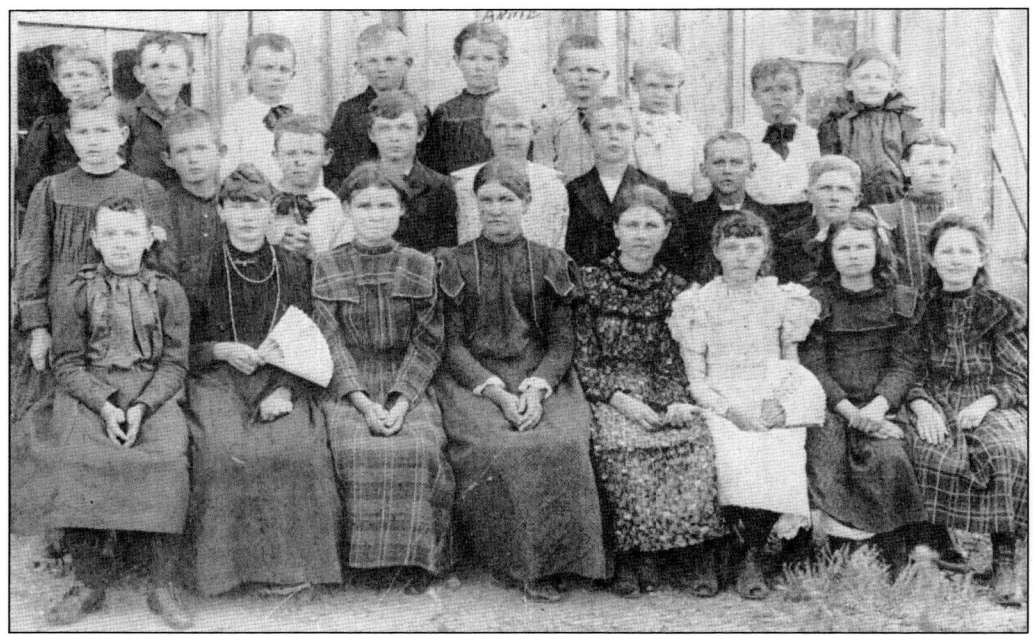

This picture of the Ranch School at the Schweers Settlement was taken in 1890. The typical class picture includes Amalie Oefinger, Angelina Rohlf, Hulda Schweers, Annie Heyen, Ida Schweers, Josie Rohlf, Lizette Schweers, Martha Schweers, Emma Brucks, Adolph Brucks, Hugo Schweers, E.W. Balzen, Mary Balzen, Rosina Balzen, Arnold Balzen, Ernest Oefinger, Edgar Balzen, Annie Brooks, E.W. Brucks, George Schweers, and Bertha Oefinger.

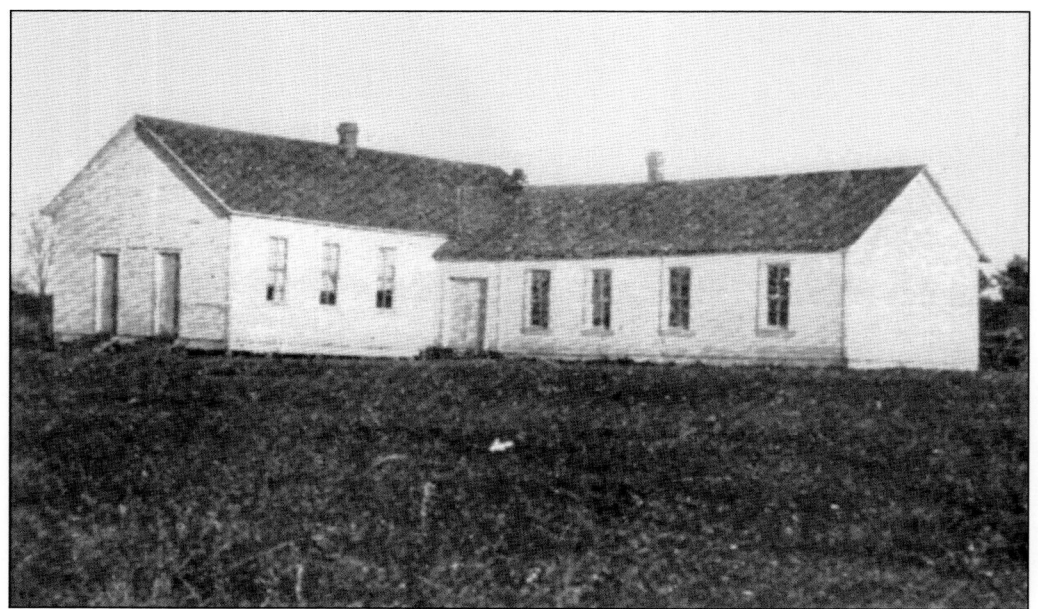

The Black Creek School was composed of about 30 miles of territory. As in many rural communities, the majority of the patrons were farmers. In 1911, two schools were combined and moved to the site pictured above, which consisted of two rooms.

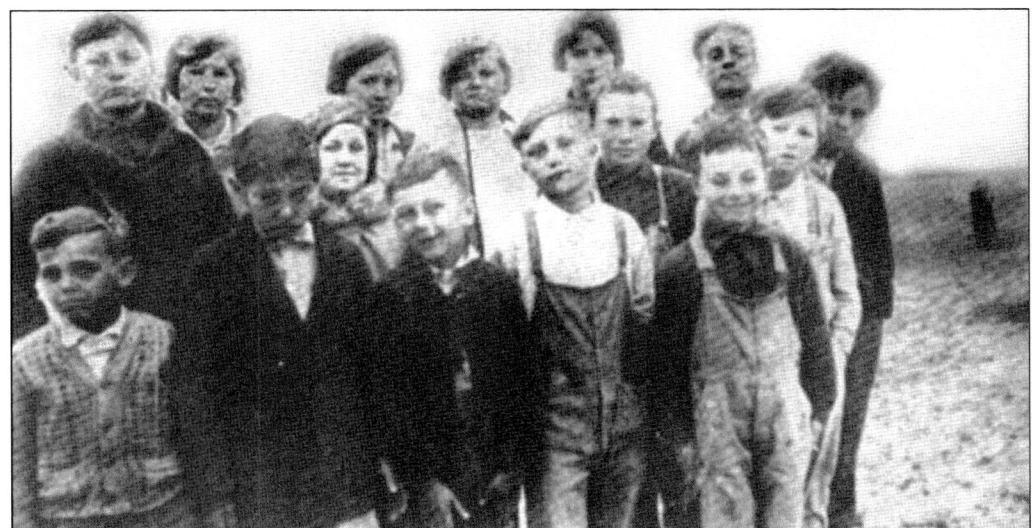

This Rio Medina School class picture was taken about 1920. Bess Turner was the teacher. Rio Medina was the center of a prosperous farming community. The residents were primarily of German descent.

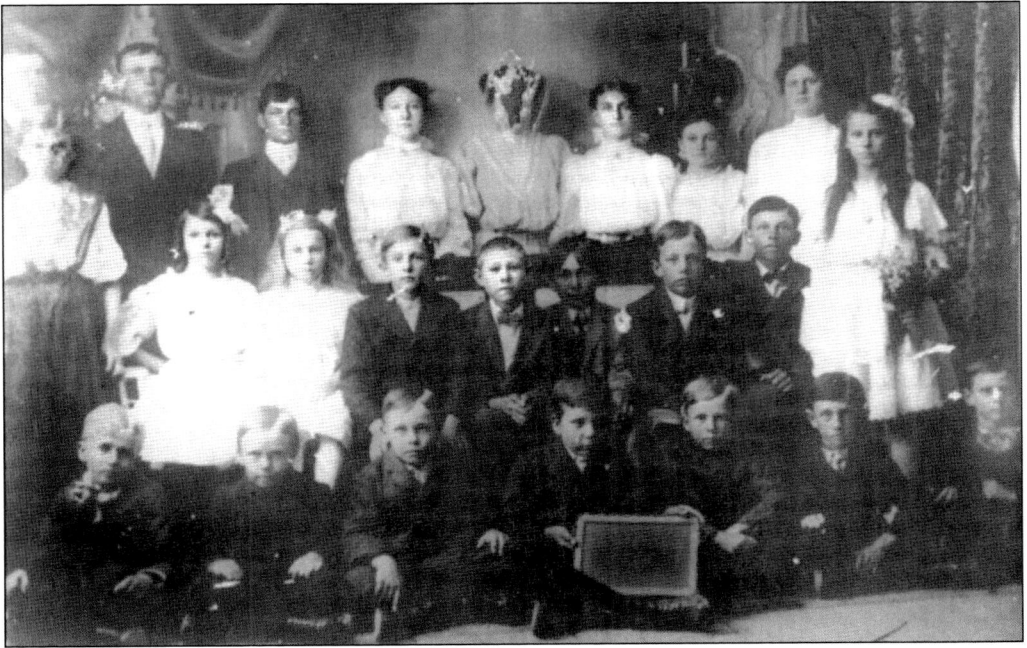

Vandenberg School Organization was formed in the community in 1876 to promote education, and the first school was erected at a cost of about $200. Included in this photograph from May 1908 are, from left to right, (seated) unidentified, Marshall Saathoff, Arthur Schlentz, Ernest Britsch (holding the slate) Herbert Decker, Alfred Winkler, and Ernest Mumme; (second row) Katie Winkler, Mary Mumme, Clara Decker, Walter Winkler, Frank Westfall, Anton Reitzer, George Britsch, John G. Britsch, and Lorine Decker; (third row) Alfred Schlentz, Emil Britsch, Robert Mumme, Emma Britsch, unidentified, Mary Saathoff, Amilia Mumme, and Viola Hoog (teacher from Uvalde).

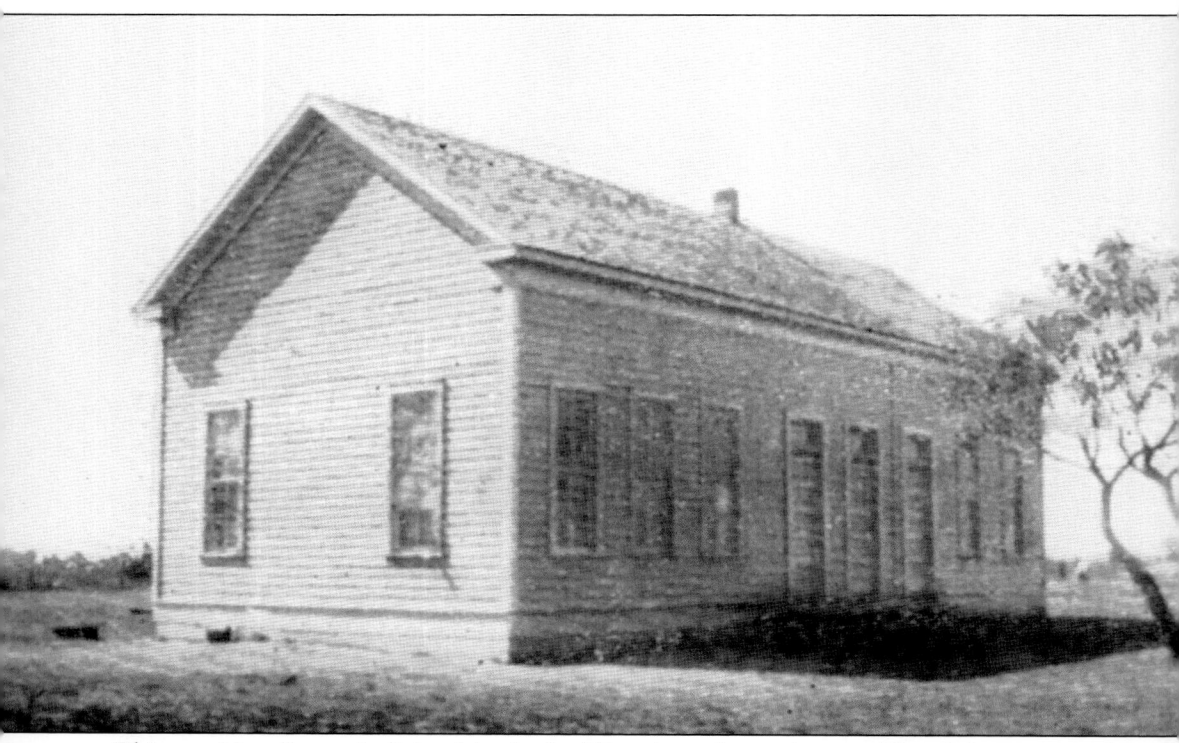

This was New Fountain School in the budding days of resettlement. Elsie Schweers was the principal, and Marie Foster was her assistant. New Fountain was settled because the water in Vandenberg was depleted.

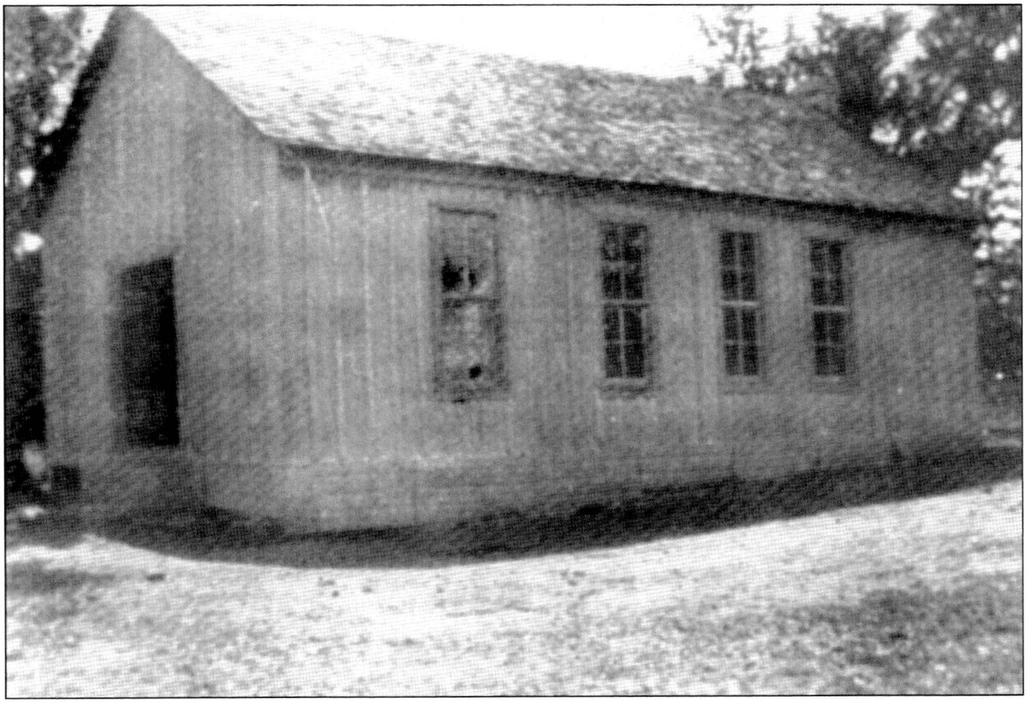

Land around the Rothe School had the best scenery in the county. It was surrounded by canyons, ravines, bluffs, mountainsides of seasonally changing colors, and the richest farming lands in all of Medina. The first part of the school, pictured above, was built in 1903.

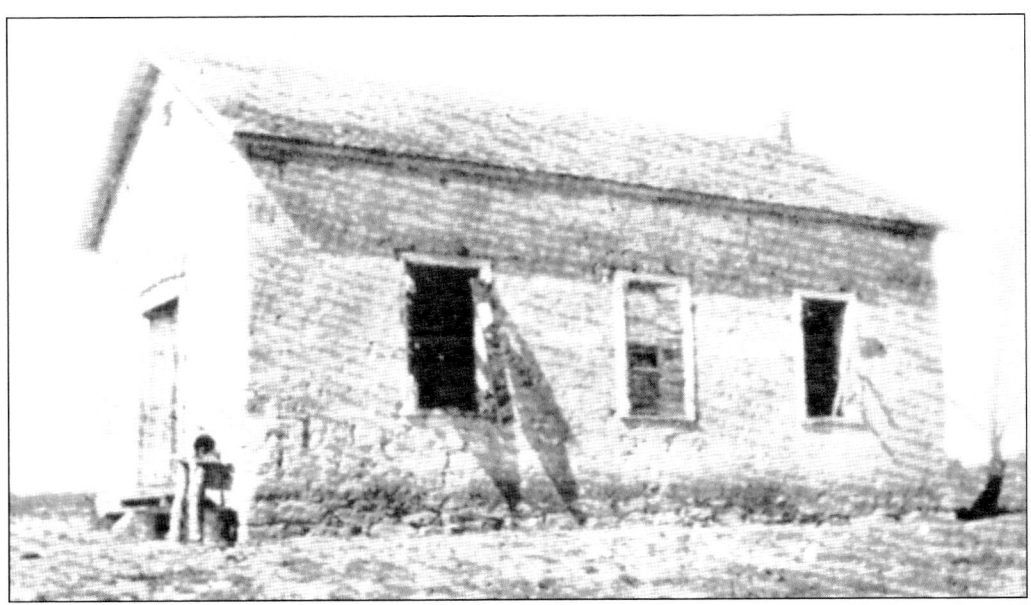

Old Seco School (*seco* is Spanish for "dry") is pictured here. The creek was usually dry and could be walked across on the way to school.

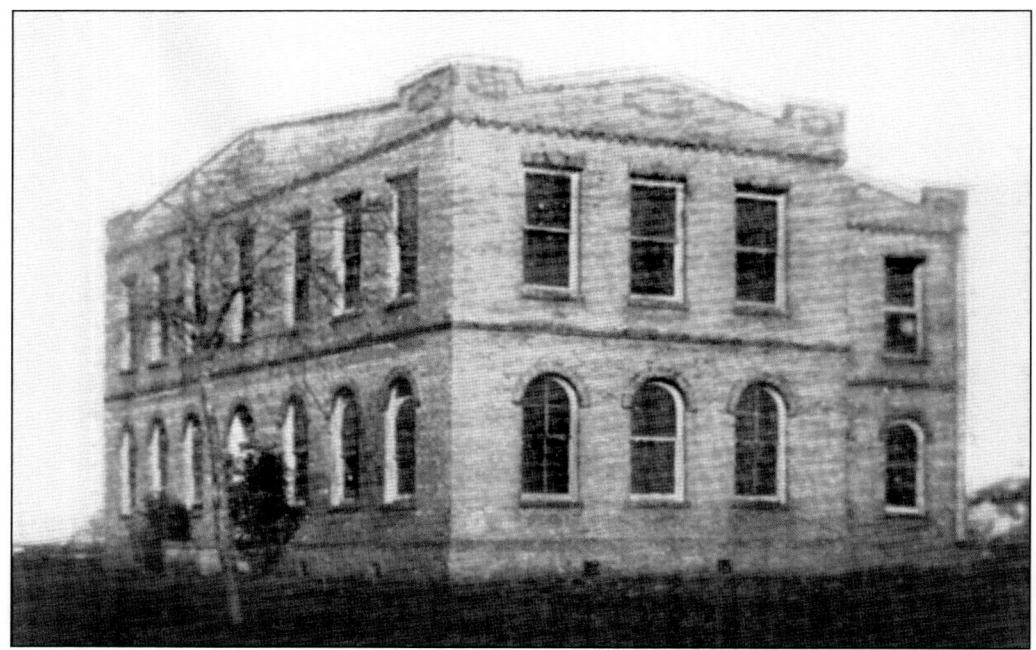

Yancey Consolidated School is in the southern end of Medina County and includes some of the northern end of Frio County. The village of Yancey, with its two churches and its school, lies in a valley surrounded by hills. The community's spirit was centered on the school and the churches. For many years, there were three schools in the community: the Community School to the north, the Styles School to the west, and the Tehuacana School to the south. They consolidated in 1912.

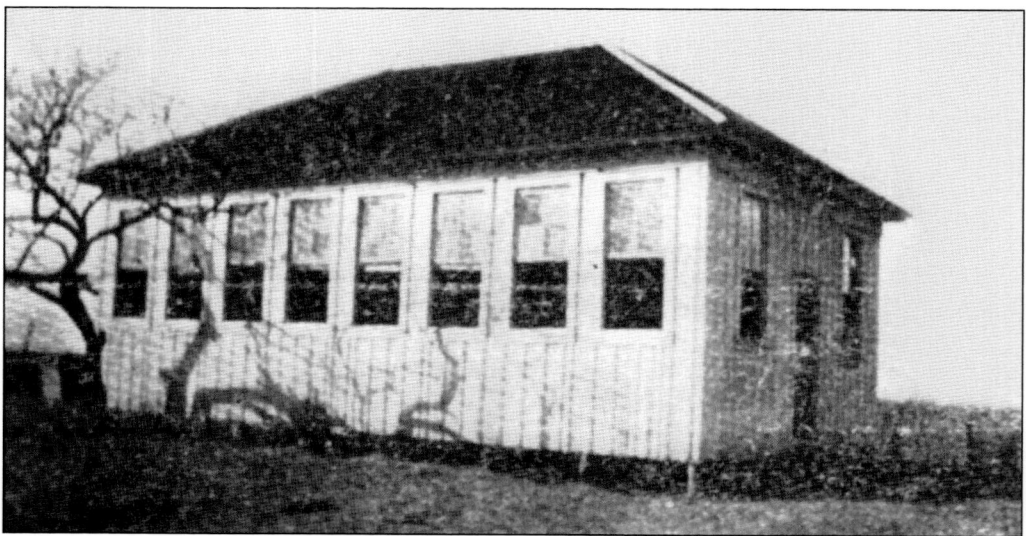

Live Oak School was built in 1907. A piano and an organ were used to teach music. One of the teachers remembers that they taught from October to March so that the students could work on the farms with their parents. The school had no water or electricity. Water was carried from the well, and they had to climb a stile over the fence to reach the school, but all of the students did exceptionally well in their future schooling.

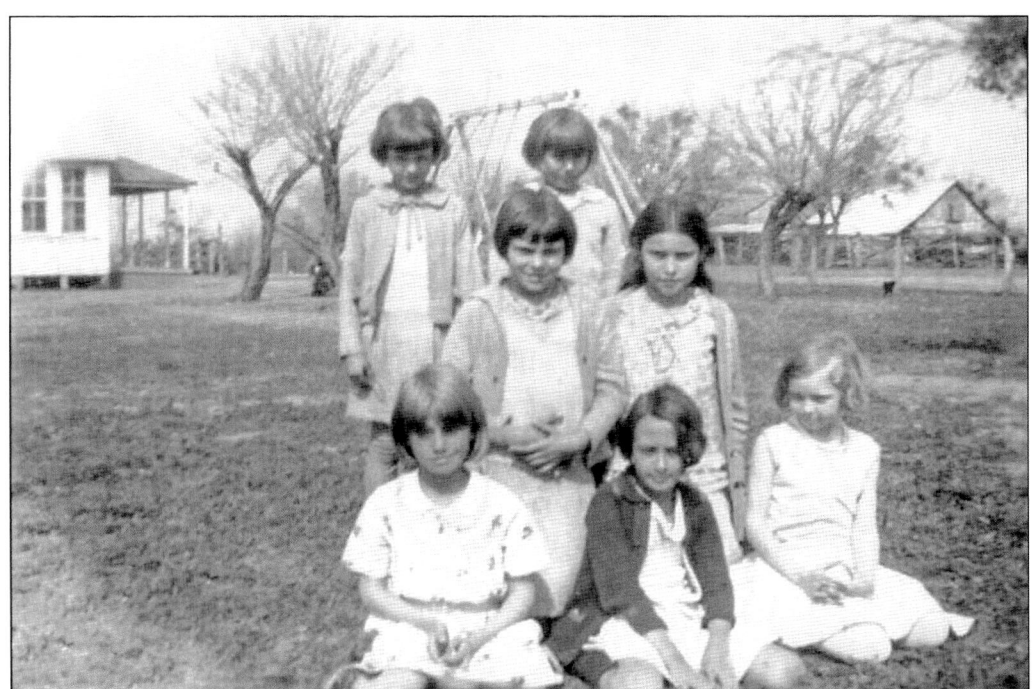

This picture of Murphy School students is from some time around 1920. The children shown are, from left to right, (first row) Lorine Neuman, Darlene Wendland, and Elsie Boehle; (second row) Frances Wiemers and Olivia Wiemers; (third row) June Wiemers and Edna Henrickson.

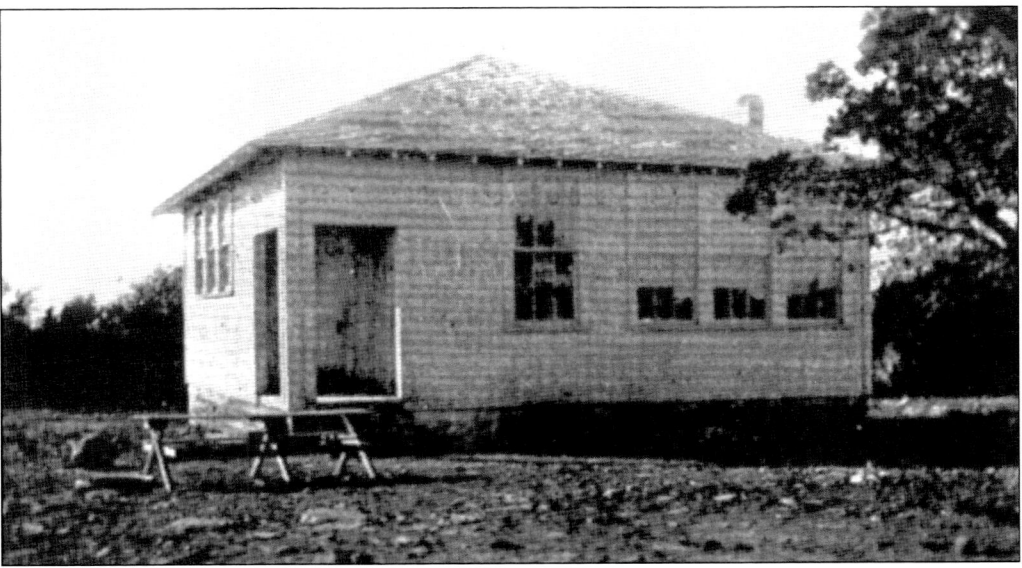

Medina Lake School was built in 1922 on a two-acre plot donated to the district by the Seekatz family. The district was a farming and ranching community—Holstein and Jersey cows were the dairy breeds, while Hereford and Durham were found on the range. The school owned a splendid piano, and public-school music lessons were given to all the children before such lessons became mandatory.

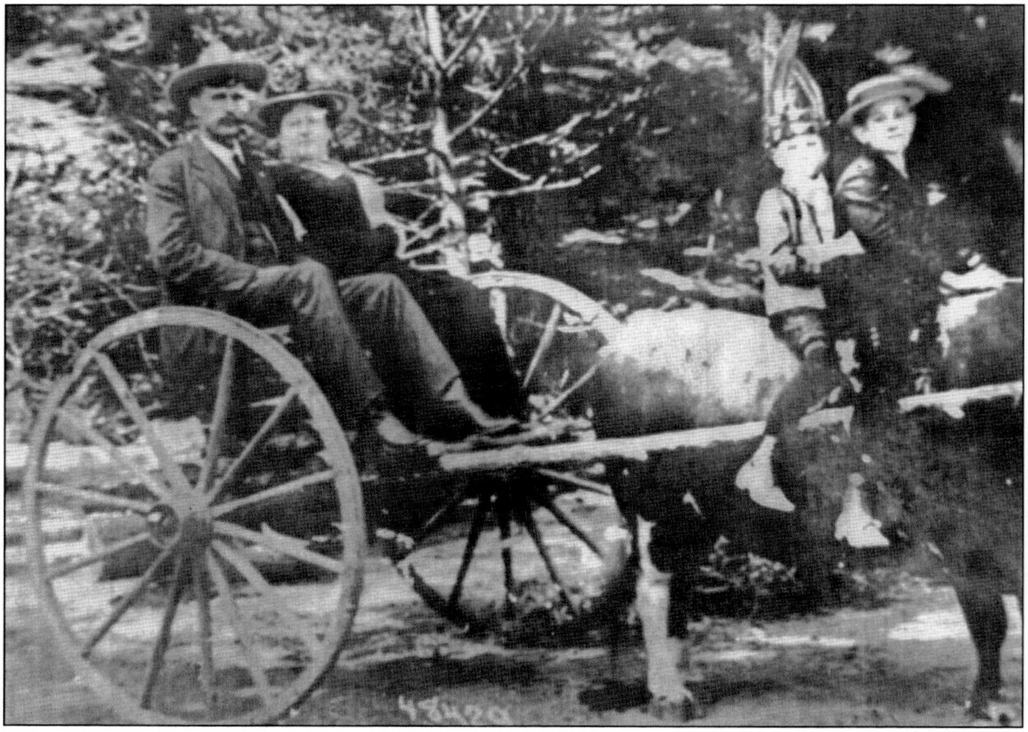

Wagons were the most popular mode of transportation until the automobile was invented. The man and woman aboard the wagon and children riding the horse are unidentified. The second boy from the right is wearing a pretend Indian headdress.

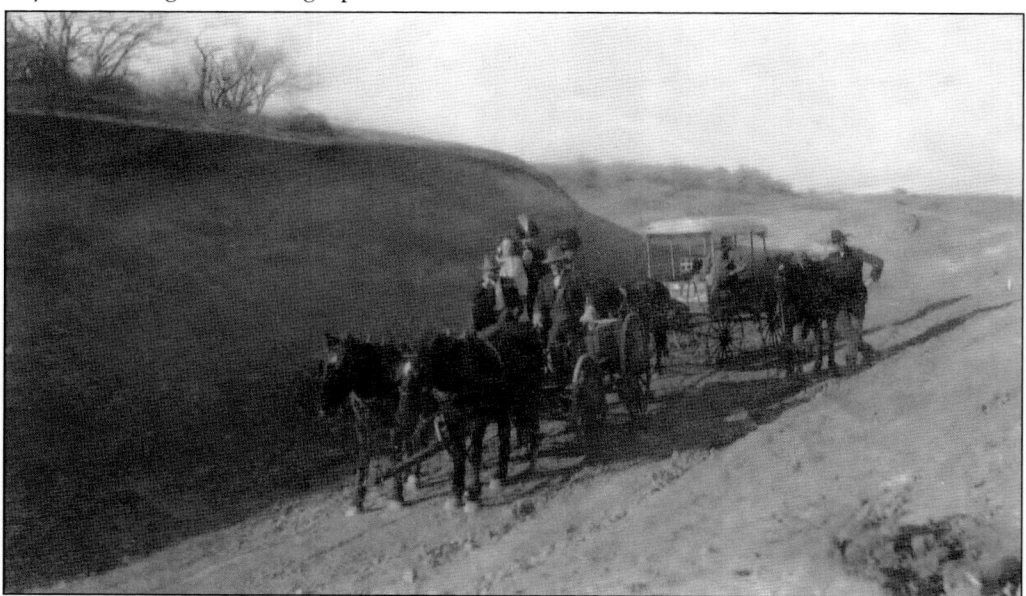

In this photograph from 1800, everyone is ready for the trip from Castroville up the river toward Del Rio. Two men are driving a wagon with two unidentified ladies and a little girl in the back. (Courtesy of Bonnie and Lester Ludwig.)

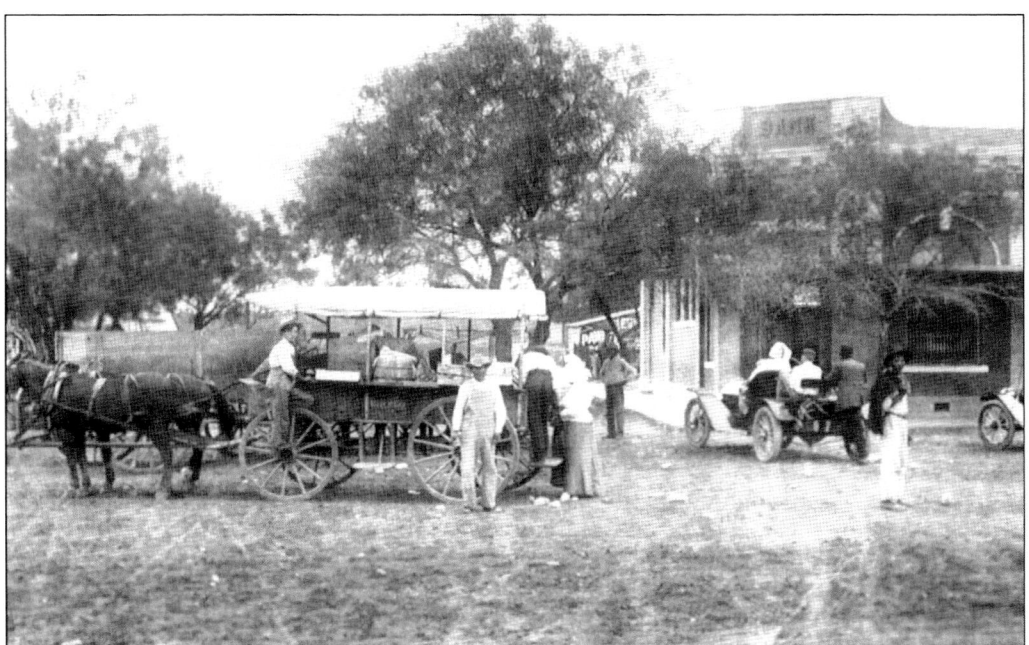

This photograph of the Front Street Bank of LaCoste was taken in the early 1900s. A wagon on the left is loaded with produce that has been brought into town to sell.

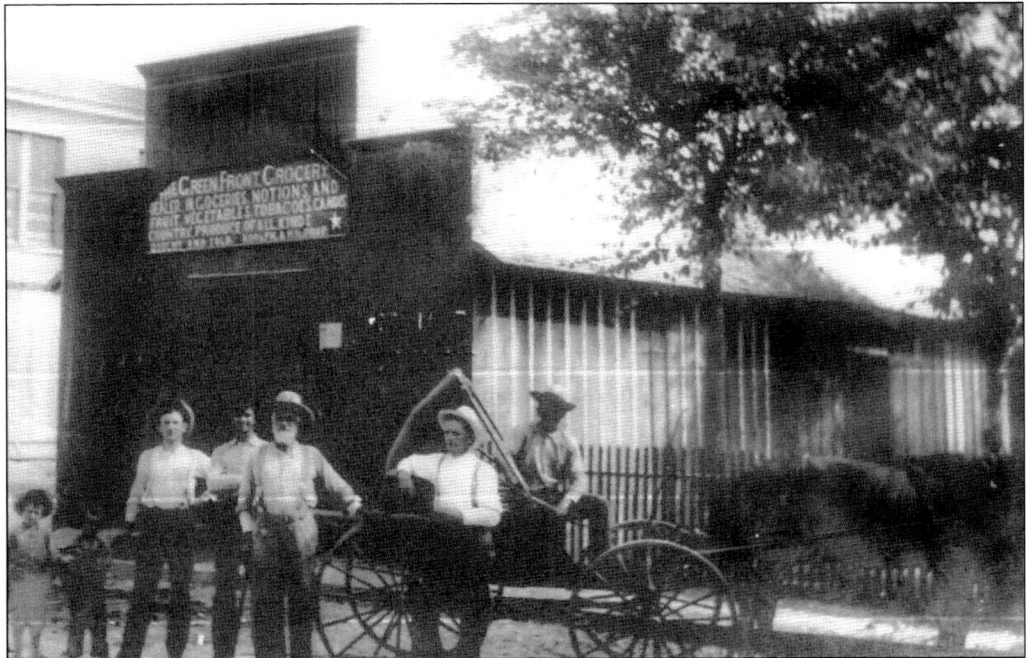

Pictured in front of the Greenfront Grocery Store in Castroville is a group of unidentified patrons. The sign above the store reads as follows: "Dealer in groceries, notions, fruits, vegetables, tobacco, and country produce of all kinds."

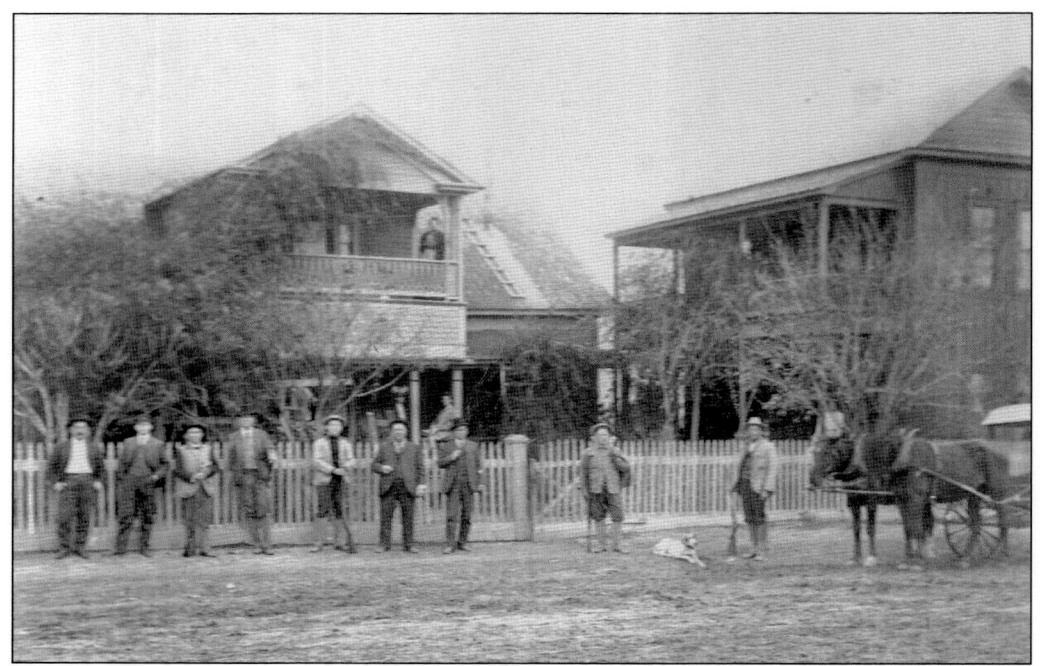

This photograph was taken in front of Rose Lodge Hotel in Devine. A party of hunters is about to leave on a hunt, and friends are there to see them off. The owners of the hotel were Mr. and Mrs. J.A. Whitfield. The first man on the left, holding a gun, is George D. Whitfield, the owners' son. (Courtesy of the Mary and Henry Briscoe family.)

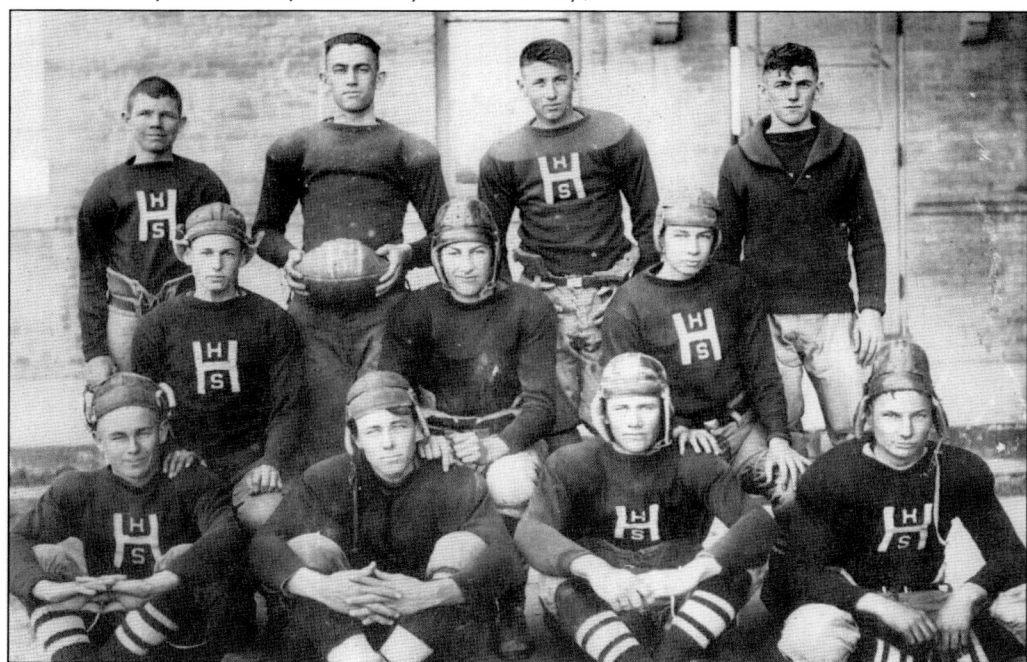

The Hondo football team of the early 1920s poses for a picture. Football games on Friday nights were as popular then as they are today.

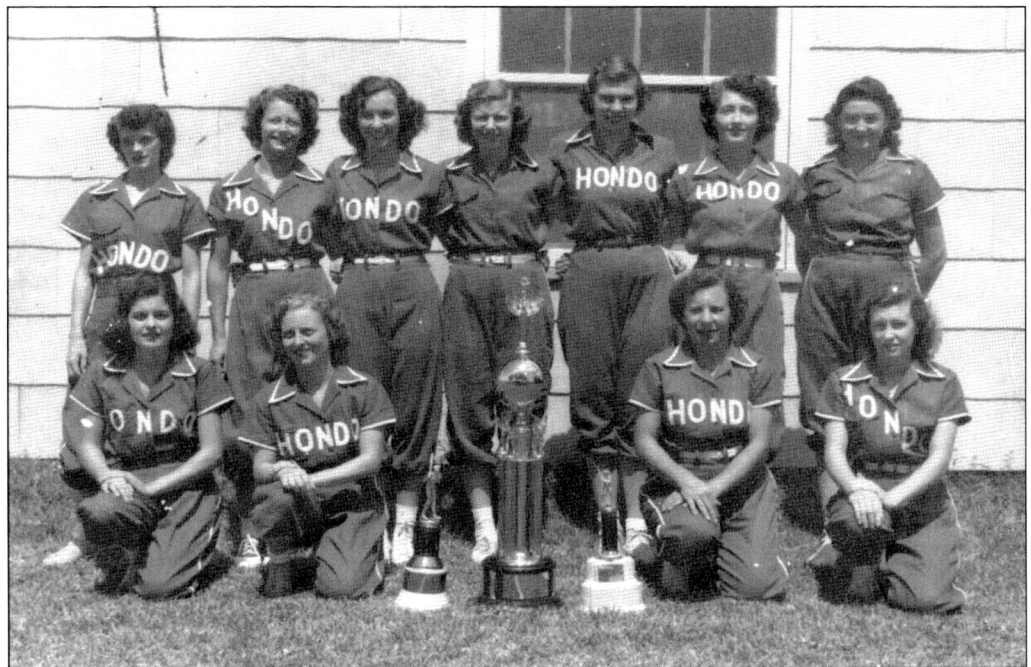

In 1950, Hondo's girl's softball team won the league and made the *San Antonio Express News*. This was quite an auspicious event.

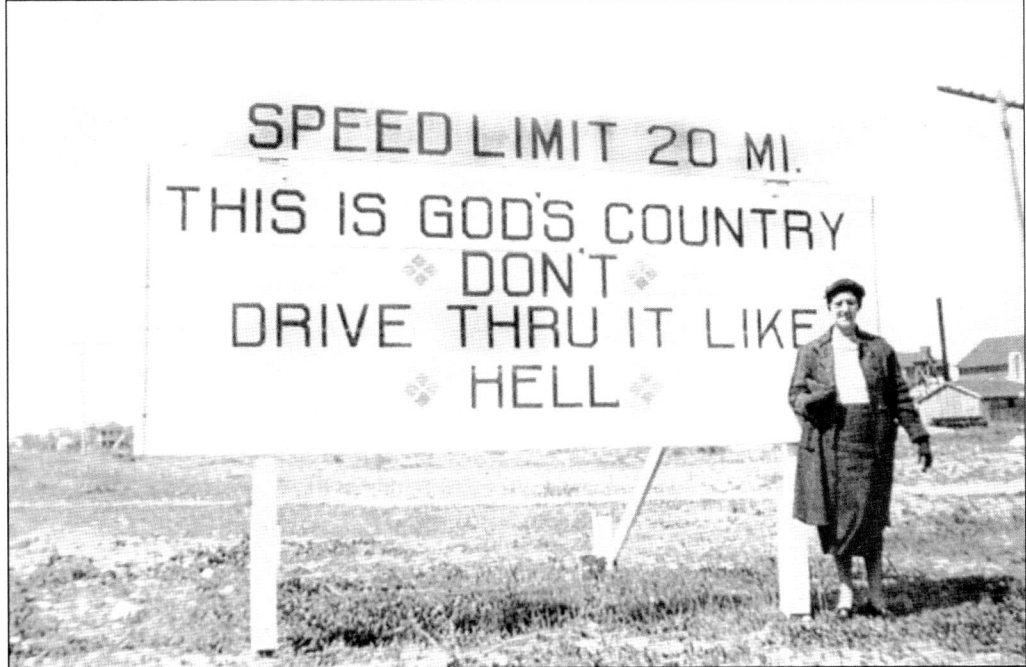

In 1940, this photograph was taken along Highway 90 in Hondo and put on a postcard. A likeness of this sign still stands in the same place. Tourists enjoy having their picture taken next to the sign.

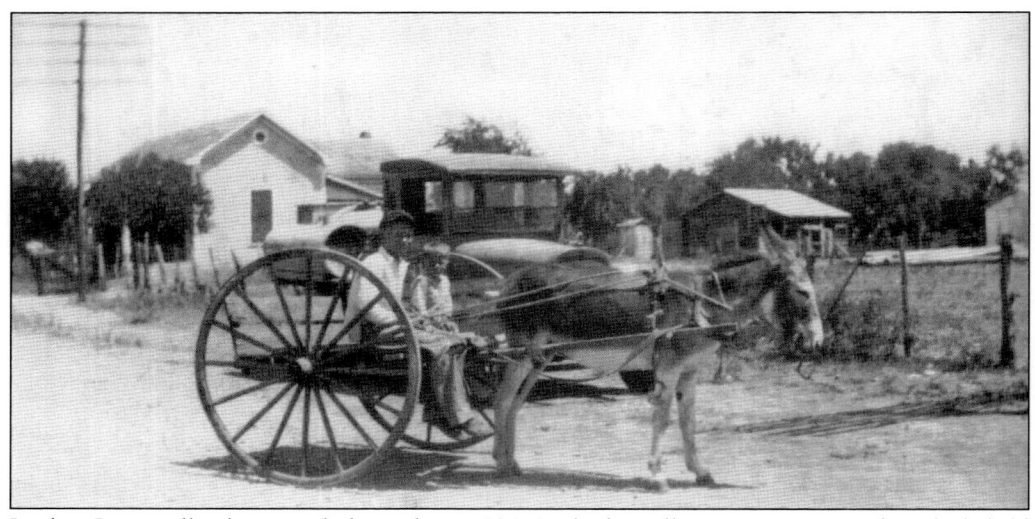

In this Castroville photograph from about 1936, Paul Christilles is giving an unidentified child a ride. A gasoline delivery truck is visible in the background.

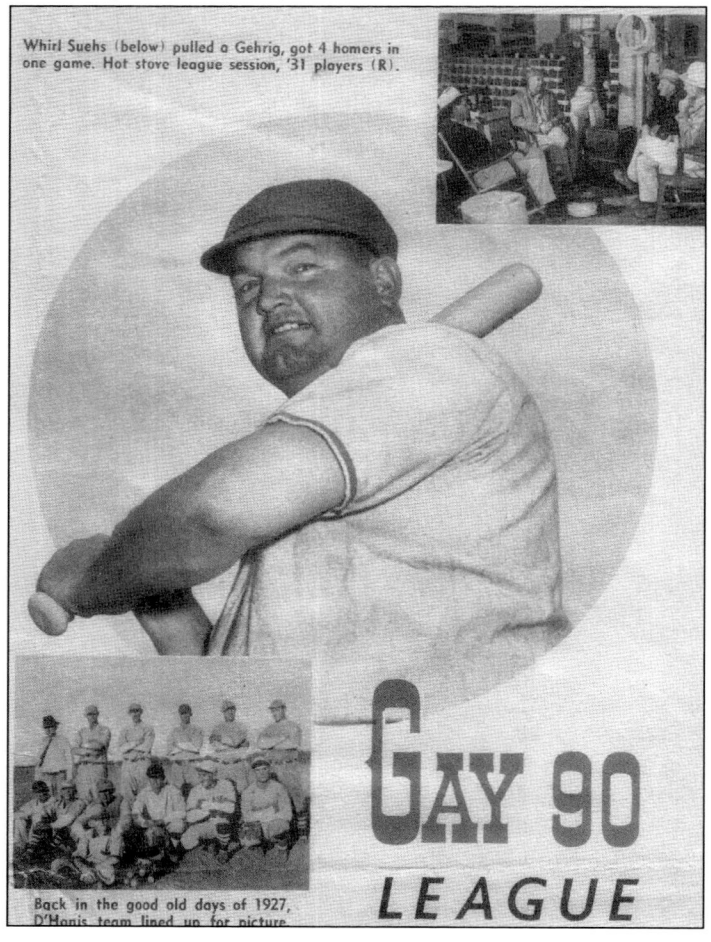

Oscar William Sues, pictured here, was a star of the Highway 90 League, composed of members of Bexar, Medina and Uvalde Counties in 1950. (Courtesy of the Oscar Suehs family.)

Three
Agriculture, Industry, Medina Dam, Golden Medina Valley Farms, Happy and Sad Times

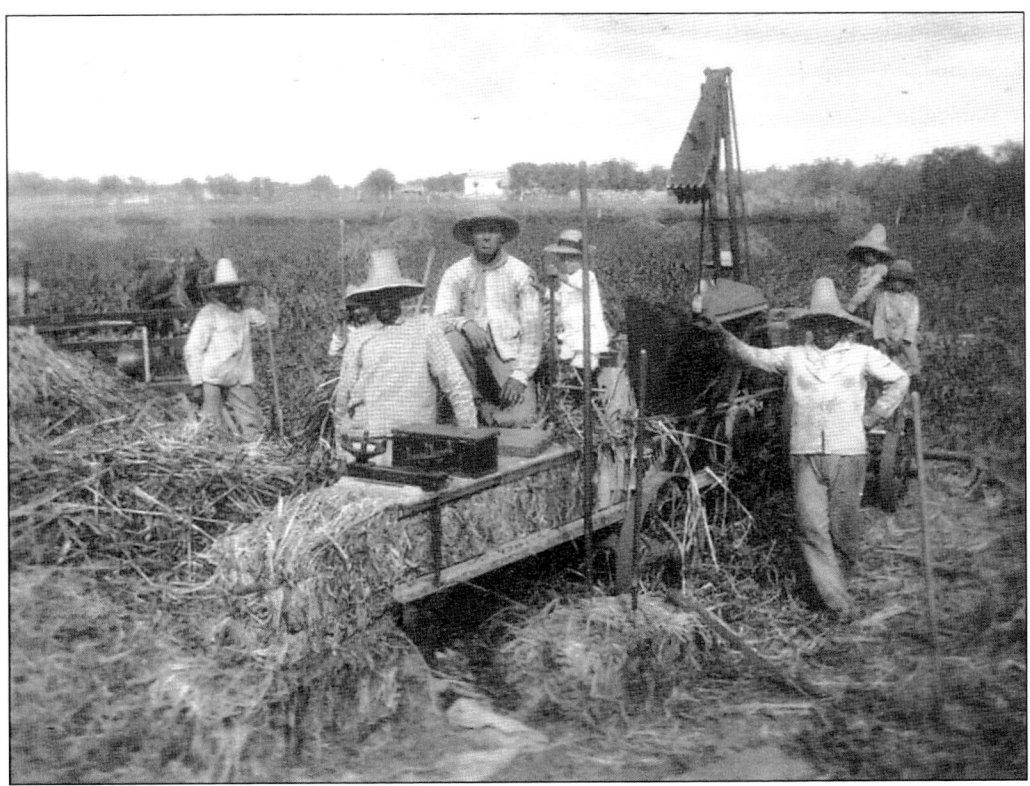

These workers are bailing hay in 1900 on a dry-land farm. They planted the crops, created boundaries of brush fence or trench fence to keep cattle and wild life out, and then waited for rain. Corn produced on a dry-land farm was about 75 bushels per acre.

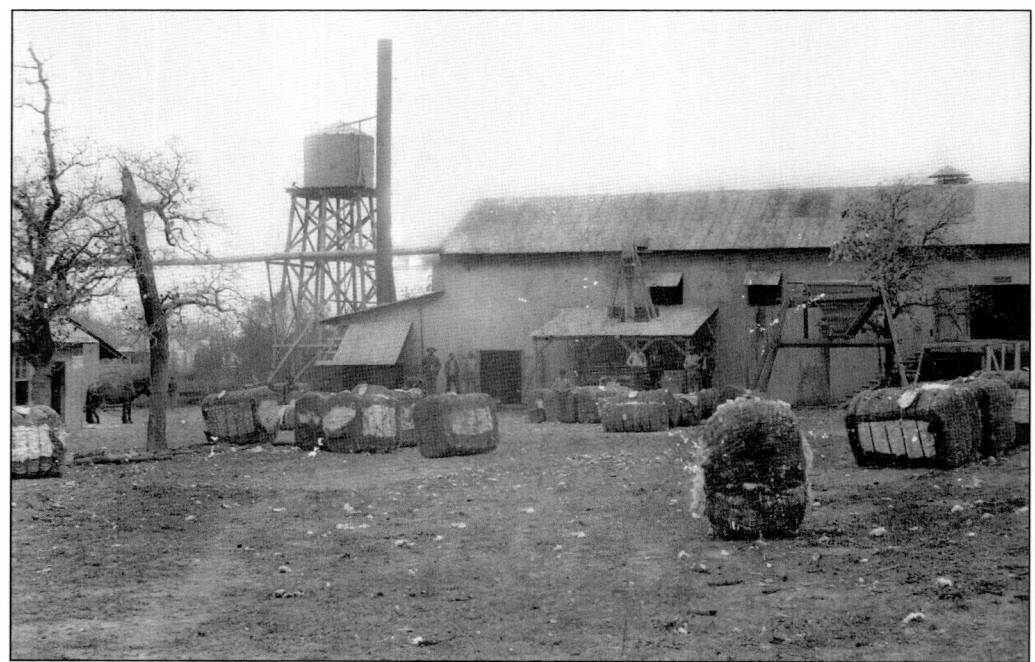

In 1900, when cotton was the major cash crop for all farmers in Medina County, the Courand Cotton Gin in LaCoste was owned by Joseph Courand of Castroville. Many workers came to Medina County from Mexico to work.

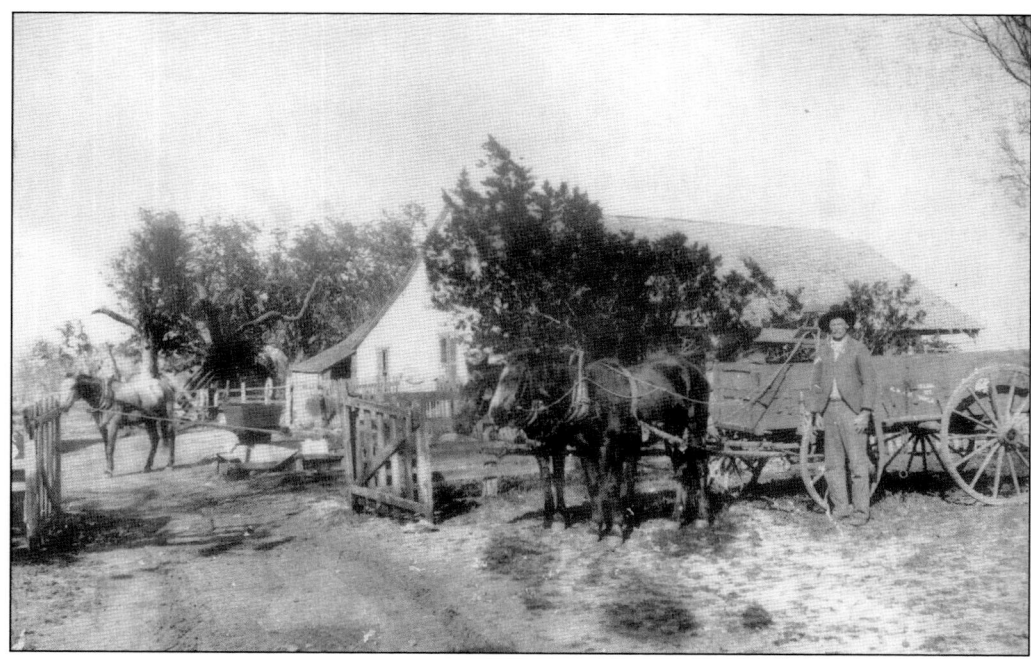

George Heyen's home was built in the late 1800s at Quihi. This picture shows a horse grinding grain for cornmeal in front of Heyen's house. The settlers were innovative in many ways. (Courtesy of Myrtle Schulte Schneider.)

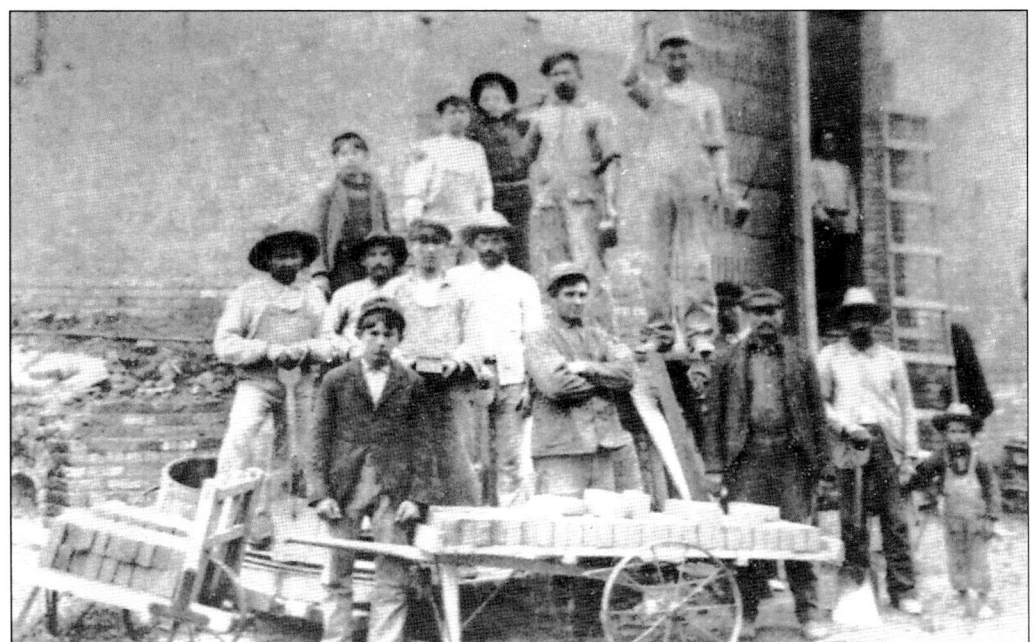
On a hill in D'Hanis, a new kind of clay was discovered. The Seco Pressed Brick Company was started in 1910. The plant shipped products all over southwest Texas. Later, the D'Hanis Brick and Tile Company grew from the banks of Seco Creek. This photograph was taken in 1930 at the D'Hanis Brick factory. The workers were farmers and people from Mexico. Work in the county was scarce, and this factory was a boon to the entire county.

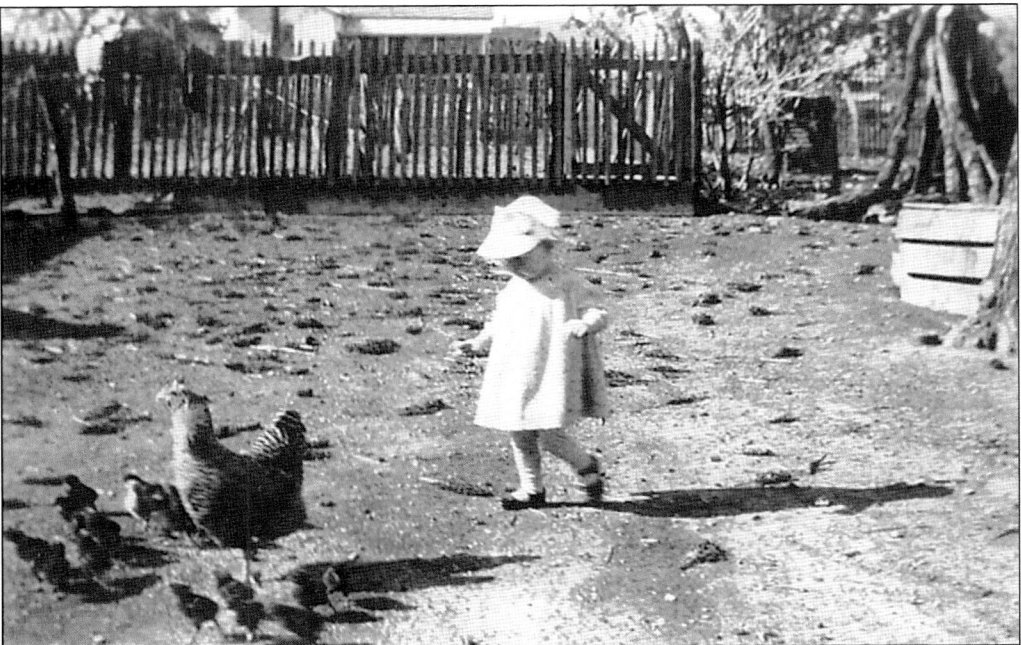
Every farm had a chicken yard. In this photograph from 1904, Percylee Chandler is chasing a hen and chicks in the chicken yard in LaCoste. (Courtesy of Bonnie and Lester Ludwig.)

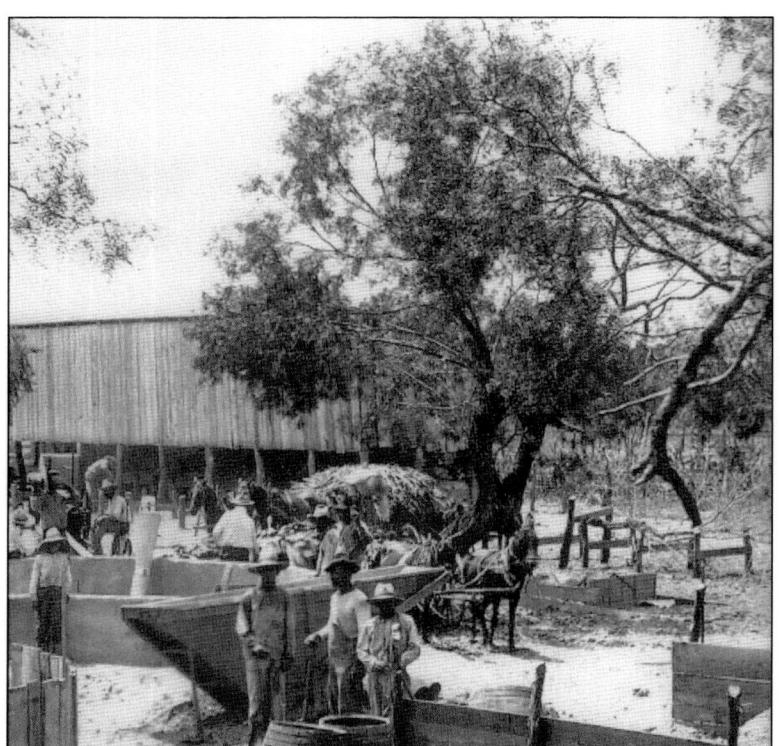

This photograph shows a pit where lime is being mixed to build a rock structure. Most farms and ranches had such a structure. In the early days, cactus juice was added to the lime mixture, and it worked quite well. It is believed that this picture was taken in LaCoste.

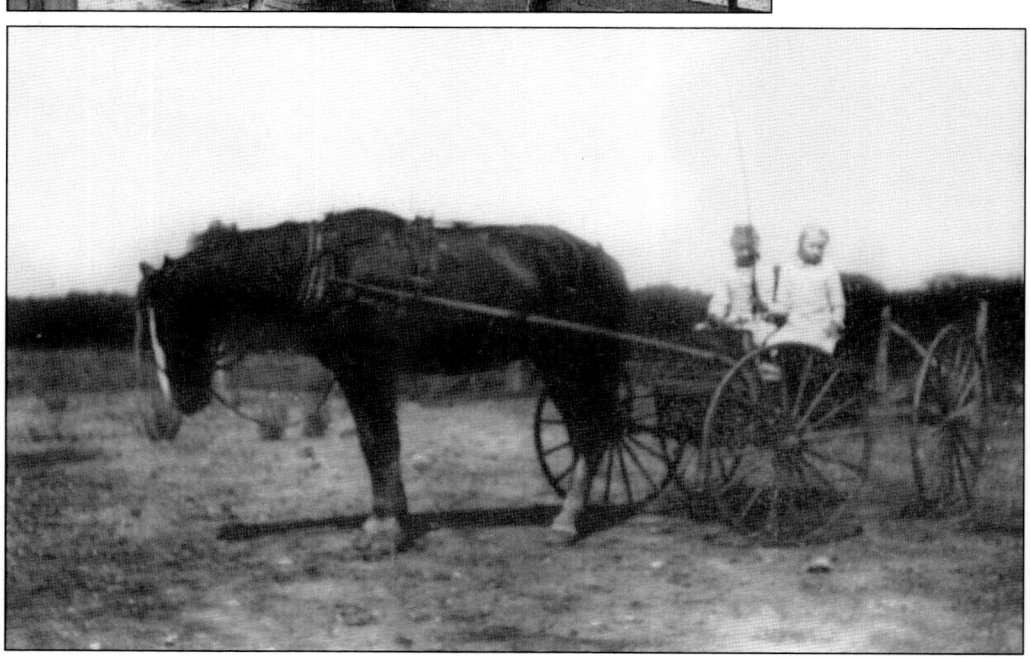

On a ranch near Pearson in 1910, two little girls are seated on a horse and buggy. To the left is Lorine, and to the right, holding the whip, is Oma Kauffman. In those days, this mode of transportation was the only one available if one didn't wish to ride a horse, mule, or donkey. (Courtesy of Bonnie and Lester Ludwig.)

Medina County has a vast reserve of oil, gas, and coal. In the mid-1970s and through the 1980s, many landowners signed leases with oil companies that allowed the companies to extract oil from the land.

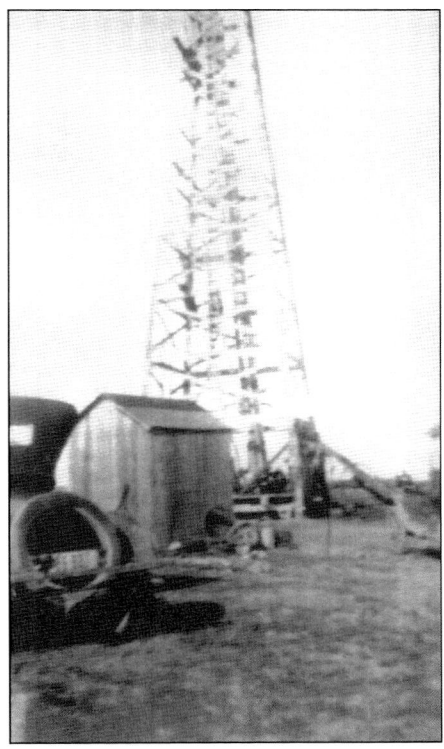

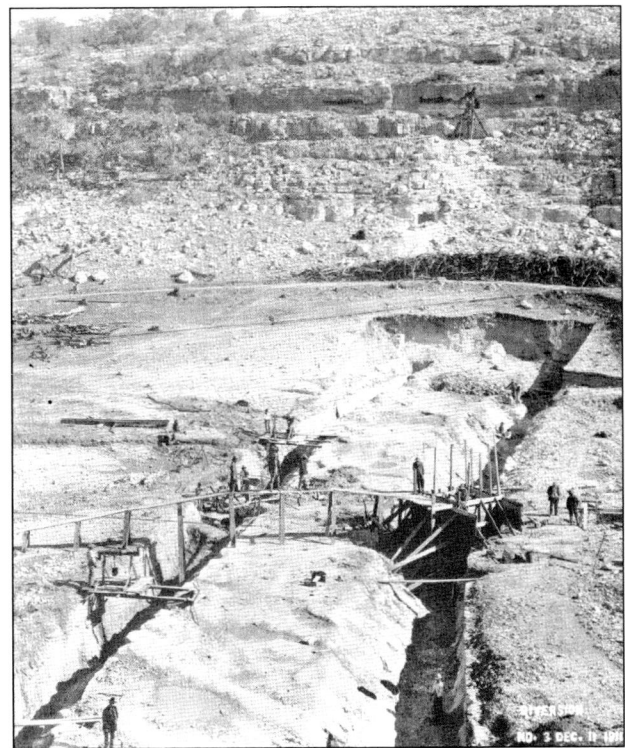

This picture, from December 1911, was taken while building the Diversion Dam. Twenty-three men excavated holes for the pier foundations. Work on Medina Dam started in 1911 and was completed in 1912. It was the largest dam in Texas and the fourth largest in the United States at that time.

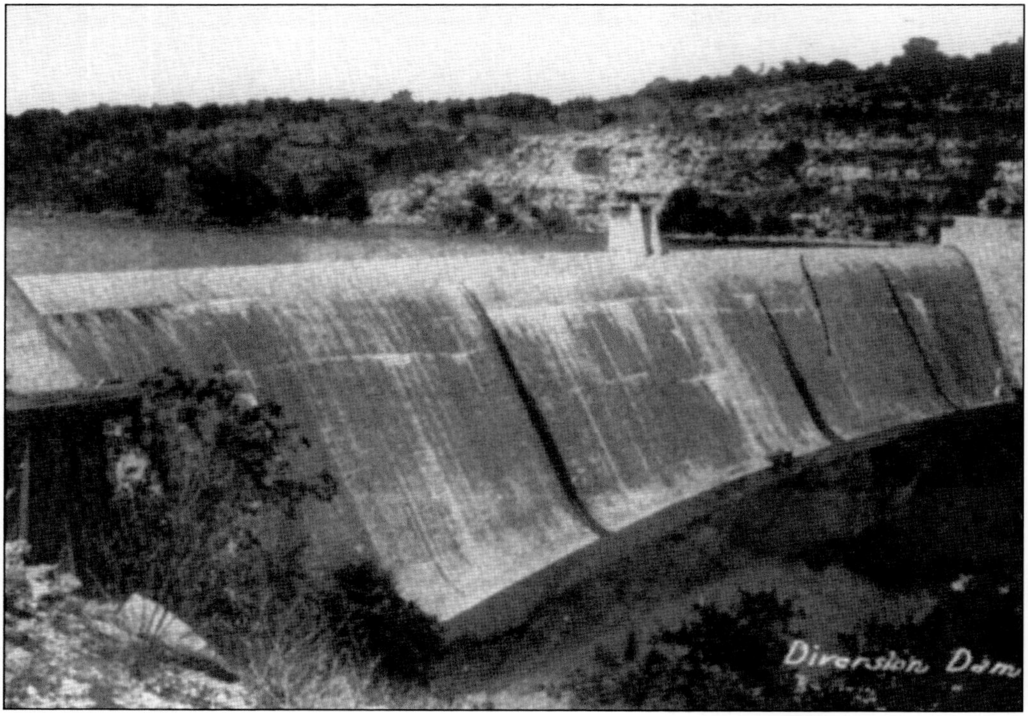

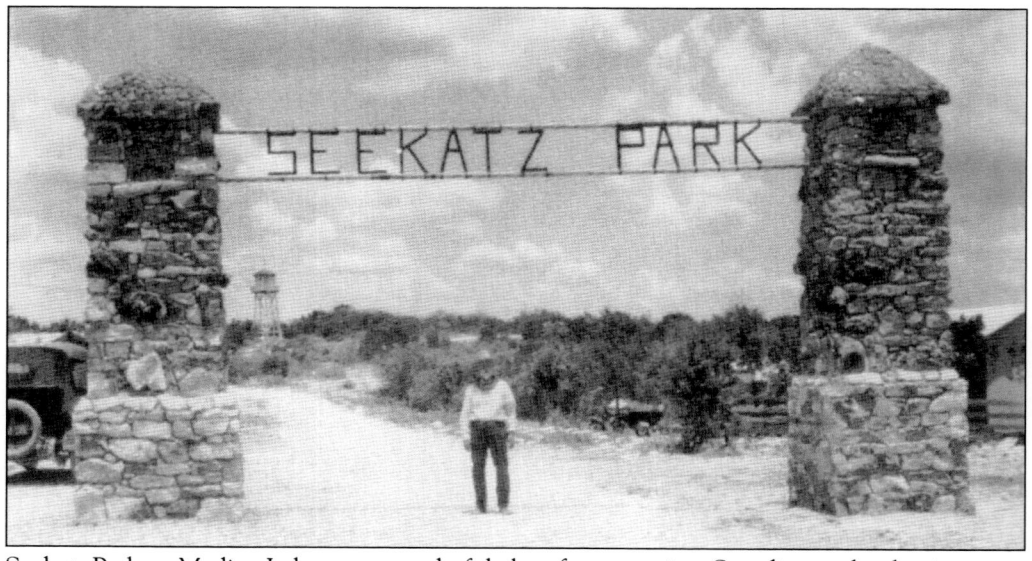

The Diversion Dam, four miles below the Main Dam, is made of solid concrete. It is 50 feet in height, 50 feet in width at the base, and 440 feet in length. Its foundation is anchored into solid rock for its entire length. The reservoir between the Main Dam and the Diversion Dam covers about 400 acres.

Seekatz Park on Medina Lake was a wonderful place for a vacation. Standing under the sign some time around 1926 is Fred Seekatz. Families loved to camp out, but the places to camp were few and far between. It would take Pres. Franklin Roosevelt and the conservation forces of the Depression to build and construct parks for the populace. (Courtesy of Bonnie and Lester Ludwig.)

Many of the workers' families traveled with them to the dam site. Pictured about 1917 at the Medina Dam site, underneath their temporary tent home, are William Collins and his family. (Courtesy of Ruby Vera.)

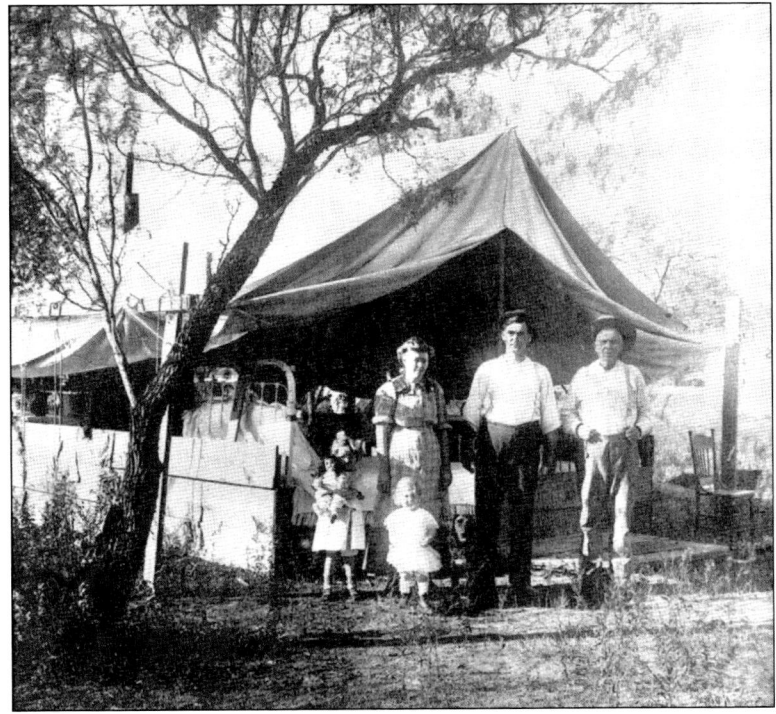

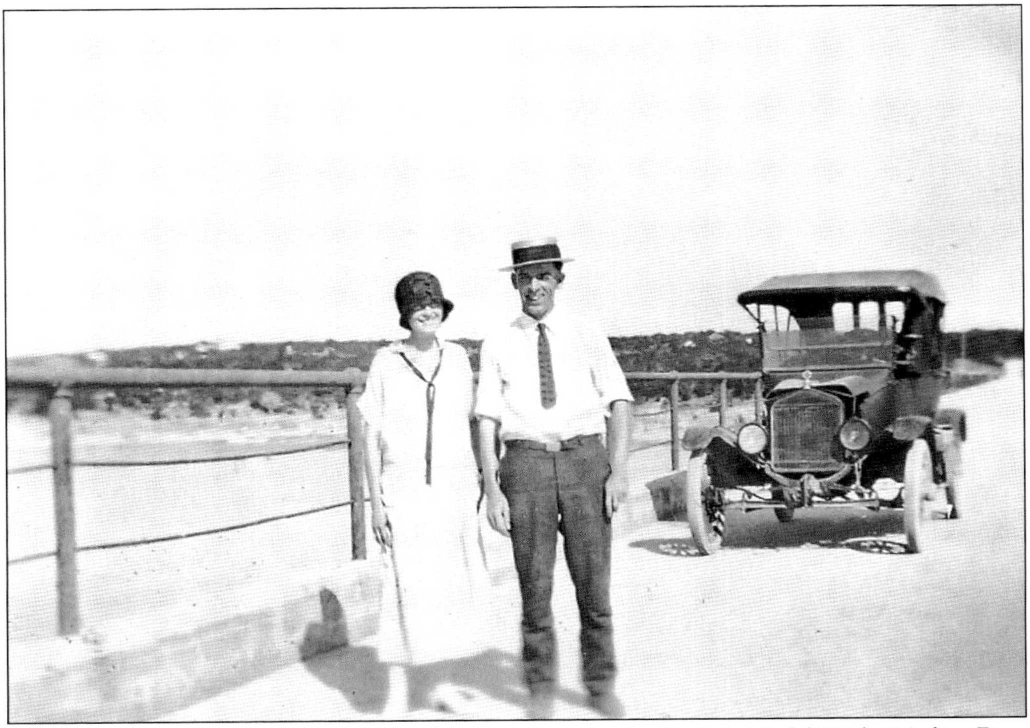

This unidentified couple has come to Medina Dam for an outing in their Model T. The Medina Dam was quite innovative for the time, and people came from far away to view the achievement.

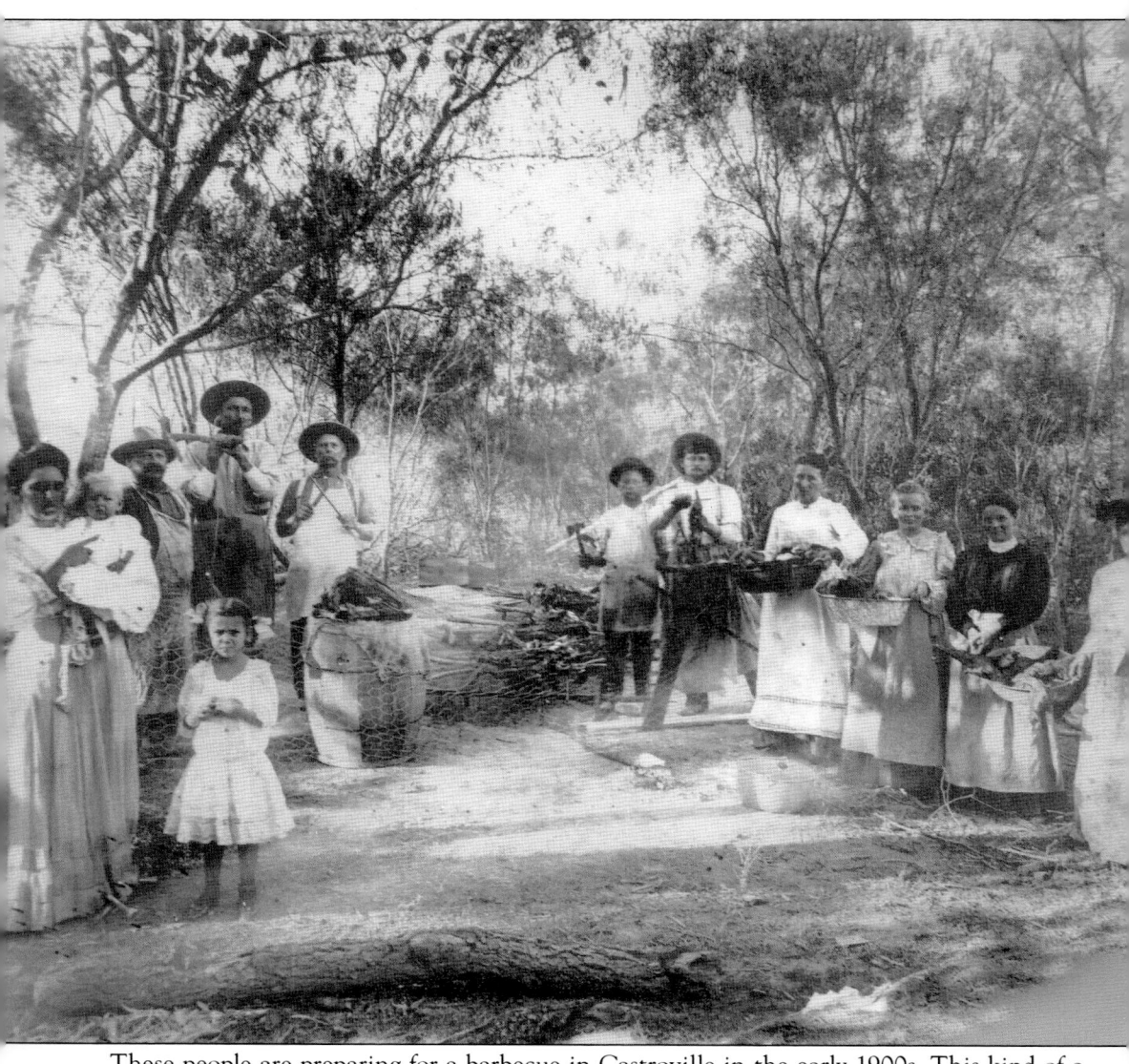

These people are preparing for a barbecue in Castroville in the early 1900s. This kind of a celebration was almost always a family affair. Notice that very young children are included. (Courtesy of Bonnie and Lester Ludwig.)

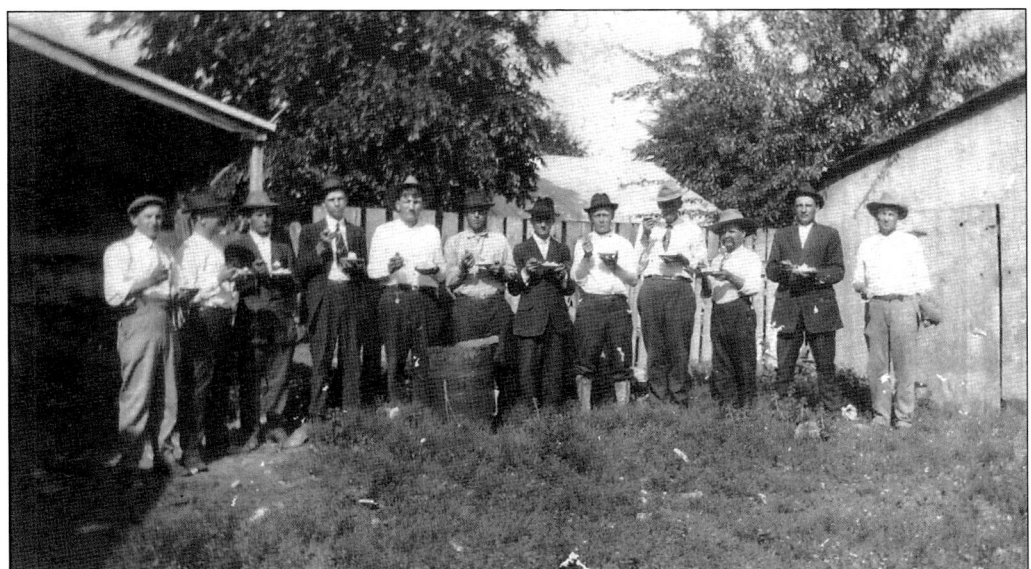

Every band had a picnic. This is Castroville's brass band about 1915. Before this band was formed, there was a band called the Five Hundred Club Band. Many of these bands played in the churches for special occasions, just as local bands do today.

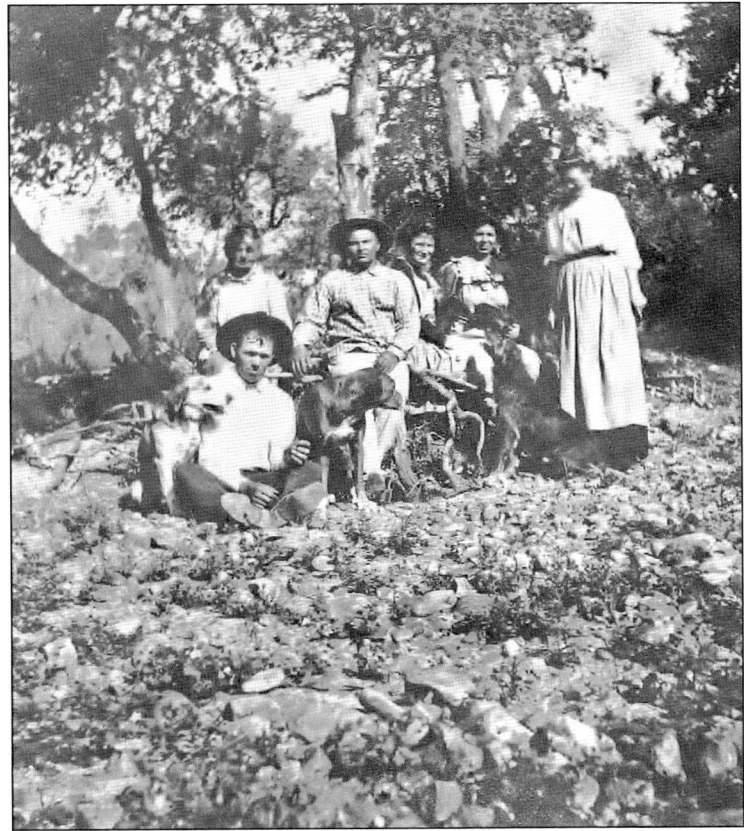

In front, Adolph Ihnken sits with his dog. Behind Adolph are, from left to right, Marie Pichot Ihnken (his grandmother), Albert Ihnken, Mamie Schulte Ihnken, Adella Seekatz, and an unidentified woman. This picnic was a celebration and gave the ladies a break from their wood-burning cooking stoves. (Courtesy of Bonnie and Lester Ludwig.)

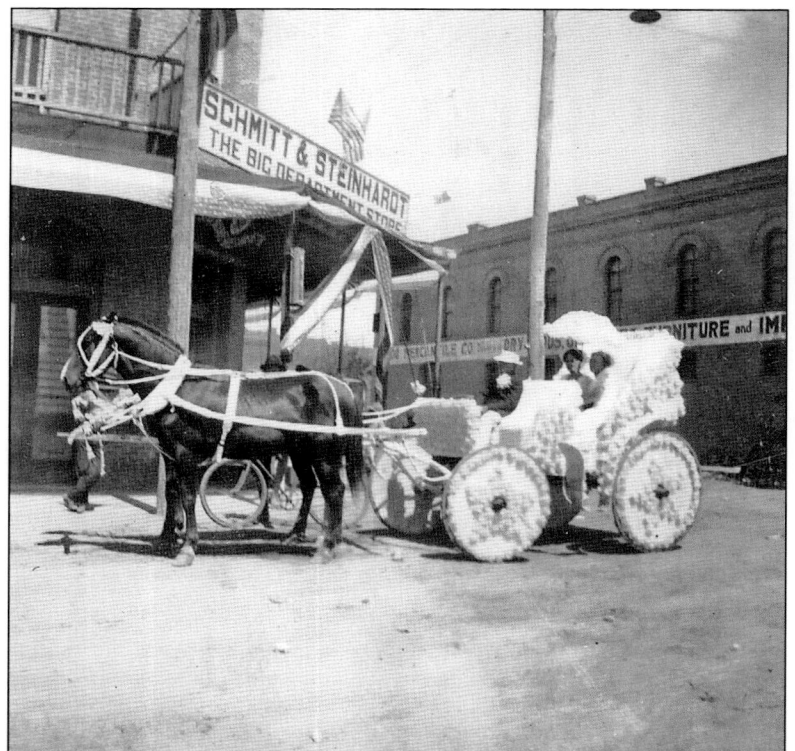

Medina County loved a fair. This picture shows a decorated buggy with a driver in front and two ladies seated in the back under a parasol. Medina County continues to have a yearly fair every summer.

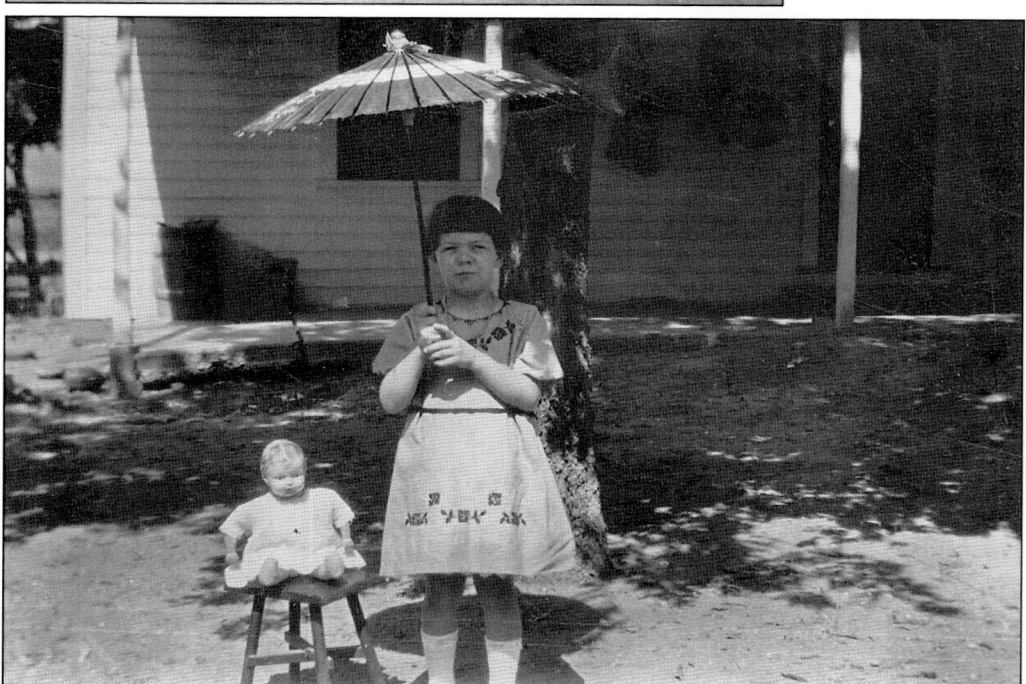

Little Margarete Kauffmann stands beside her doll. Women and girls often shaded themselves from the sun because, in those days, fair skin was the fashion. (Courtesy of Bonnie and Lester Ludwig.)

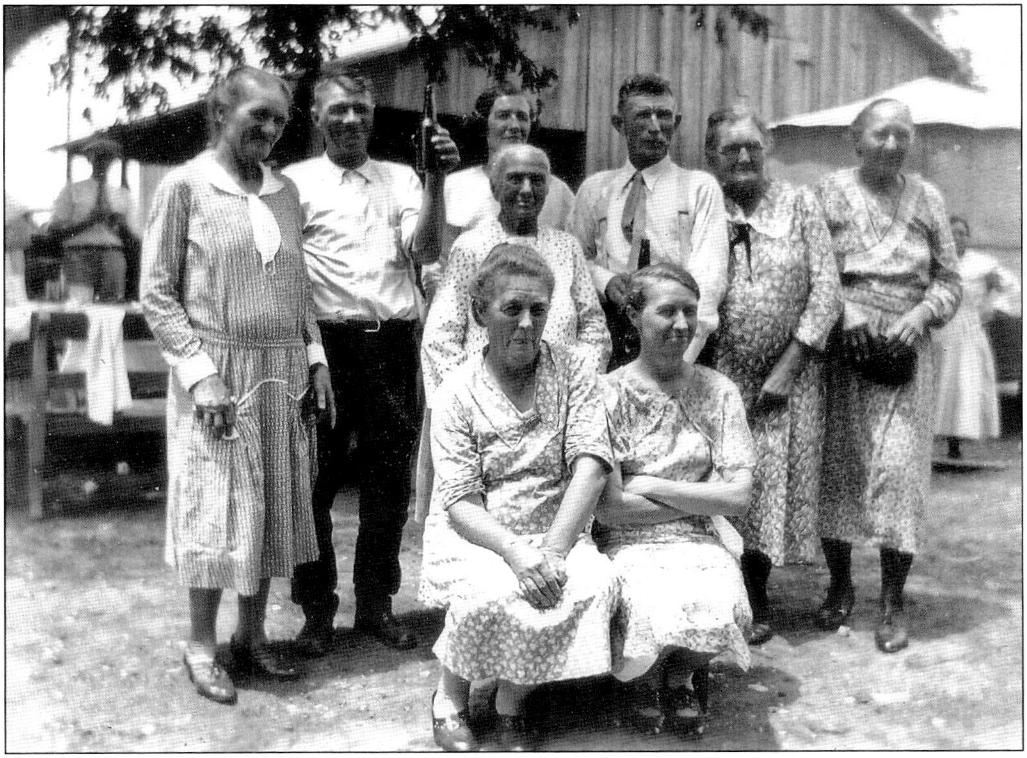

In the mid-1900s, the Kauffman family gathered for this photograph. Included are, from left to right, (standing) Matilda Haass, Henry Kauffmann, Ida Kauffmann, and Joe Kauffmann. The others are unidentified. (Courtesy of Bonnie and Lester Ludwig.)

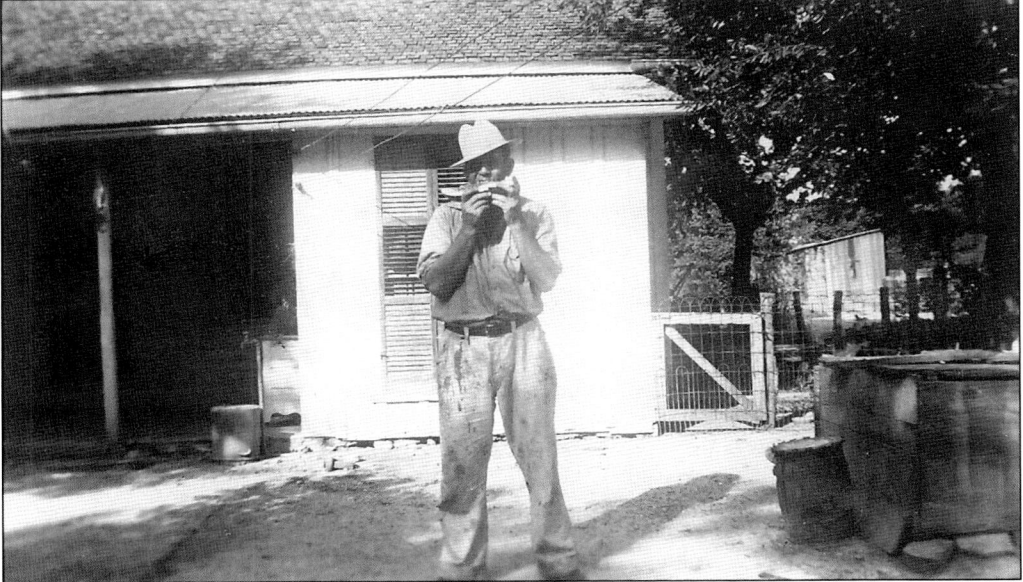

In this image from about 1935, Walter Koehler is seen eating watermelon at someone's yard picnic in LaCoste. (Courtesy of Bonnie and Lester Ludwig.)

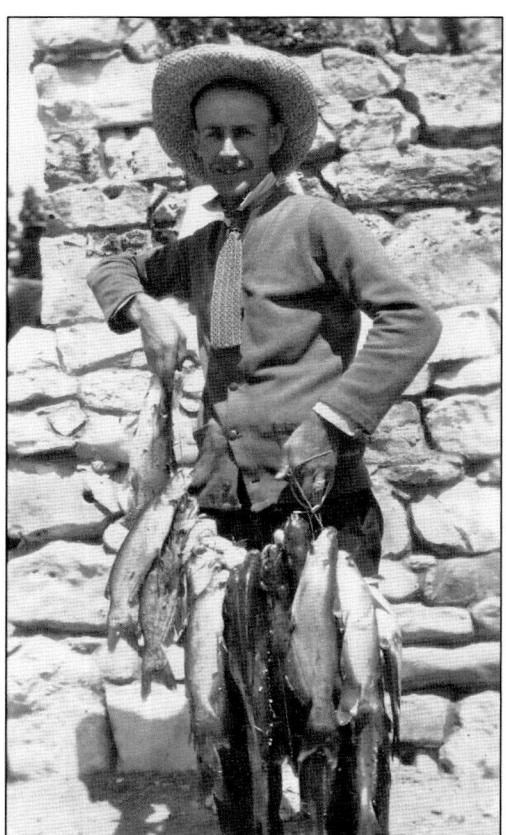

Fred Seekatz had great day fishing in Medina Lake. It looks like 13 fish were caught. Medina Lake continues to offer great fishing to all who will wet a hook. (Courtesy of Bonnie and Lester Ludwig.)

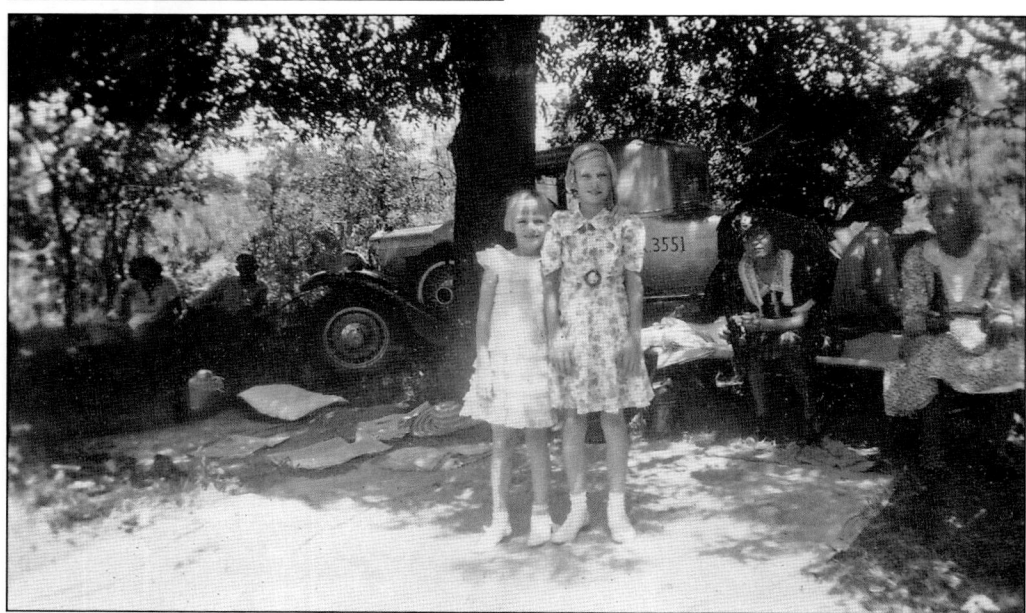

Two little Chandler girls stand in the yard of a farm in 1907. A wrecker truck of the age is parked behind the tree. (Courtesy of Bonnie and Lester Ludwig.)

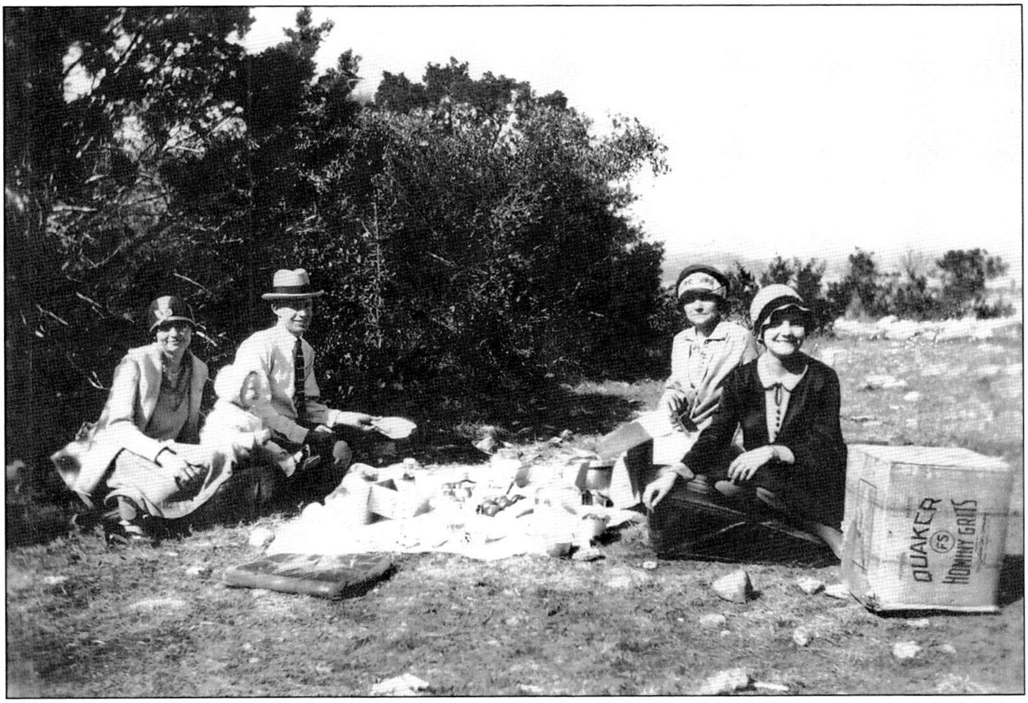

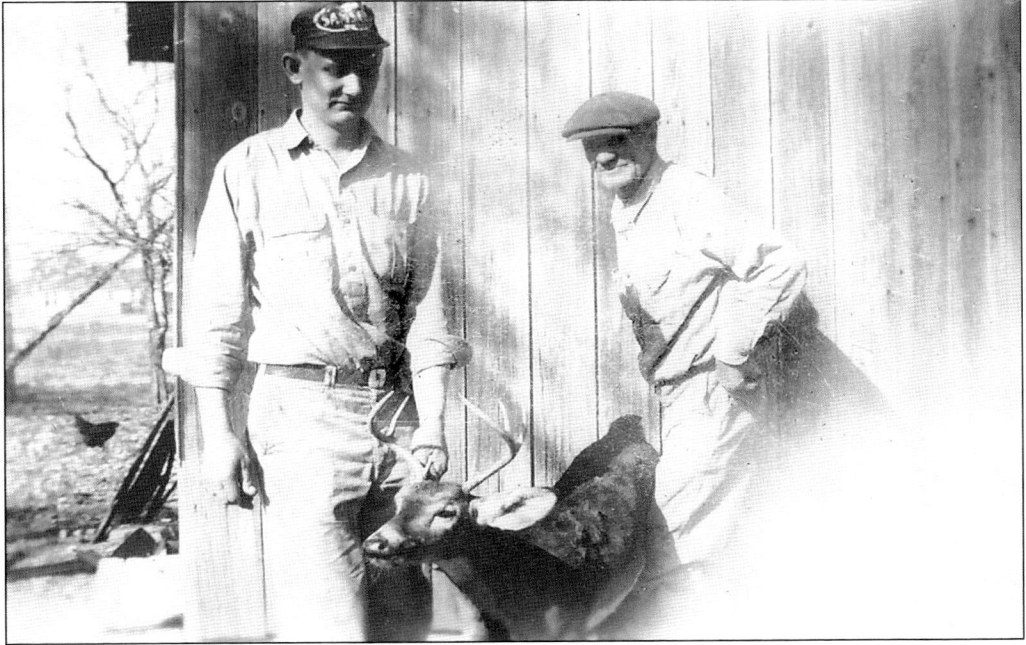

These folks are well dressed for a picnic in the early 1900s. A Quaker Oaks box appears to be the way food and goods for the picnic were transported.

Hunting native game has always been a welcome sport for farmers and ranchers. Hunting provided meat for the table. In this picture from 1930, Hugo Adam and Henry Kauffman show the deer they felled. (Courtesy of Bonnie and Lester Ludwig.)

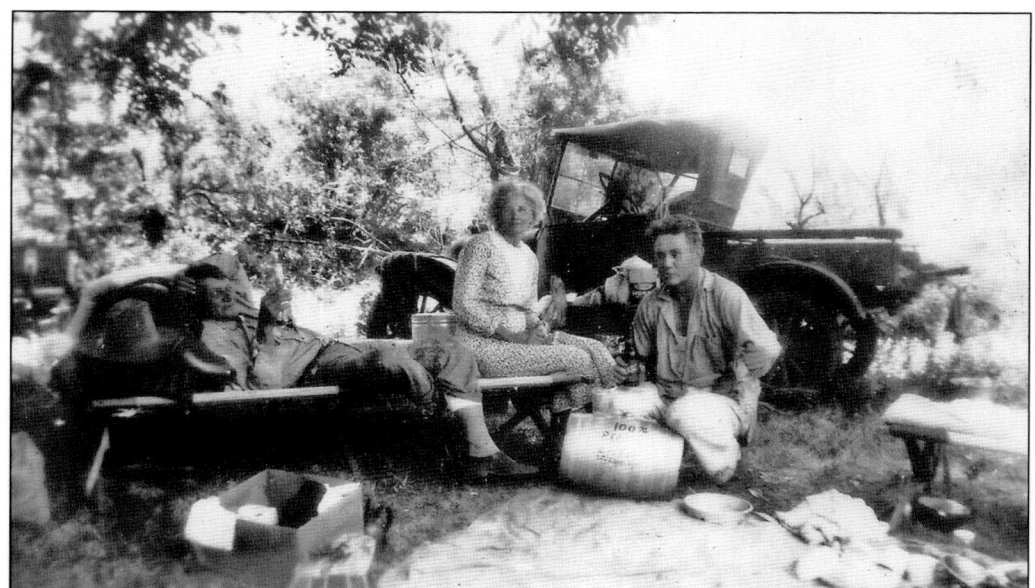

Pictured camping out on their land are Mollie and Henry Kauffman in June 1936. Notice the truck behind the couple. The man lying on the cot is unidentified. (Courtesy of Bonnie and Lester Ludwig.)

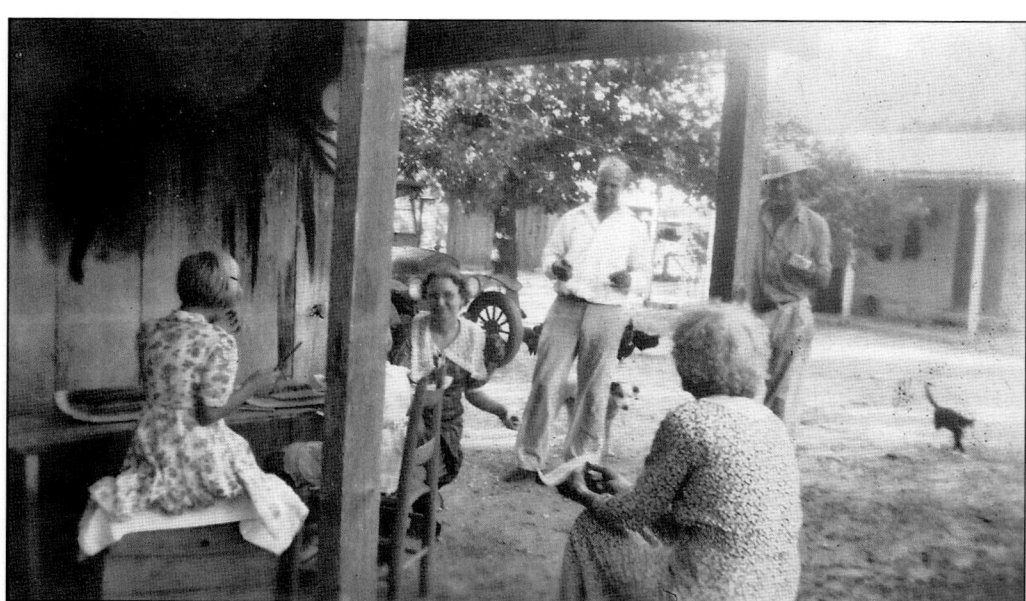

Seen enjoying watermelon about 1936 are, from left to right, Percylee Chandler, Lorine Chandler, Percey Chandler, and an unidentified gentleman. Seated on the right is Yvonne Chandler. (Courtesy of Bonnie and Lester Ludwig.)

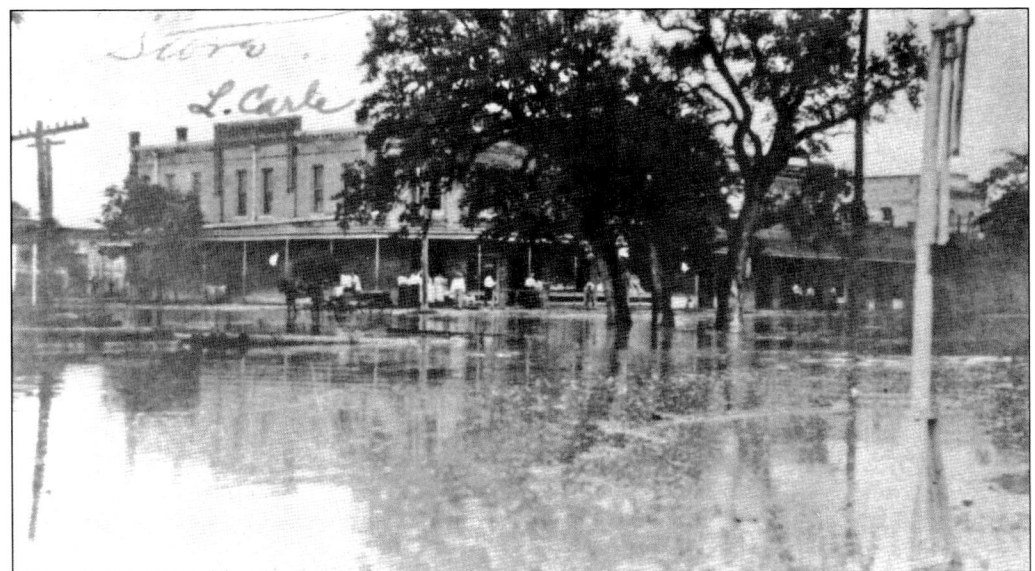

The flood in D'Hanis in 1935 did a lot of damage. The old hanging tree can be seen on the far right. This scene (without the water) can be viewed in D'Hanis today, just on the right side of the railroad tracks and Highway 90 West.

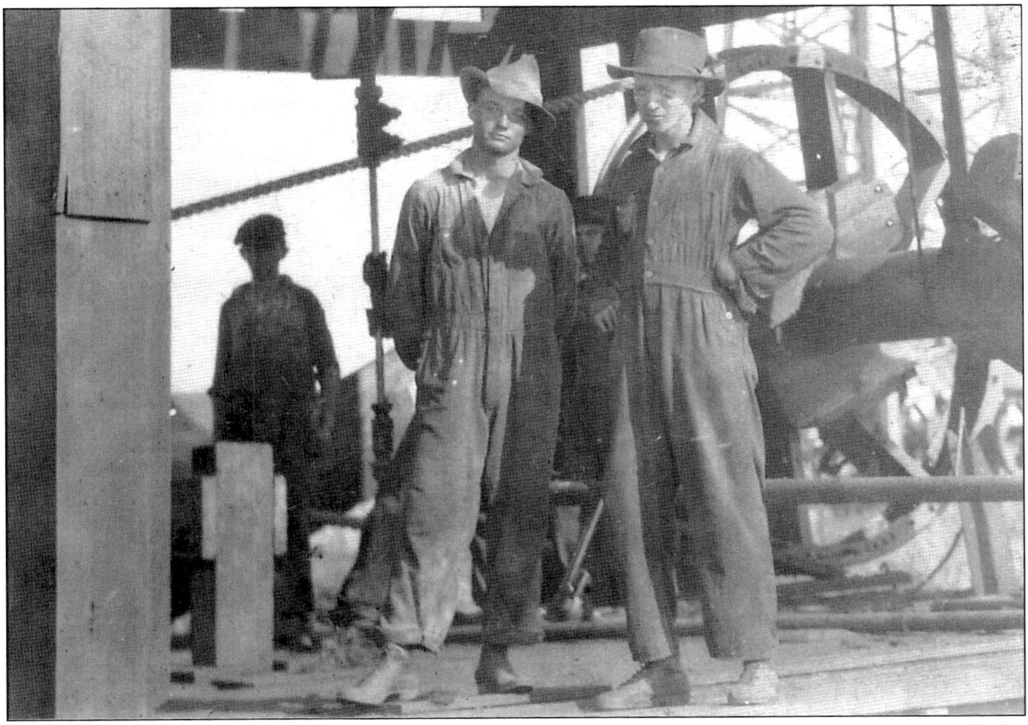

The oil fields of Texas and in much of the nation drew many workers from around the states. Pictured are two workers, Ernest Brown (left) and Bob Brown of Devine. (Courtesy of Laurel D'Osogna.)

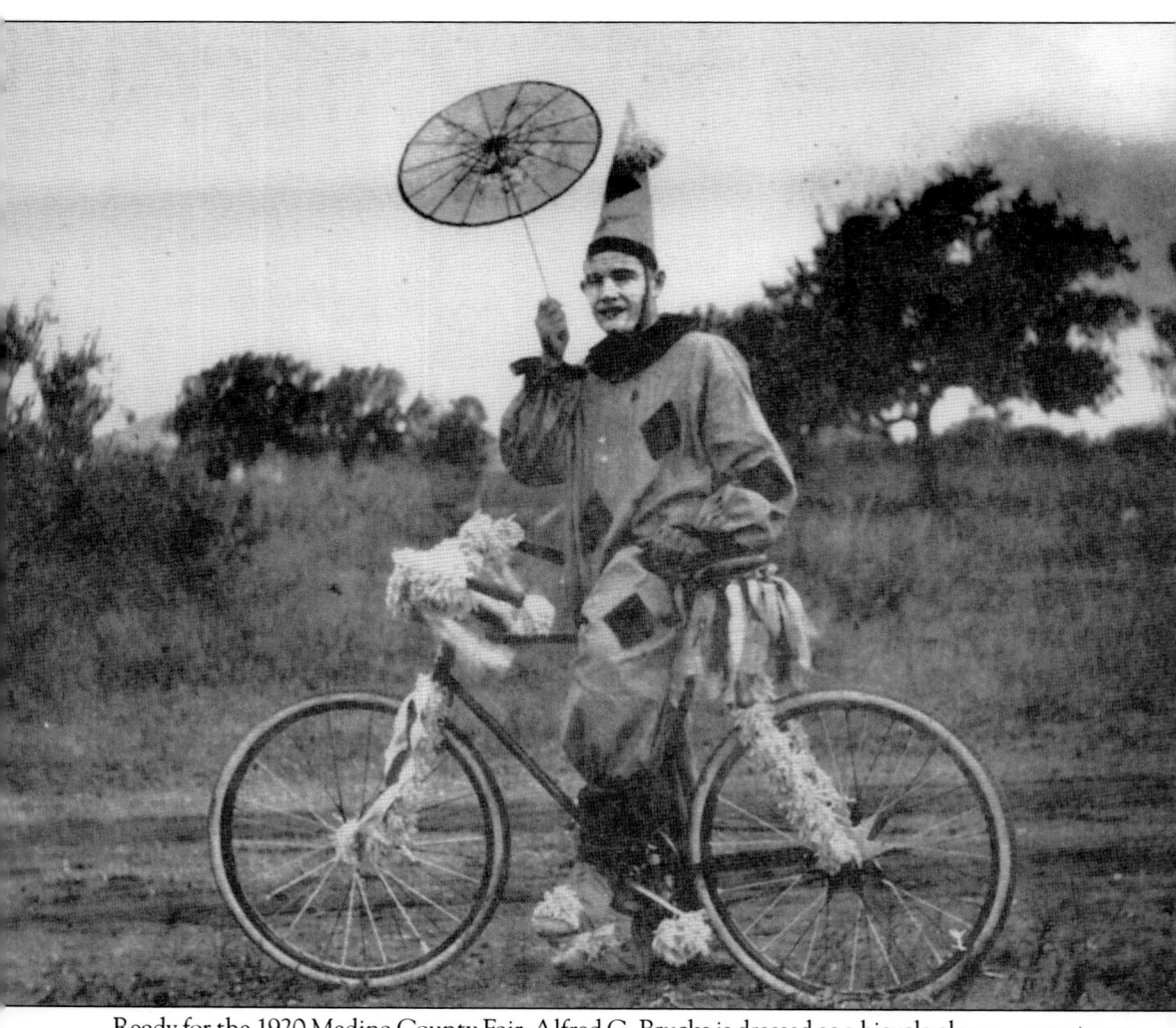
Ready for the 1920 Medina County Fair, Alfred G. Brucks is dressed as a bicycle clown—a costume to be admired any day!

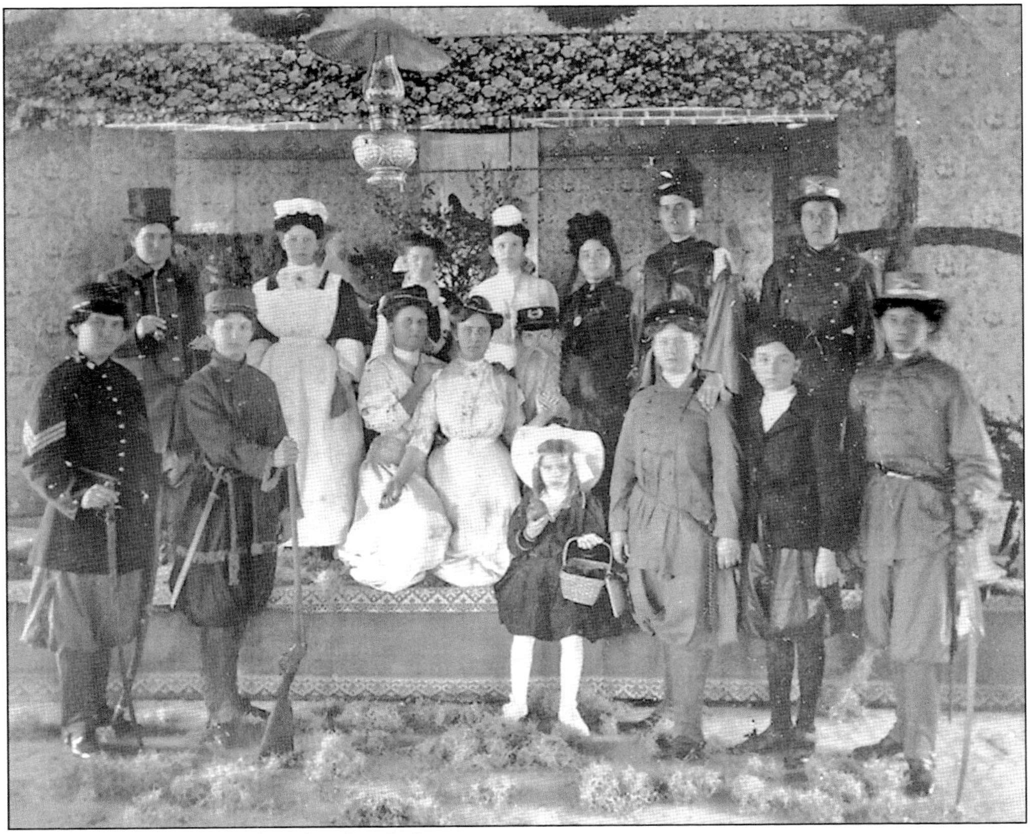

A St. Louis Catholic Church school play was the scene for this photograph. The play was directed by the Sisters of Devine Providence. Music was considered a very important part of every child's education, making the people in the entire county very musically inclined.

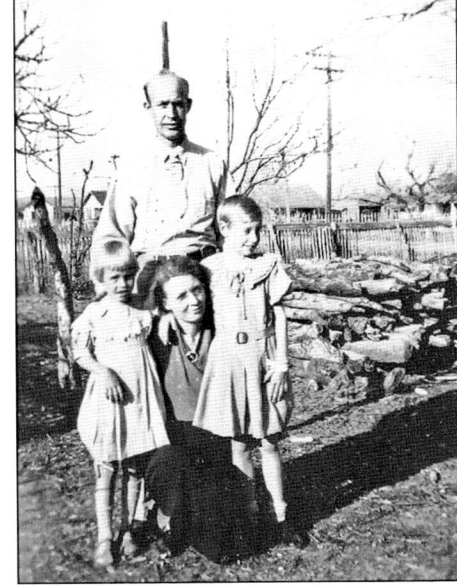

This photograph, taken about 1936 near LaCoste, is of the Chandler family. Standing is Percy Chandler; his wife, Lorine, is on her knees huddled between their daughters. On the left is Bonnie, and Percylee Chandler is at right. (Courtesy of Bonnie and Lester Ludwig.)

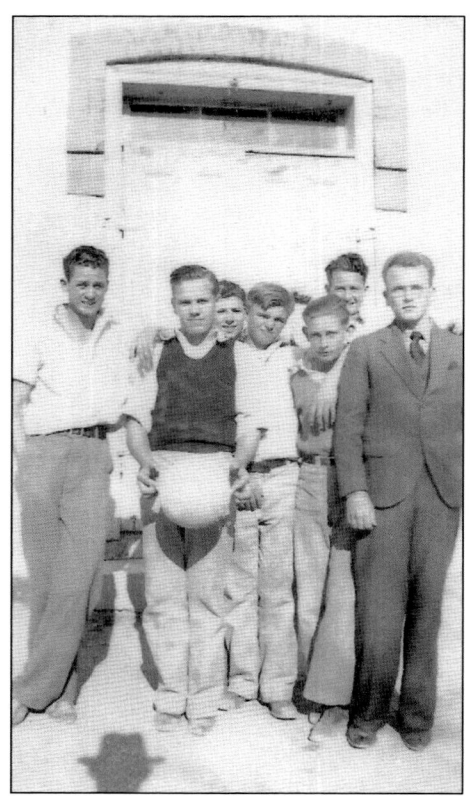

This group photograph was taken around 1940. The boys pictured are, from left to right, "Little Boy McVay," Charlie Suehs, Alvin Bippert, Herbert Weik, August Penk, "Big Boy McVay," and Albert Vance (wearing a suit). This picture was probably taken during a city celebration.

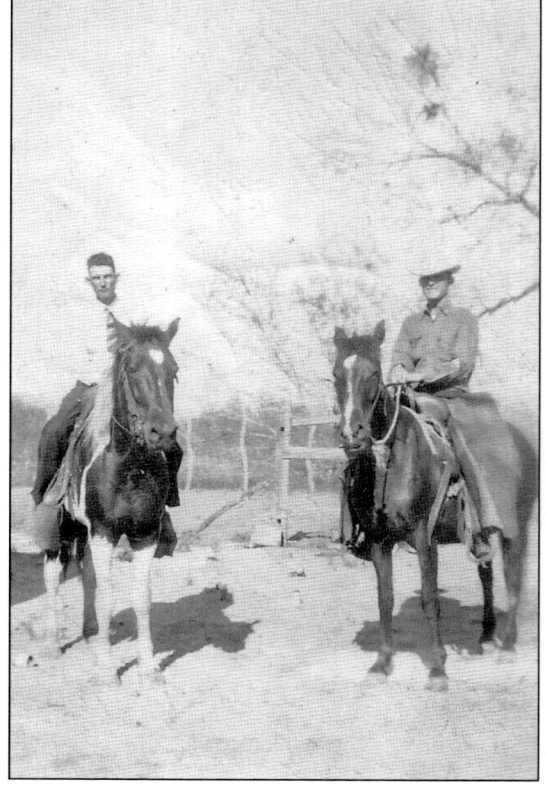

This photograph was taken near Devine. Shown on the left is Eddie Campbell, sitting astride Lester Delbrail's favorite horse, named Paint. Lester is on the horse to the right. Boys in Medina County were taught to ride almost as soon as they could walk, and rodeos were very popular. (Courtesy of Laurel D'Osogna.)

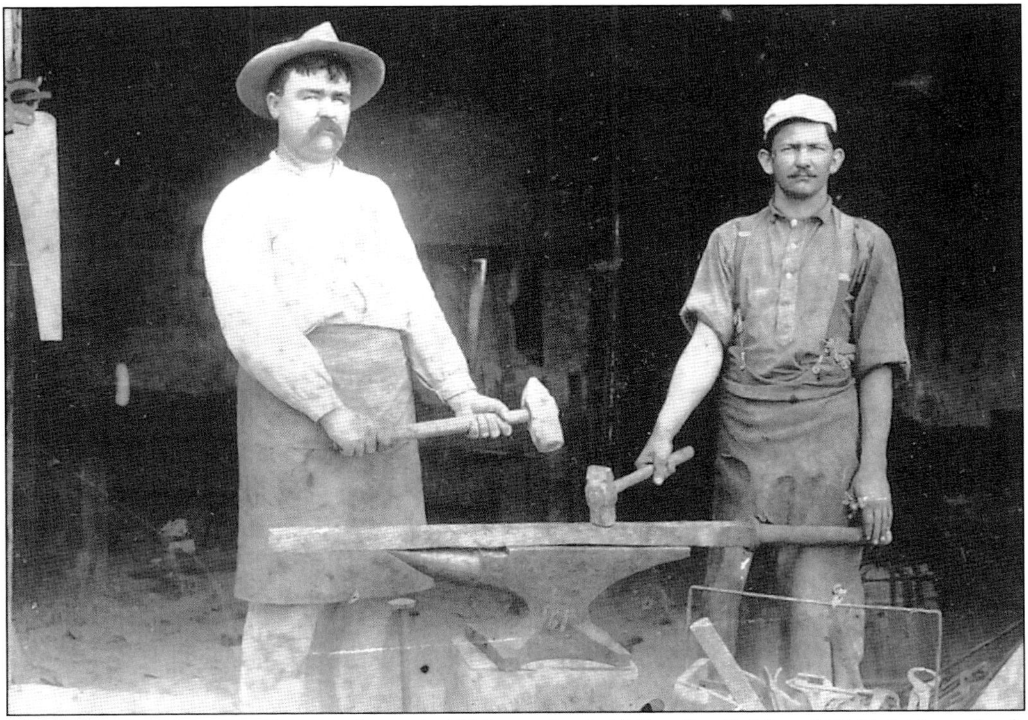

The blacksmiths pictured here in the early 1900s are Andy Halberdier (left) and Ed Tschirhart, both of Castroville. Ed Tschirhart was the third child of Nicolaus Tschirhart and Katherina Meyer. His was a large family made up of 10 boys and two girls. Both of Ed's parents came from Lothringen, Alsace, and are buried in Castroville. Ed married Mary Katherina Jungman, and they had two children. Four years after they were married, Mary Katherina died due to the rigors of pioneer life. Later, Ed married Anna Franciska Stepanek. Anna emigrated from Holitz, Germany, and they had three children. She had studied medicine in Innsbruck, Austria, where she received her doctor's license. She tried to establish her practice in San Antonio but was not accepted because she was a female doctor. After settling in Castroville, she became a highly respected midwife.

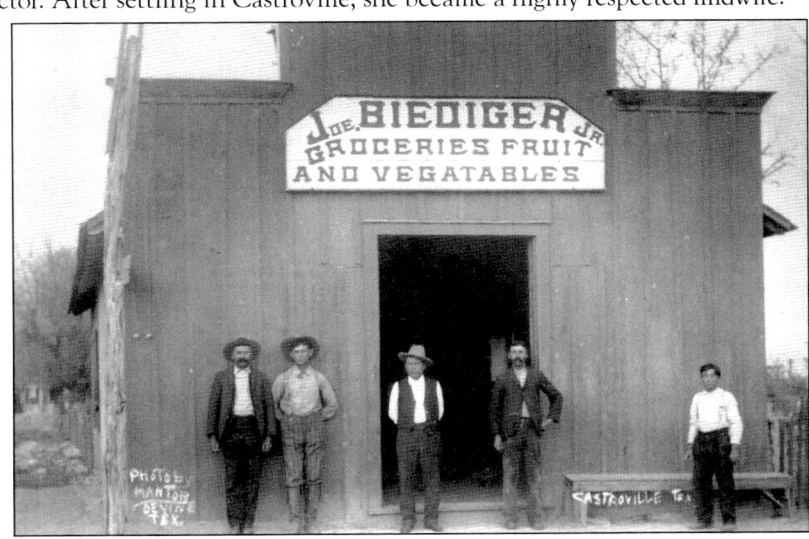

Joe Beidiger Jr. stands to the left in front of his store along with four unidentified men. The grocery was located Castroville and is pictured here in 1908. As the sign reads, his store specialized in groceries, fruit, and vegetables.

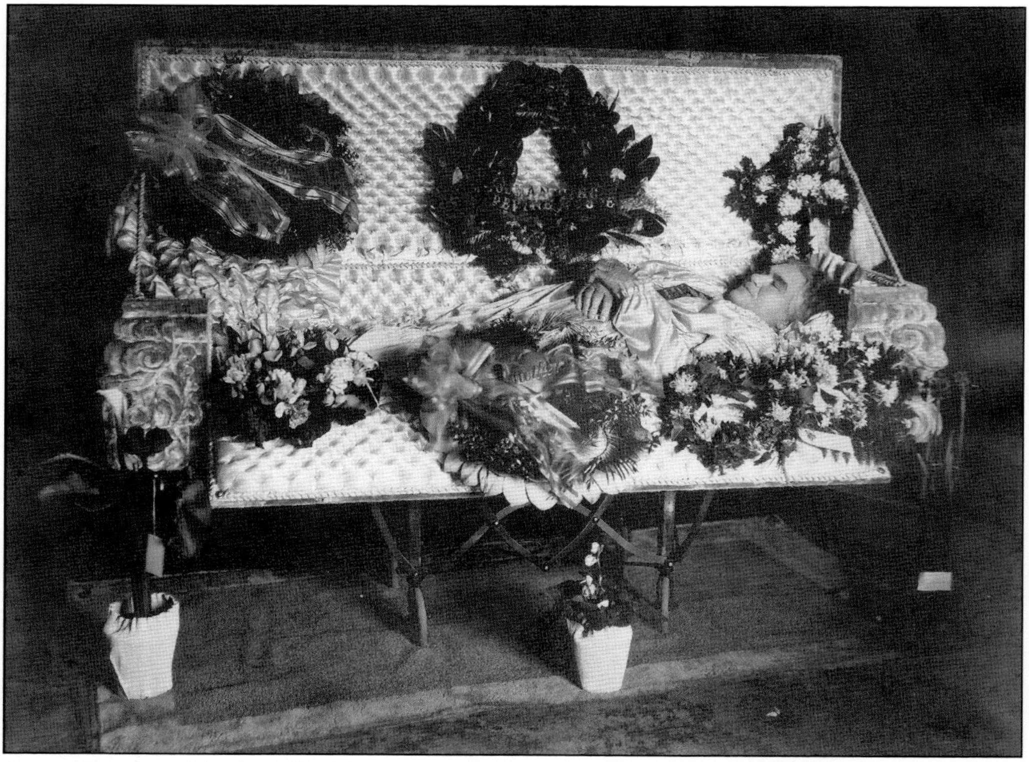

Pictured is Anna Elizabeth Walch Ludwig at her death in 1919. Life was very hard for the pioneer wives; Anna was only 43 years of age. (Courtesy of Bonnie and Lester Ludwig.)

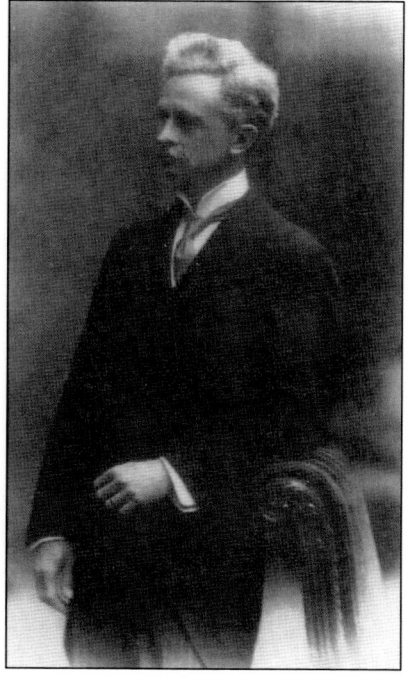

Dr. Fred Stark Pearson, the internationally known engineering genius from Tufts College in Medford, Massachusetts, built Medina Dam with British capital in 1911. Both he and his wife were on the SS *Lusitania* on their way back to England when the ship was torpedoed by a German submarine on May 7, 1915. (Courtesy of Ruby Vera.)

This young woman was the daughter of Dr. Pearson, Natalie Pearson Nicholson. She married in England and never saw the town—Natalia—that was named in her honor. (Courtesy of Ruby Vera.)

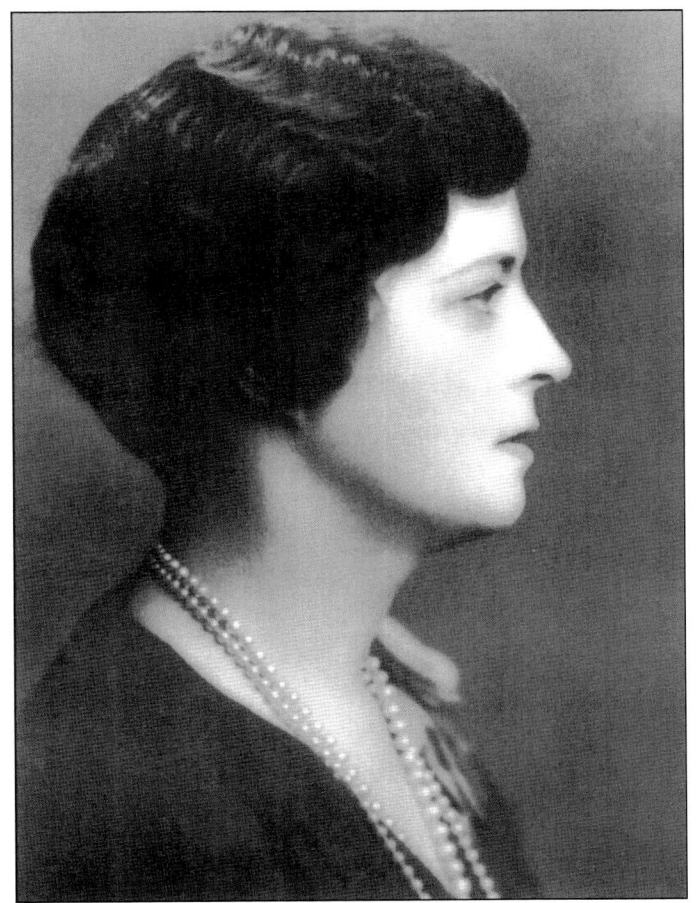

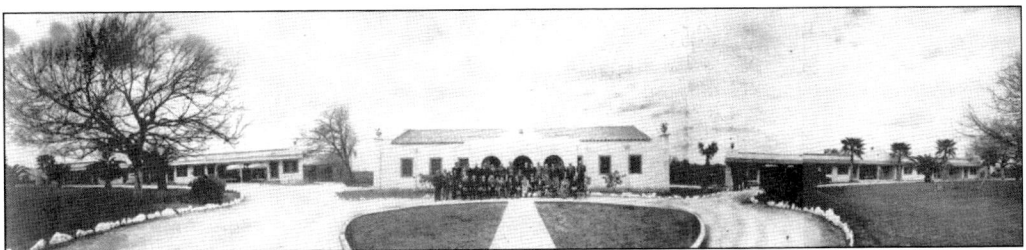

Pictured is the headquarters of Medina Irrigated Farms, Inc. Located in Natalia, the headquarters are shown after irrigation began, when people from all over the United States flocked to Medina County to buy the newly irrigated farmland. (Courtesy of Ruby Vera.)

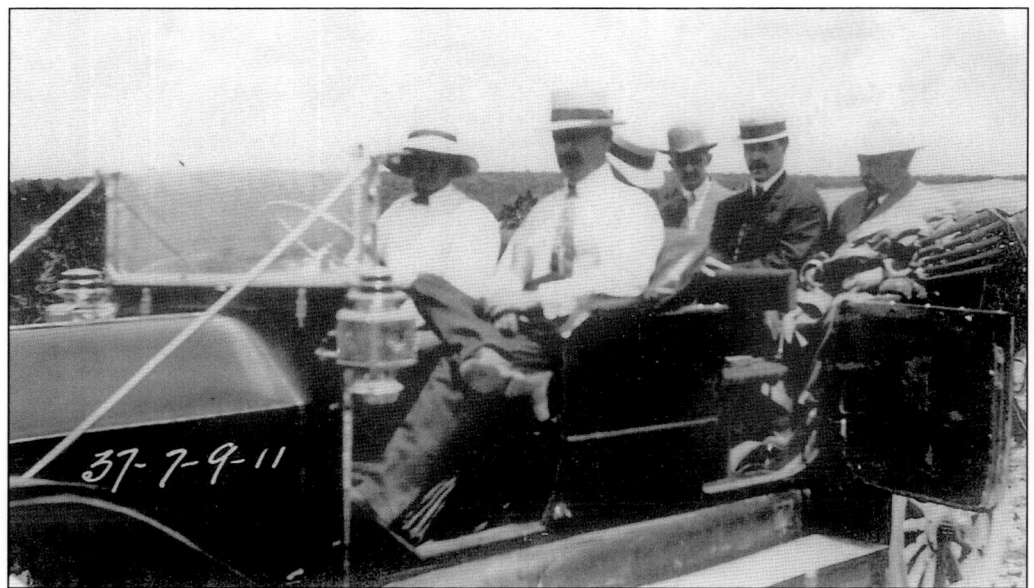

Pictured in this touring car are the engineers for Medina Dam. Dr. Pearson is in the back, seated to the far left. The work done on Medina Dam made it the largest in the state of Texas at that time. (Courtesy of Ruby Vera.)

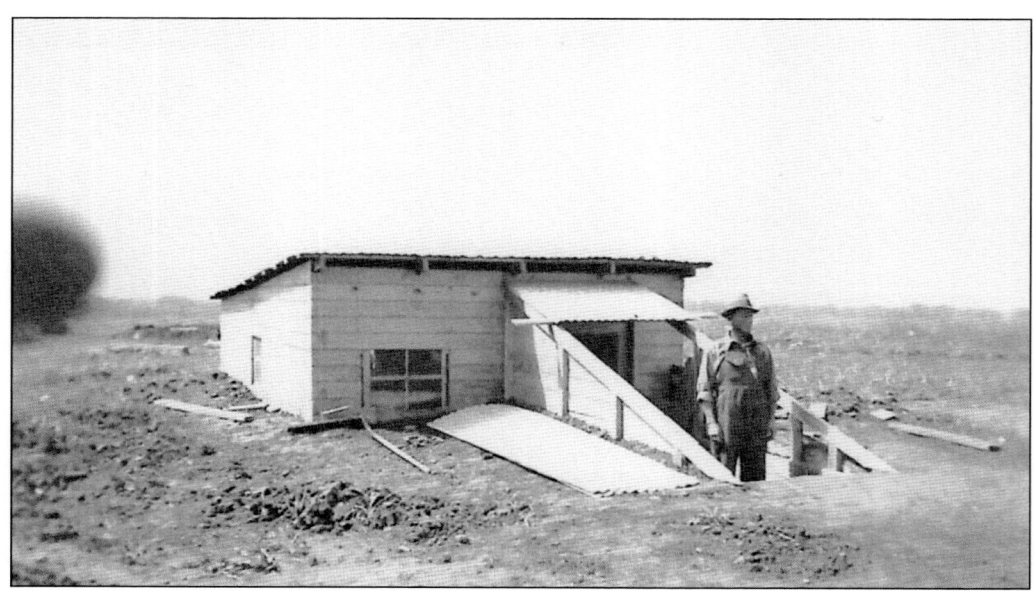

This picture was taken of J. Sam Martin's dugout on his irrigated land. J. Sam came from Oklahoma, where his farm had not produced a single crop. (Courtesy of Ruby Vera.)

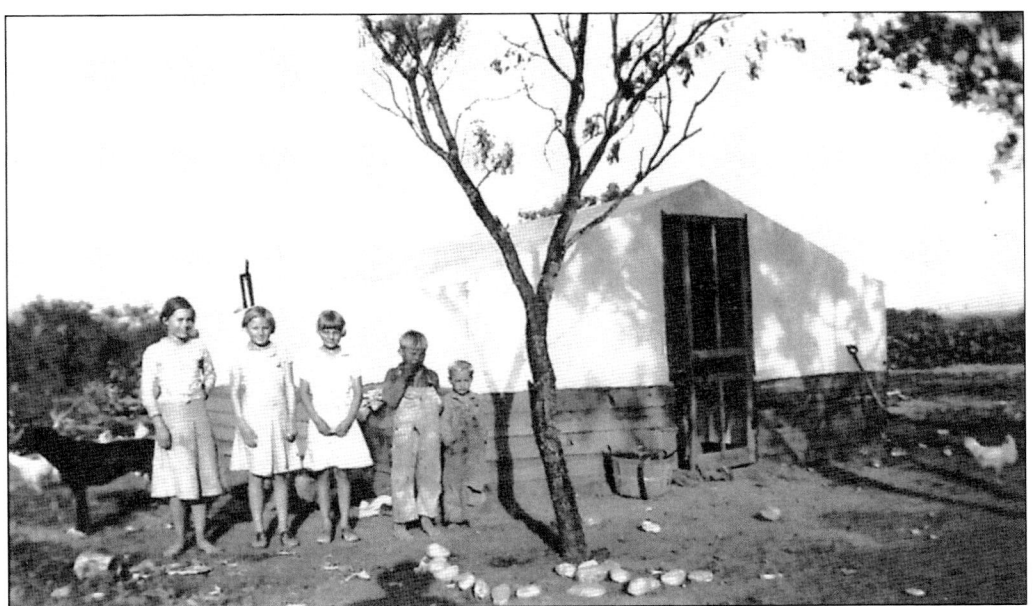

The H.C. Carter family and their seven children came from the plains region of Texas. He rented 160 acres in the plains over a seven-year period with nothing to show for it. (Courtesy of Ruby Vera.)

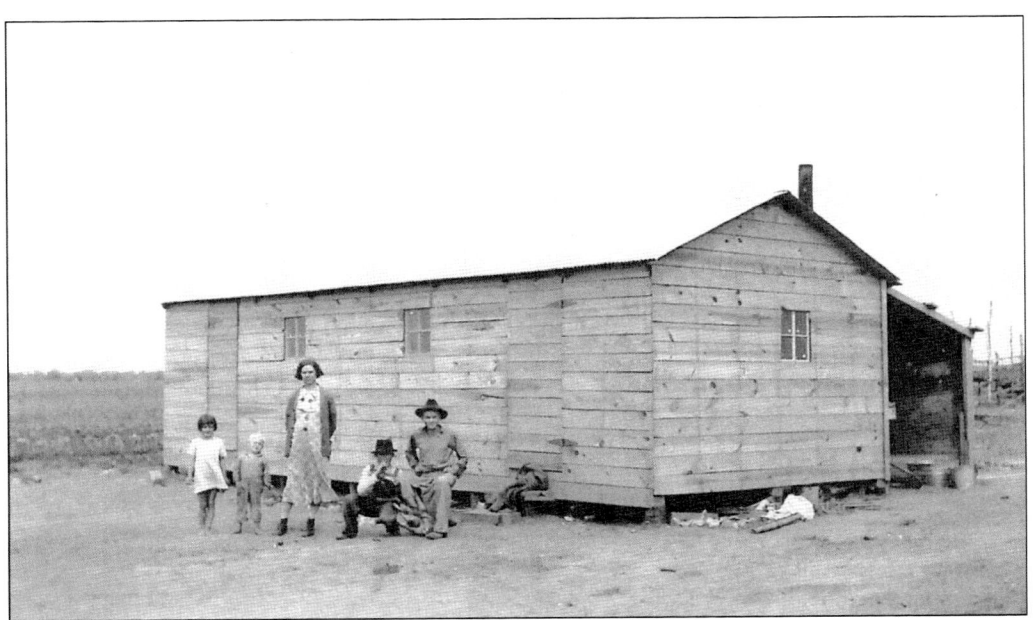

G.F. Bell, with his wife and nine children, came from Wellington, Texas, where they suffered three dry years prior to moving to Medina Irrigated Farms. He regarded his 21 acres as sufficient to make a living. (Courtesy of Ruby Vera.)

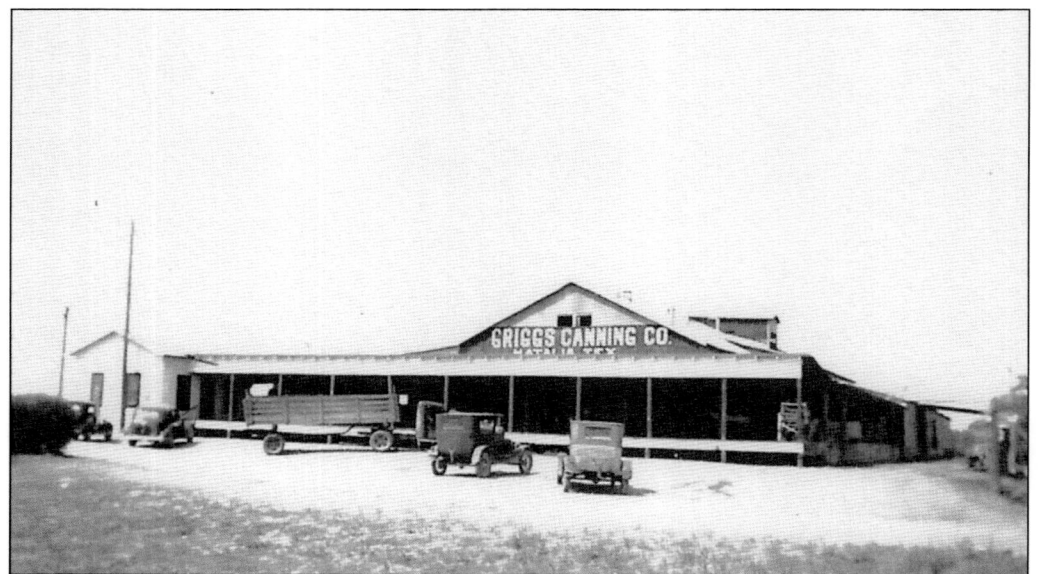

This is a picture of the Griggs Cannery, which was built for Medina District farmers and assured a market for a wide variety of crops. (Courtesy of Ruby Vera.)

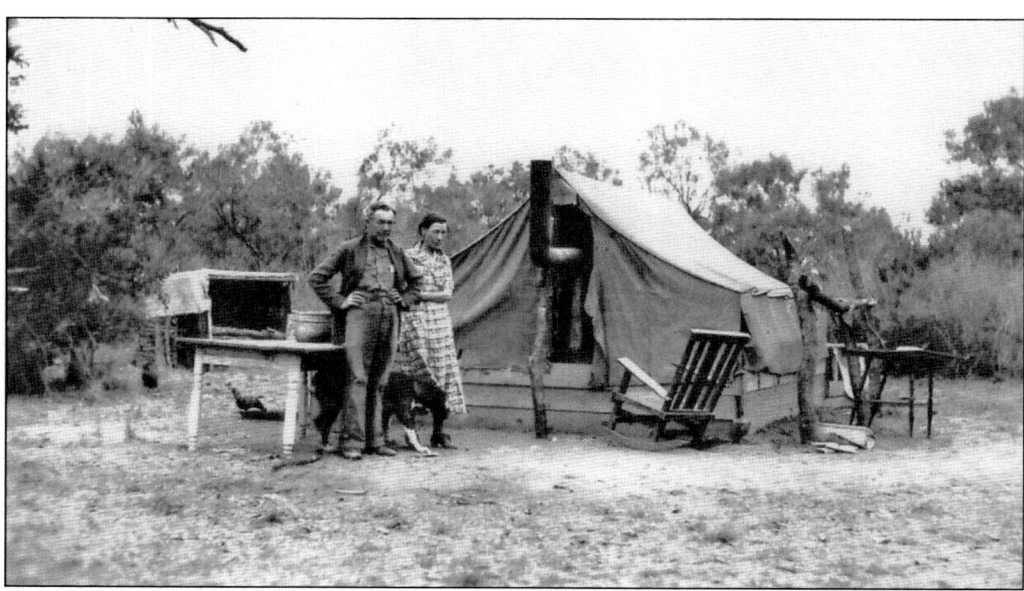

W.C. Dodd came from Ford County with his wife and one child. They arrived in January 1936 and planted beans and corn. The land he left in Ford County had been rendered worthless by dust. (Courtesy of Ruby Vera.)

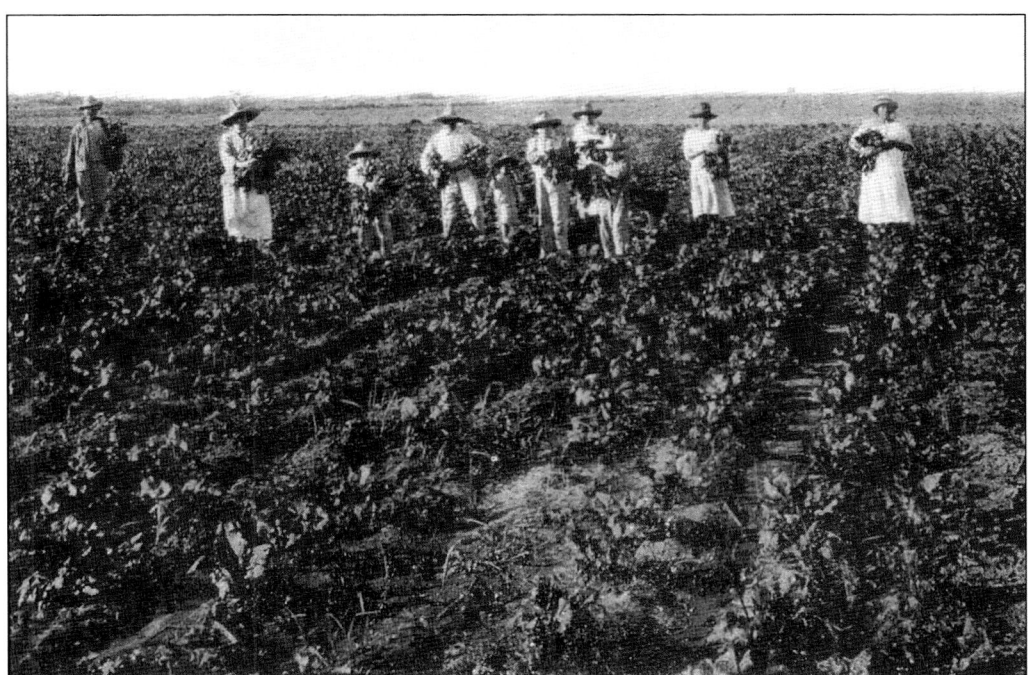

Pictured is a crop being harvested in the irrigated land. In 1930s, some crop was harvested almost every month of the year. (Courtesy of Ruby Vera.)

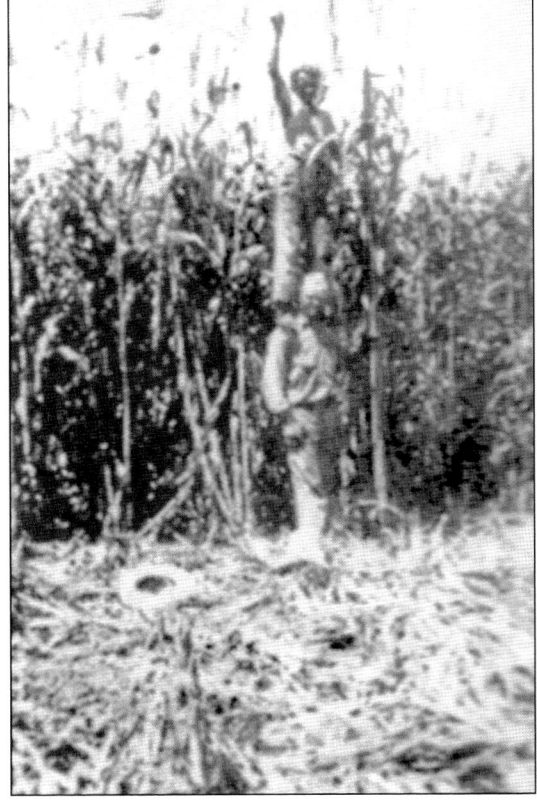

The corn stands two men tall in this image. Water from Medina Dam worked like magic. The farms in the area produced great bounties, and the people who invested in land in Medina County were well rewarded for their efforts. (Courtesy of Ruby Vera.)

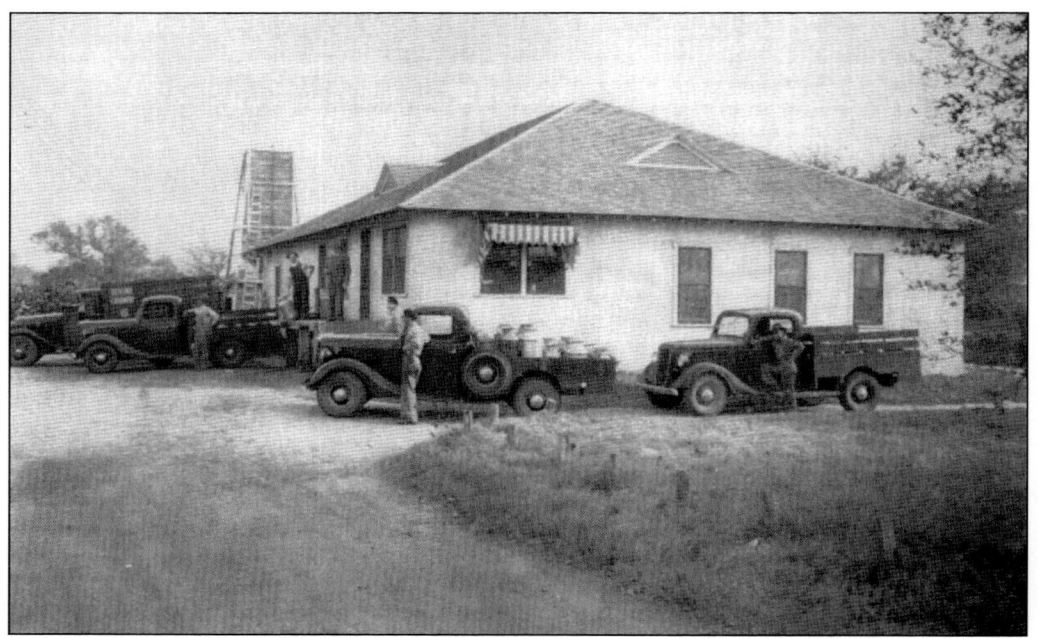

In 1935, the Devine Creamery and Cheese Company contracted for milk and cream and manufactured a fine grade of cream cheese. (Courtesy of Ruby Vera.)

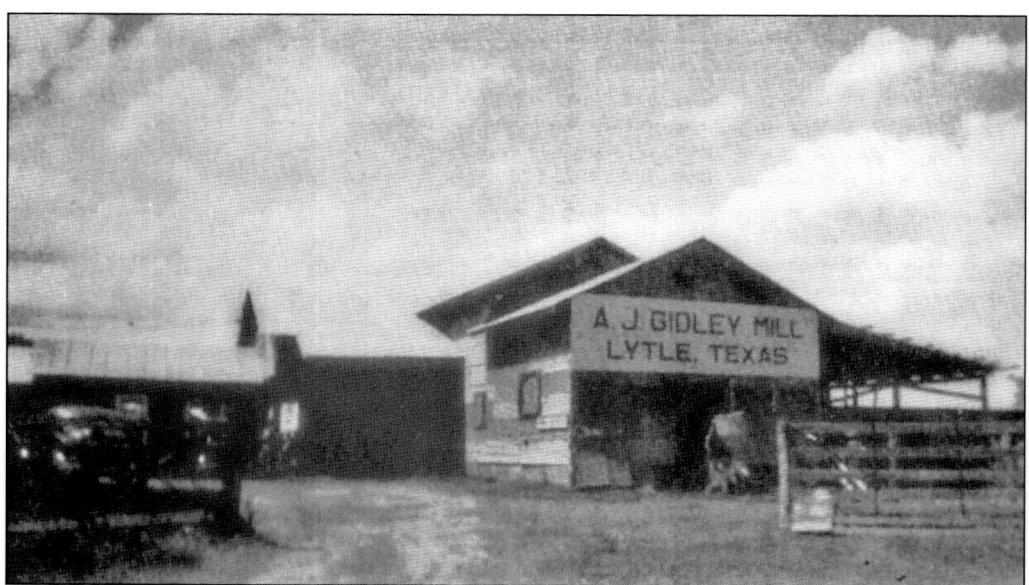

Pictured here is the A.J. Gidley Mill in Lytle, Texas, after the Medina Dam allowed water to flow to the Medina Valley farms. (Courtesy of Ruby Vera.)

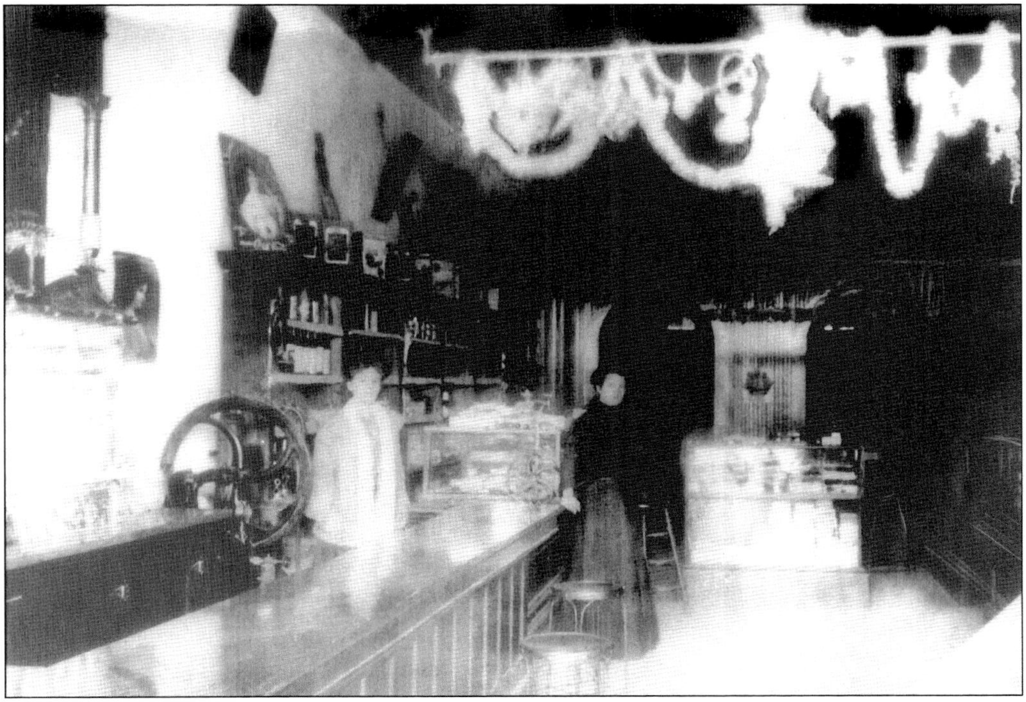

Pictured is Sadie Hutzler's Confectionery in Hondo. All kinds of good things to eat, such as candy, cakes, and delicacies of fruits and nuts, were sold. The lady in black on the right is Hutzler, and a Miss Meirman is standing on her left. This store was in business from 1906 to 1922.

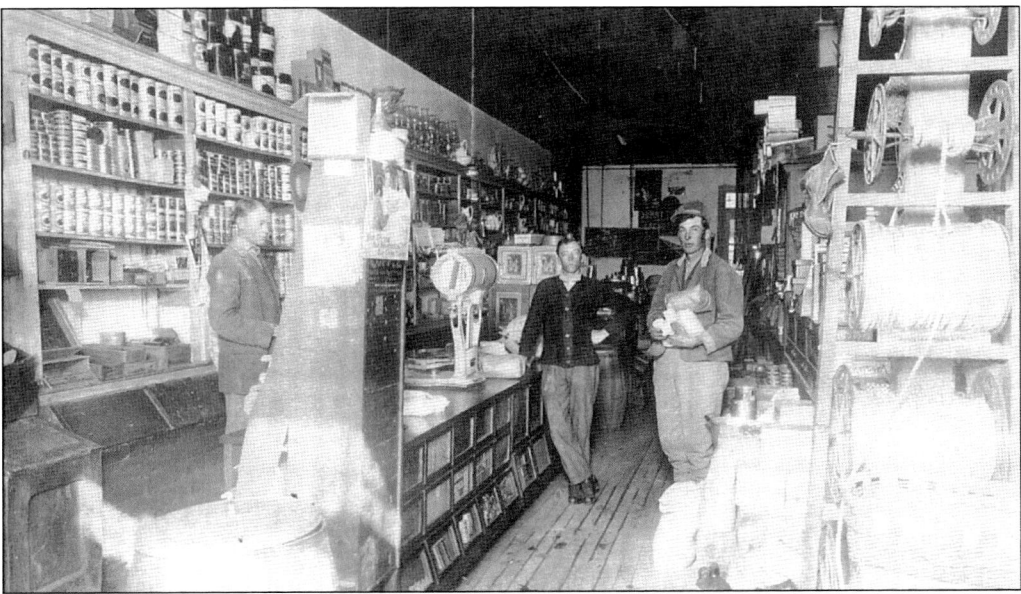

This picture from 1915 is of an early D'Hanis mercantile store that was moved to Hondo. The store was called Fohn-Bless Store. The family lived upstairs. Everything was for sale or trade in this store—horse tack, rope, canned goods, clothes, hats, watches, scales, shoes, cloth, hardware, books, seeds, and many other items. The building received a Texas Historical Marker in 1974.

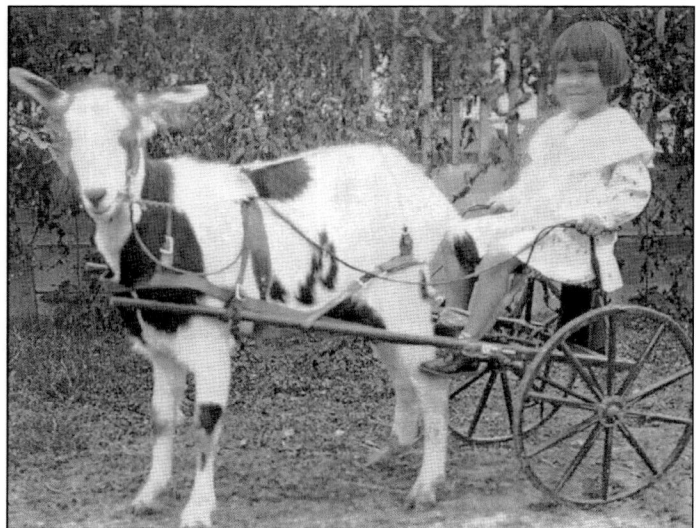

This little girl had no problem getting around Medina County in her goat cart!

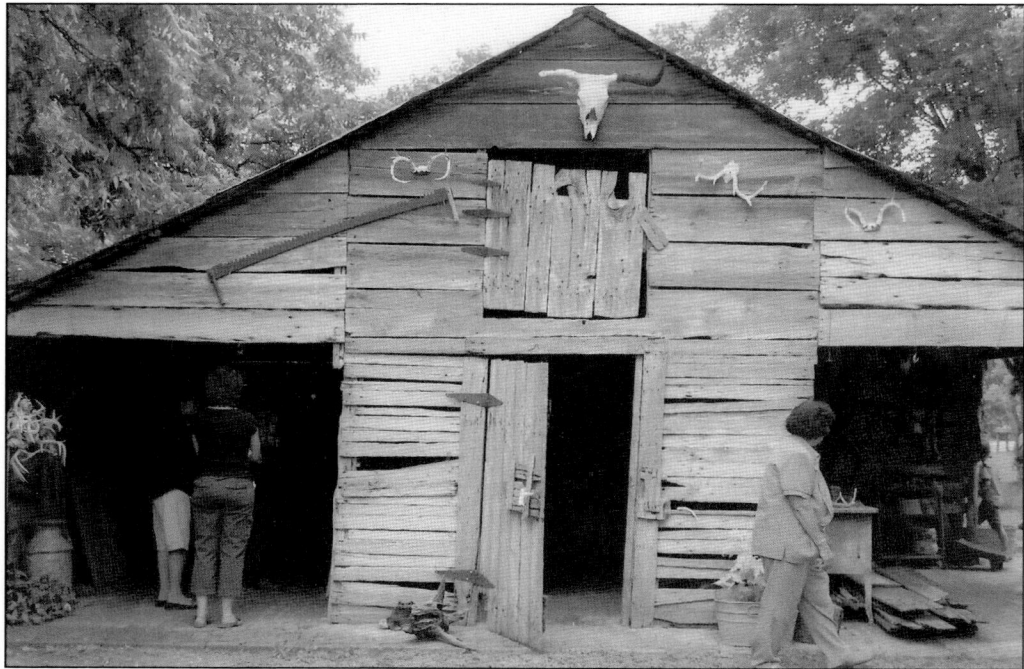

The Rothe line camp was on the Rothe brothers' ranch, which contained approximately 95,000 acres and covered most of the northwest quadrant of Medina County. The brothers constructed line camps throughout their ranch to round up and manage their herd in preparation for the drive up the Chisholm Trail. The line camp is a wood-frame building made of wide, hand-sawed cypress boards and handmade square nails. The roof would be made of hand-hewn cedar shakes. This building contained one room for cooking, a loft for sleeping, a covered porch, and an attached horse stall. The Chisholm Trail was a series of feeder trails that converged for the long drive to the Kansas railheads. The location of the line camp was based on its proximity to the spring-fed turkey roost, an arc-shaped, mile-long waterhole on Comanche Creek in Medina County. (Courtesy of the author.)

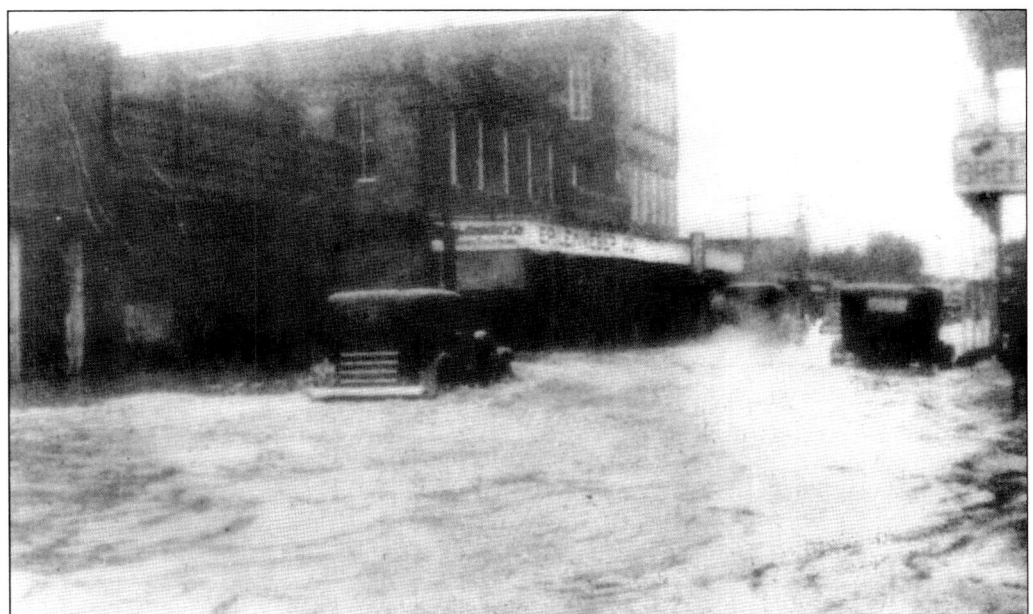

Downtown Hondo looked like this on May 31, 1935, after 18 inches of rain flooded the area. This photograph shows Avenue M and Eighteenth Street. Modern drainage projects had not yet reached this far west.

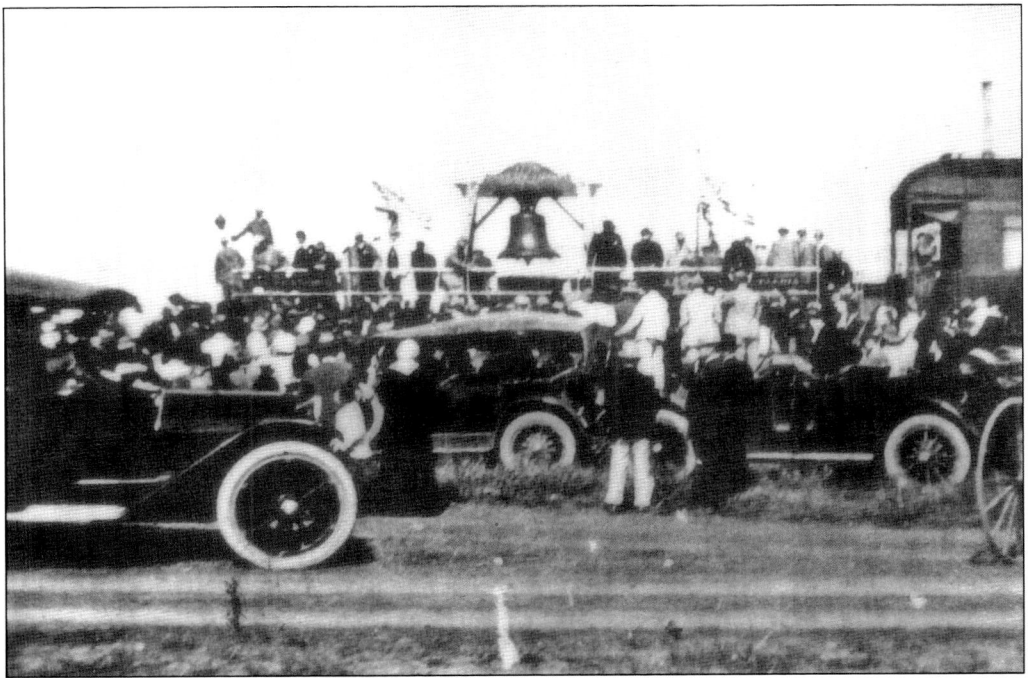

The people in Medina County have always been very patriotic. In 1917, a great event took place in Hondo. The Liberty Bell toured the country and made a stop in Medina County. It was a very lively occasion, and it is said that people were allowed to touch the bell. Soon after, Medina County would be asked to supply able-bodied young men for World War I.

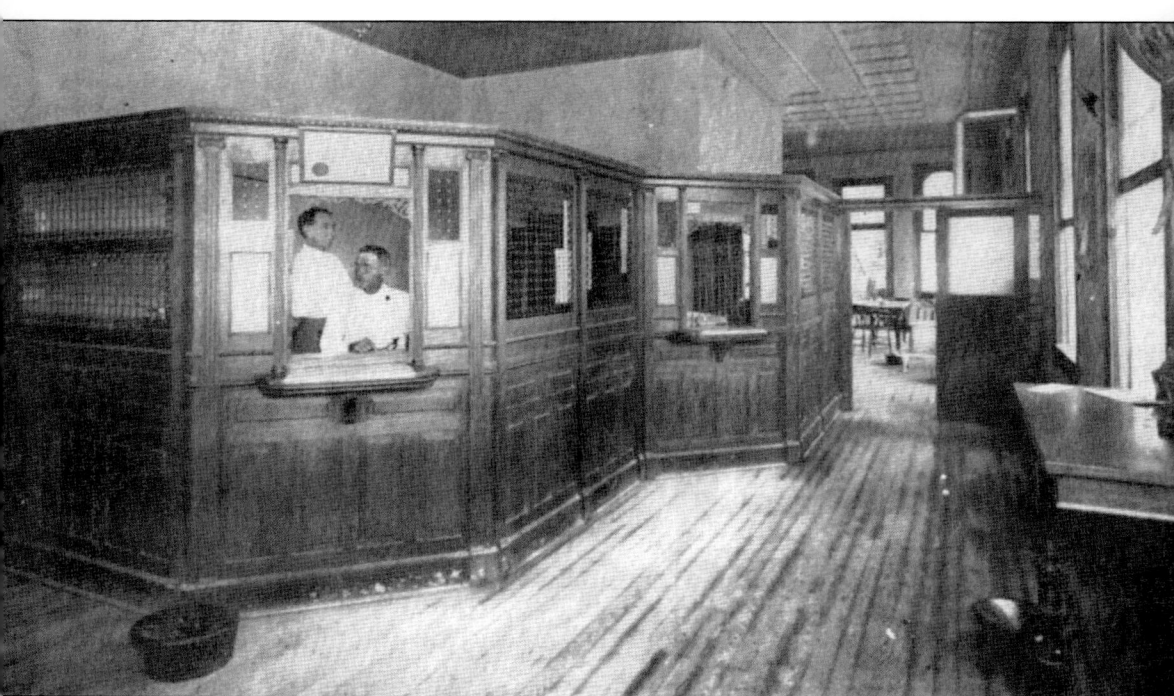

Shown in the window of the State Bank in Hondo are Henry Rothe (left) and Fisher King. In 1921, two banks in Hondo were robbed in one night by the Newton Gang. While the gang detained the bank watchman at the railroad station, they used a crowbar and TNT to break into the banks. The gang was eventually caught and served time. The railroad station in which they held the night watchman is now the Medina County Historic Museum. The infamous crowbar can be viewed there.

Four
Memories of a Few of Medina County's Patriots, and Hondo Army Air Field

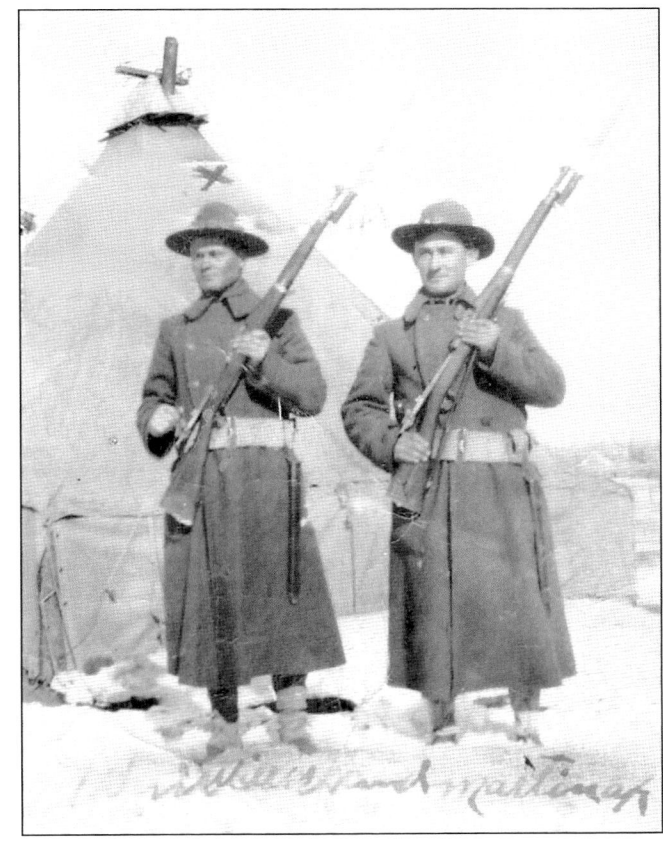

Willie Winters (left) of Devine and a friend are pictured in front of a tent while stationed in Europe during World War I. Willie returned from the war, lived an eventful life, and is buried in Hondo.

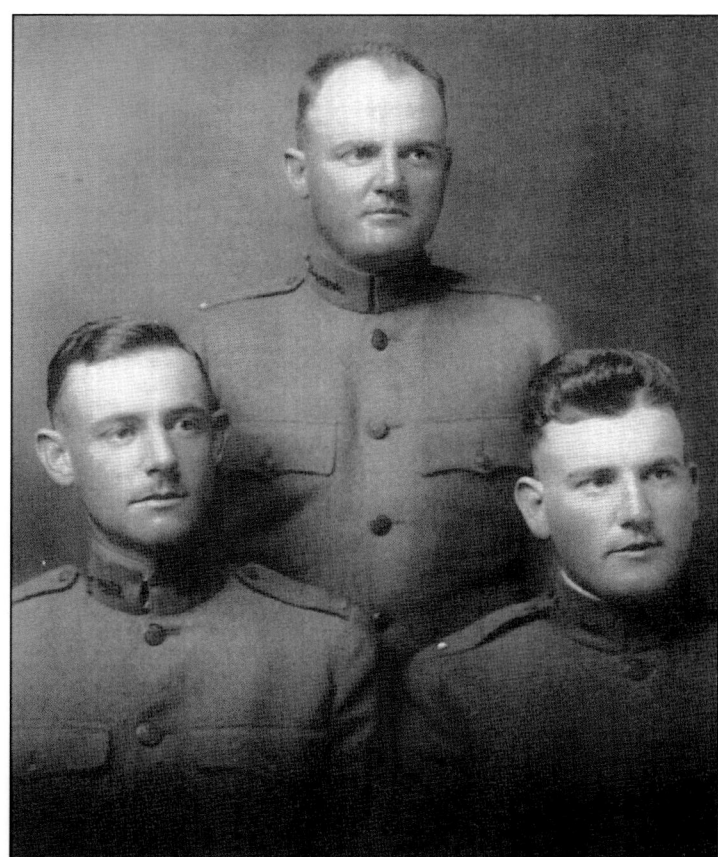

The three well-educated sons of Edmond and Fannie De Montel—grandsons of the famous Charles De Montel who was a surveyor, engineer, rancher, and soldier during the days of the Republic of Texas—are pictured here. They are, from left to right, Emmet, Elmer (Govie), and Elbert De Montel. They served their country during the perilous days of World War I. Even though fighting the countries from which their forbearers came, Medina County supported the United States in each world war. Several men were dropped behind enemy lines to infiltrate enemy countries, and several were used as translators at the Nuremberg Trials after World War II.

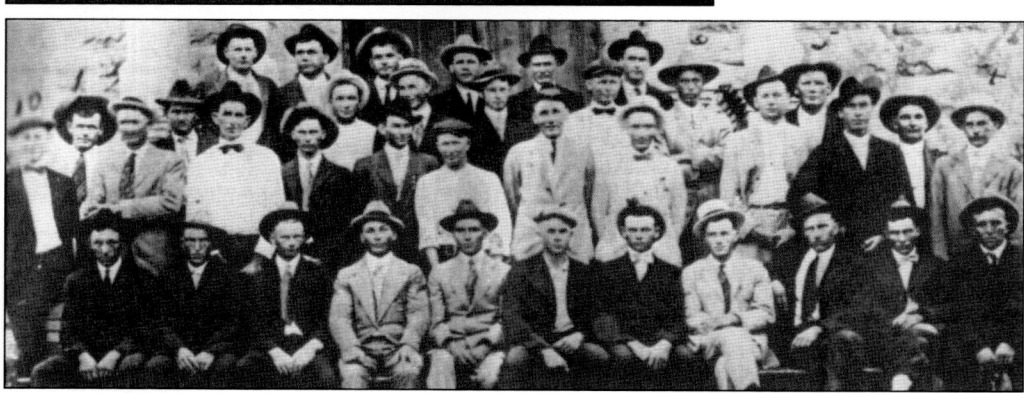

All of these young Medina County men signed up to fight for their country in World War I. These brave men are, from left to right, (first row) Elmer P. Jungman, Joseph F. Haegelin, Guido Richter, John E. Belzung, Guenther H. Rothe, Phillip Karrer, Bill Schott, Louis Franger, James Gibson, Albert Griffin, and Walter Scheile; (second row) Oscar B. Taylor, Louis H. Pichot, C.J. Peters, Archie Schuchart, Henry Brown, Fritz Eli Burgin, Edward H. Weynand, J.W. Thompson, Henry Langfeld, Henry Biry, Rudolph A. Haby, Julius J. Haby, and Oscar E. Wurzbach; (third and fourth rows) Robert Breiten, Alfred J. Schmidt, Denman Harris, Arnold G. Haass, Alex Wendland, Frank Saathoff, John G. Faseler, Emil Nehr, Ernest Brucks, Emil Muennink, George Britsch, and Mimke F. Weimers.

The plane pictured here, a Lincoln Sport plane, was built by Ferdinand A. Tschirhart. Ferdinand was born in Castroville in May 1906. He was the grandson of one of Castroville's original immigrants, Nicholas Tschirhart. As a child, Ferdinand witnessed the infancy of aircraft development. By the time he was 20, he had developed a passion for aviation. In 1926, a full year before Lindbergh made his famous flight, he decided to order a kit from the Lincoln Aircraft Company in Nebraska and to build and fly it. A replica of this plane can be seen in the lobby of the Castroville Airport. (Courtesy of Clif Eissler.)

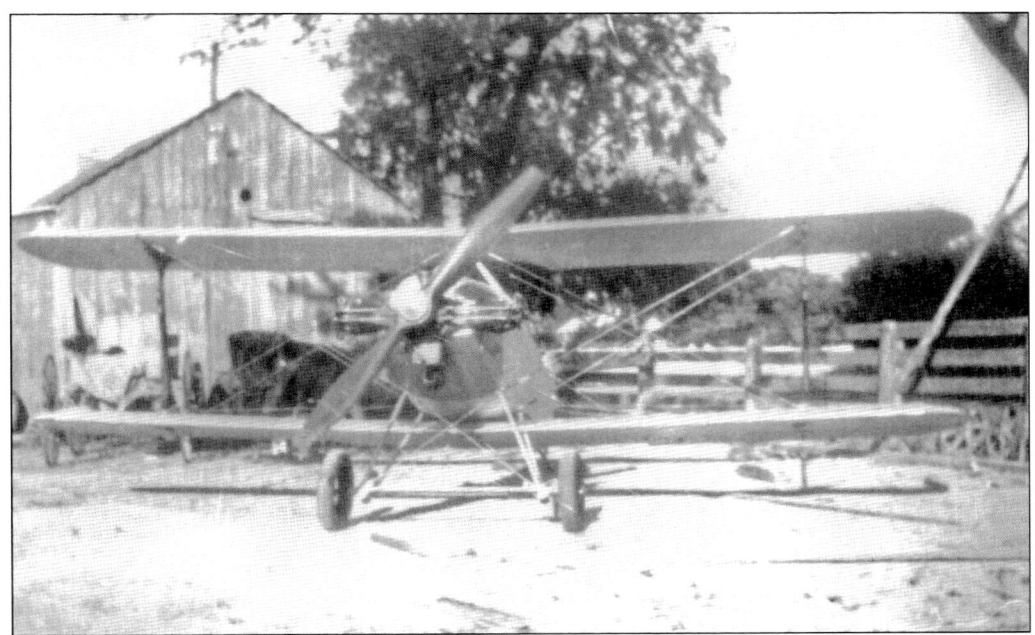

Fritz Rihn was the last surviving World War I veteran in Medina County. Fritz was born in Castroville on his parent's farm in the Biry area. Inducted into the US Army in Hondo, Fritz was sent to France, where he participated in several battles. He is pictured holding a Browning automatic, which was later used extensively in World War II. Fritz married Pauline Jungman Brown. He received the French Legion of Honor, France's highest decoration to Allied veterans.

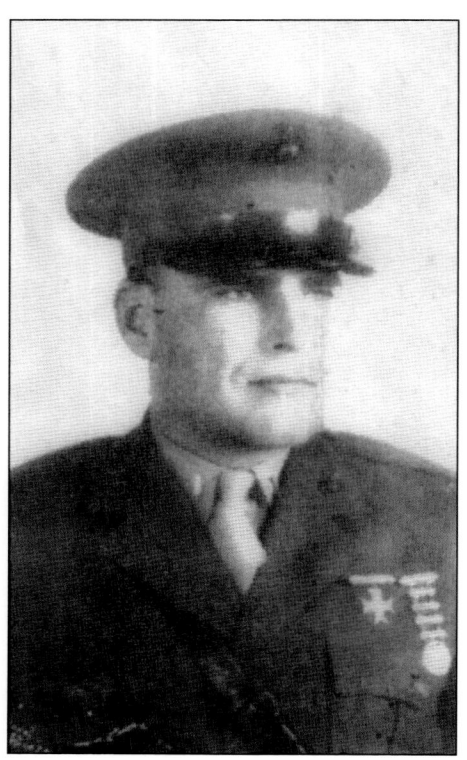

US Marine Corps first lieutenant Henry Moss is pictured here. After graduation from Texas A&M University, Henry became a teacher at Devine High School. As World War II began, he joined the Marines and was in the battle of Peleliu Island. This battle involved 10,000 Japanese troops. Injured on the beach and patched up with sulfur—the new miracle drug—he was sent to the beaches of Okinawa, where the Marines secured the island. After the war, he returned to teaching in 1946 and taught until retirement in 1982. Henry was a positive influence on hundreds of young people in Medina County. (Courtesy of the Mary and Henry Briscoe family.)

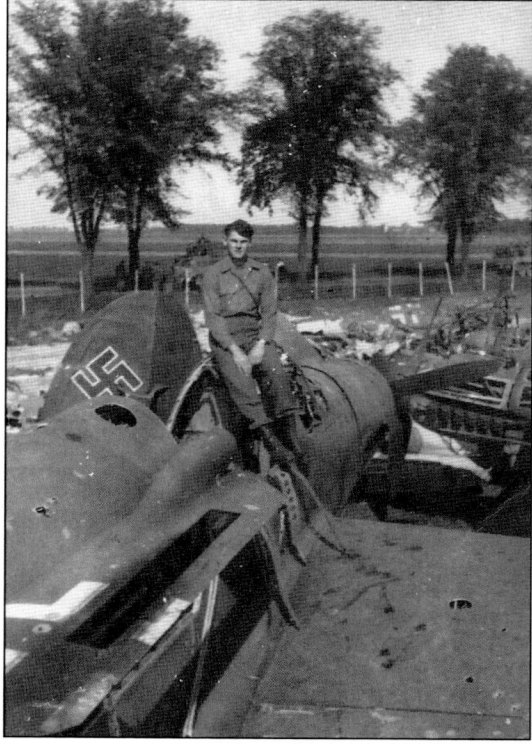

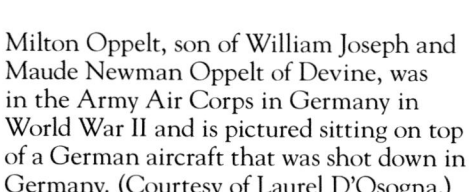

Milton Oppelt, son of William Joseph and Maude Newman Oppelt of Devine, was in the Army Air Corps in Germany in World War II and is pictured sitting on top of a German aircraft that was shot down in Germany. (Courtesy of Laurel D'Osogna.)

James Oppelt, fifth child of William Joseph and Maude Newman Oppelt, was born on a farm 10 miles south of Castroville. He graduated from Devine High School in 1947. James was a Marine who fought his way out of Chosin Reservoir in Korea in one of the bloodiest battles in history. Out of 20,000 American soldiers in the battle, only 5,000 came out unscathed—James was one of those few.

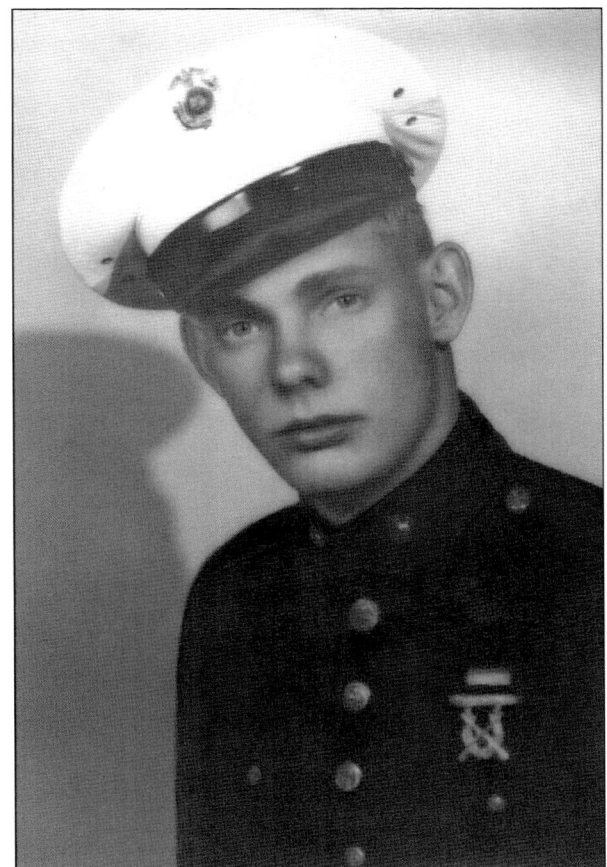

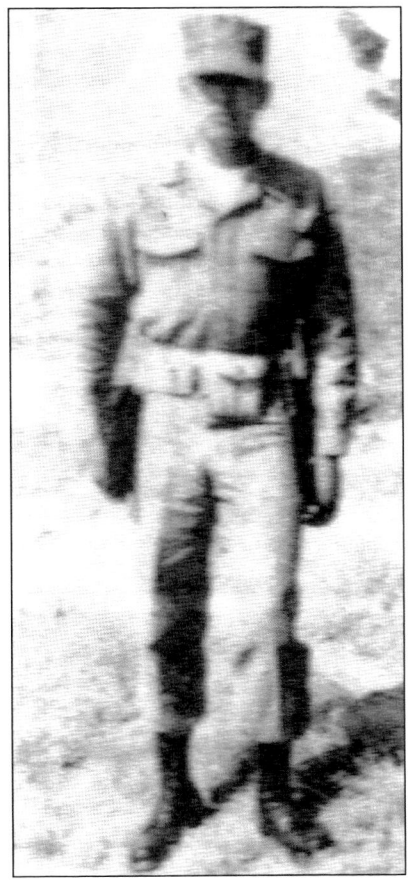

Pictured here in newsprint is a brave Medina County Purple Heart recipient, US Army corporal Gilberto Garcia. Son of Vidal and Florence Garcia, Gilberto was born on a farm and attended school in Kyotz (Padilla) in Devine. He graduated from Poteet High School. In an outpost while patrolling, Gilberto was hit by a mortar shell and took 18 stitches in the leg. He continued to lead his squadron, directing fire from just 50 meters away from enemy forces. While crossing a booby-trapped bamboo fence, Gilberto was injured again and lost both legs. He returned to his farm in Devine and married Lydia Rodriguez. With two artificial legs, Gilberto continued to farm and raise a family. The sacrifices he made for this country's freedom can never be repaid. (Courtesy of the Mary and Henry Briscoe family.)

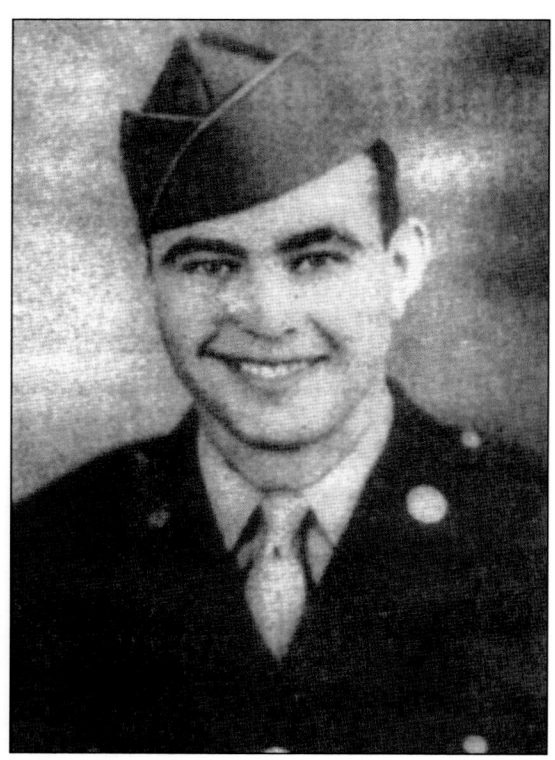

Pfc. James W. "Willie" Noblitt is pictured here. His family came to the Golden Medina Valley project from Oklahoma during the Dust Bowl and settled in Devine. He graduated from high school and worked for the Griggs Canning Company before volunteering with the Army. Willie was wounded in his foxhole in Leyte in the Philippines when shrapnel fired by Japanese snipers entered his leg above his left knee. A buddy next to him was killed. Willie survived the attack by receiving the new miracle drug penicillin by injection every three hours, but the wound would continue to plague him all of his life. Willie was awarded the Purple Heart. (Courtesy of the Mary and Henry Briscoe family.)

Leonard Wiemers, the son of George and Marie Wiemers, was born on a farm near Yancey. Leonard graduated from Yancey High School in May 1943. He was sworn into the Army at Fort Sam Houston in San Antonio. After Utah Beach was secured, he was sent in with General Patton's men at St. Lo, France, as they moved across France into Belgium. Carrying their Browning automatic rifles (BARs), K rations, ammunition, canteens, and gas masks, the men slept on the ground, exposed to enemy fire. While firing at German troops who were advancing at close range, he was struck from behind. He had a three-inch gash in his scalp and was temporarily blinded. Soon healed, Leonard was announced fit for duty while in Germany. While trying to silence a German pillbox 100 yards ahead of him, he was shot through the neck. After surgery in England, Leonard was again sent back to the front as an aircraft mechanic. After the war, in 1949, Leonard married Bernice Powell of Devine. Leonard received two Purple Hearts. Because of men like Leonard Wiemers, America enjoys freedom today. (Courtesy of the Mary and Henry Briscoe family.)

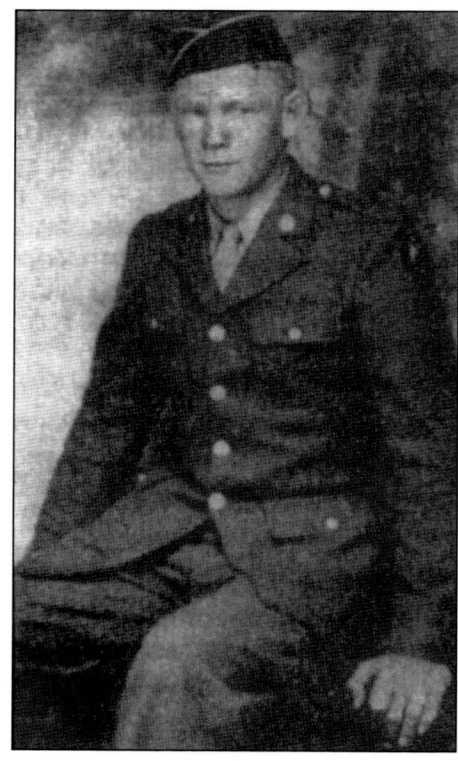

Eugene Suehs was the son of Charles William and Mary Alice Naegelin Suehs of Castroville. The Suehs family came from Alsace via a different route than most settlers. They arrived in Mexico and made their way up to the Republic of Texas. Eugene served his country in the Army Air Corps after he finished school in San Marcos at Texas State University. Eugene taught flying but was never sent overseas. He married Dorothy Ott of San Antonio in 1949. (Courtesy of the Mary and Henry Briscoe family.)

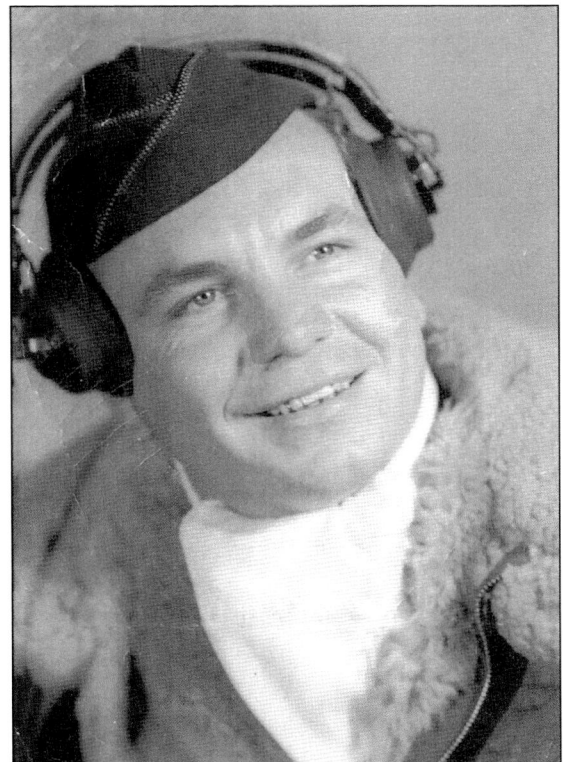

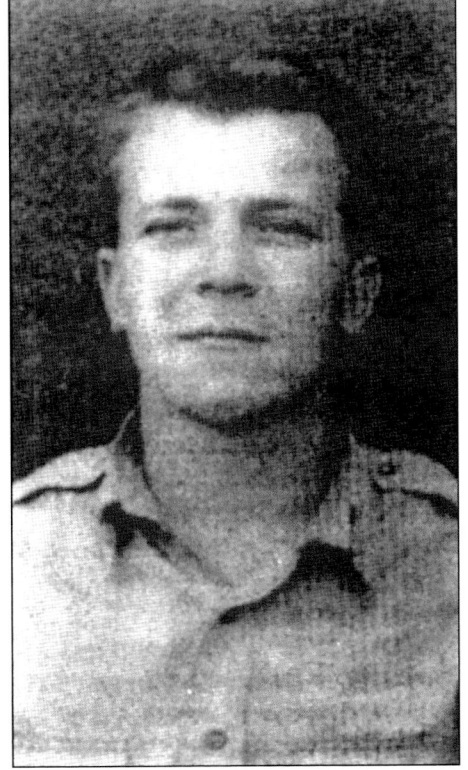

Richard J. Schott of Castroville entered World War II as a first lieutenant. In 1943, while on his eighth mission, his unit of 31 B-26 planes encountered German air fire. The plane's left engine was hit, causing the entire crew to bail out. For 23 months, until the end of the war, Richard was a prisoner of war in Germany. He was allowed to grow a small vegetable garden in the prison camp. He and another prisoner carried water to the garden daily. They shared the rare bounty with the other prisoners in his *stalag* (German POW camp). (Courtesy of Richard J. Schott.)

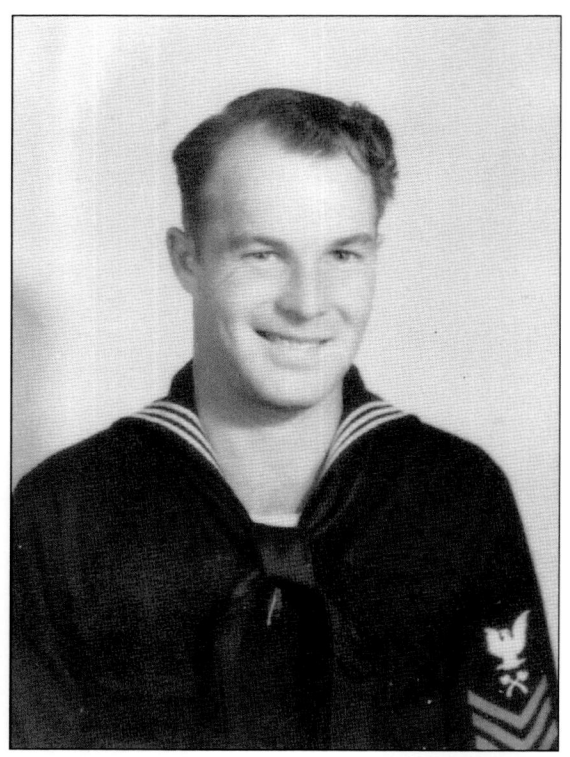

Navy chief Jack Heath of Hondo served in World War II from February 1942 to January 1946. After the war, he returned home to Texas and to civilian life. (Courtesy of Mary Ann Pringle.)

Eddie Patrick of Air Force Village II in Medina County served with Gen. Claire Chenault and his famous Flying Tigers in China before World War II was declared. After the war, he completed his education and returned to the Air Force, retiring as a full colonel. (Courtesy of the author.)

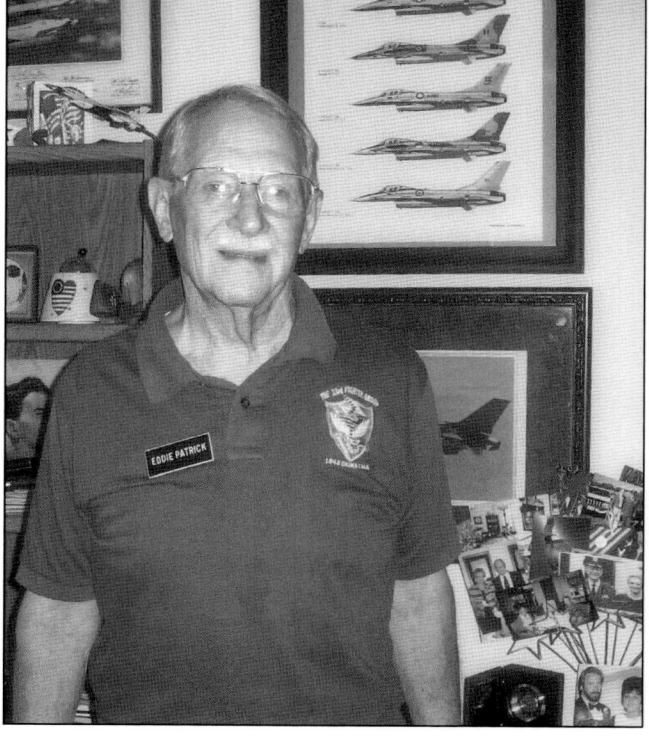

Chief Machinist Mate James Wilson Bailey (1911–1988) of the US Navy Seabees (1943–1945) graduated from Hondo High School. The son of Henry Raymond and Nora Heath Bailey, he served his country proudly during World War II. (Courtesy of Mary Ann Pringle.)

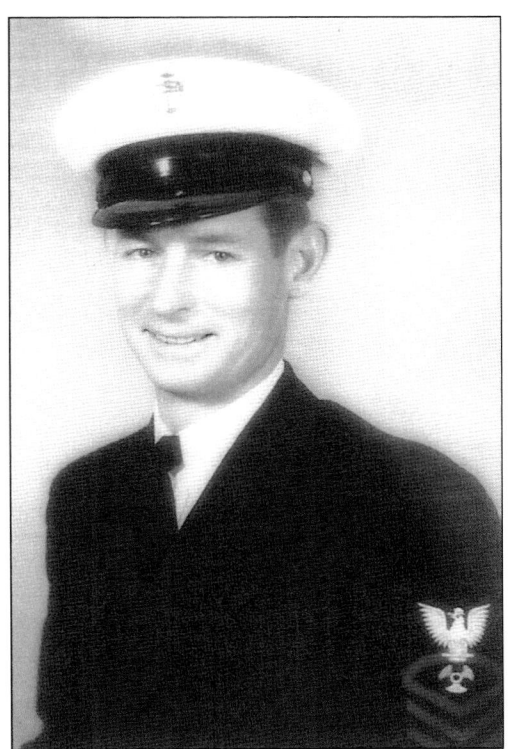

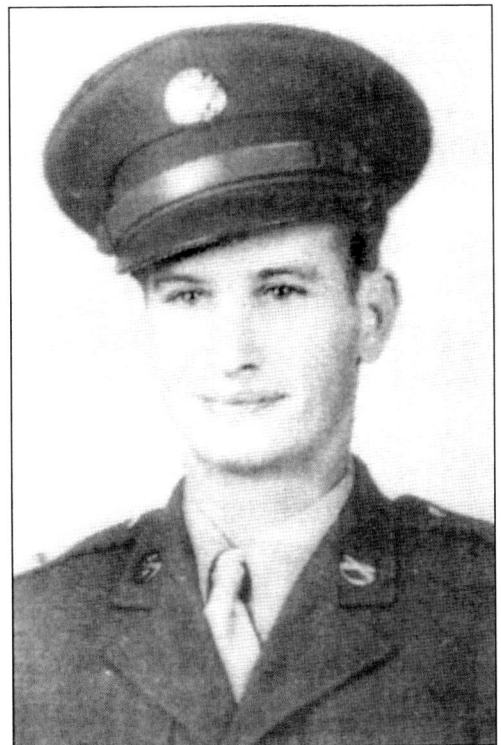

Pvt. Paul Joseph Schott of Devine, son of Edward A. and Elizabeth Ehlinger Schott, married Laura Bendele in 1940. In 1944, at the age of 28, Paul entered the Army and was sent to France. Wounded in severe weather during combat, Paul lost a leg. When he returned to Devine after the war, he became city secretary and served in that capacity for 32 years. He was awarded a Purple Heart for his service and was an inspiration to all. (Courtesy of the Mary and Henry Briscoe family.)

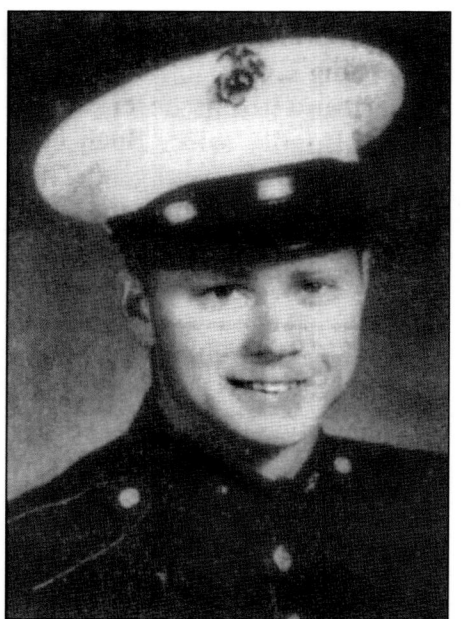

Freeman White, born in Hall County, moved with his parents to Lytle when he was eight years old. After graduating from high school, Freeman entered the Marines, and he was deployed to South Korea during the Korean War. On September 16, 1951, Freeman and a buddy were in a two-man foxhole up in the mountains where the North Koreans were attacking. Later, on the cold night patrol, he and his buddy were advancing on a pillbox, with Freeman going around one side and his buddy taking the other. There was an explosion as his buddy stepped on a land mine, losing a leg. Freeman carried his buddy back for help. His buddy lived two weeks before succumbing. Freeman continued in combat until the end of the war. He won a Purple Heart for his service to his nation.

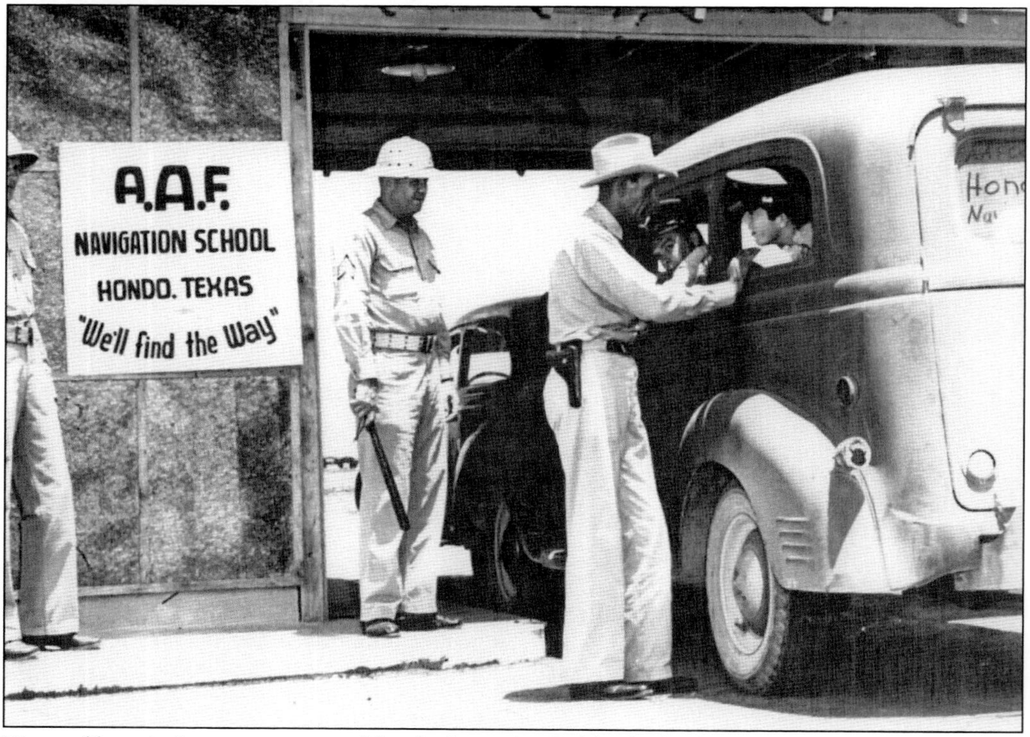

Pictured here is the main gate into Hondo Army Air Field. The field (landing tarmacs, dormitories, electrical utilities, plumbing, and water) was miraculously built in just 90 days by H.B. Zachry Company of San Antonio. This base was established to train men and women desperately needed to be Army Air Corps navigators. Between 1942 and August 1945, almost 1,500 navigators learned their craft for World War II at Hondo Army Air Field.

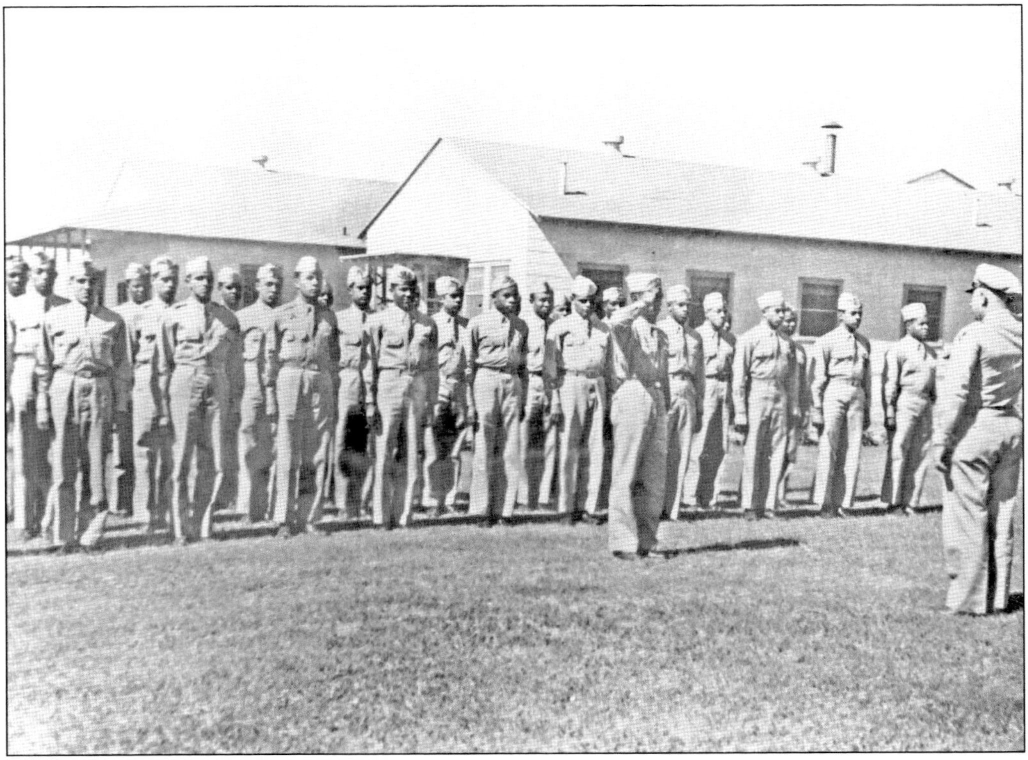

The first class of navigation cadets arrives from primary flight training at Tuskegee, Alabama, in this picture. This was a momentous occasion for the little town of Hondo.

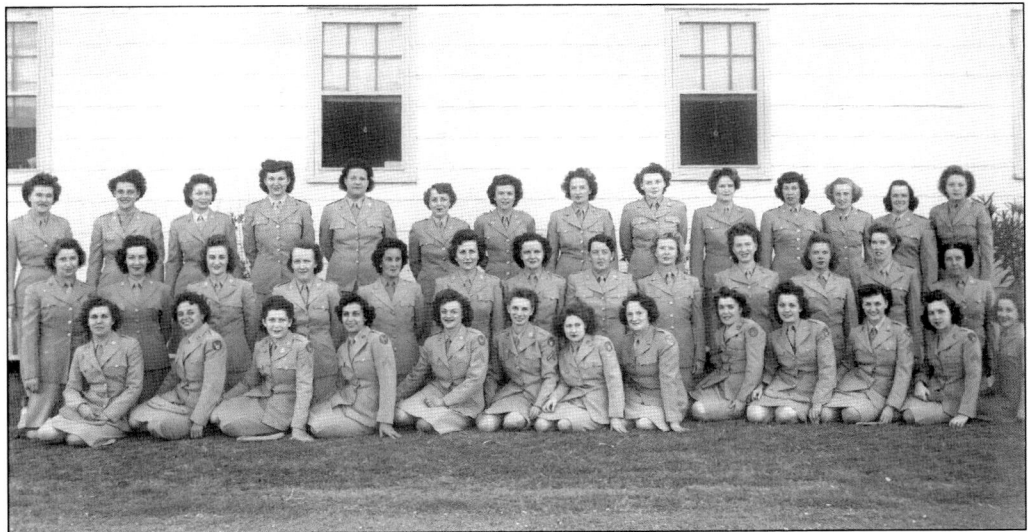

Pictured in front of the female barracks is the Women's Air Squadron (2523rd Army Air Forces Base Unit at Hondo Army Air Field), the first female unit of its kind in the world. This barrack, given to the Medina County Historical Museum, was moved off the old base but unfortunately burned down in its new location.

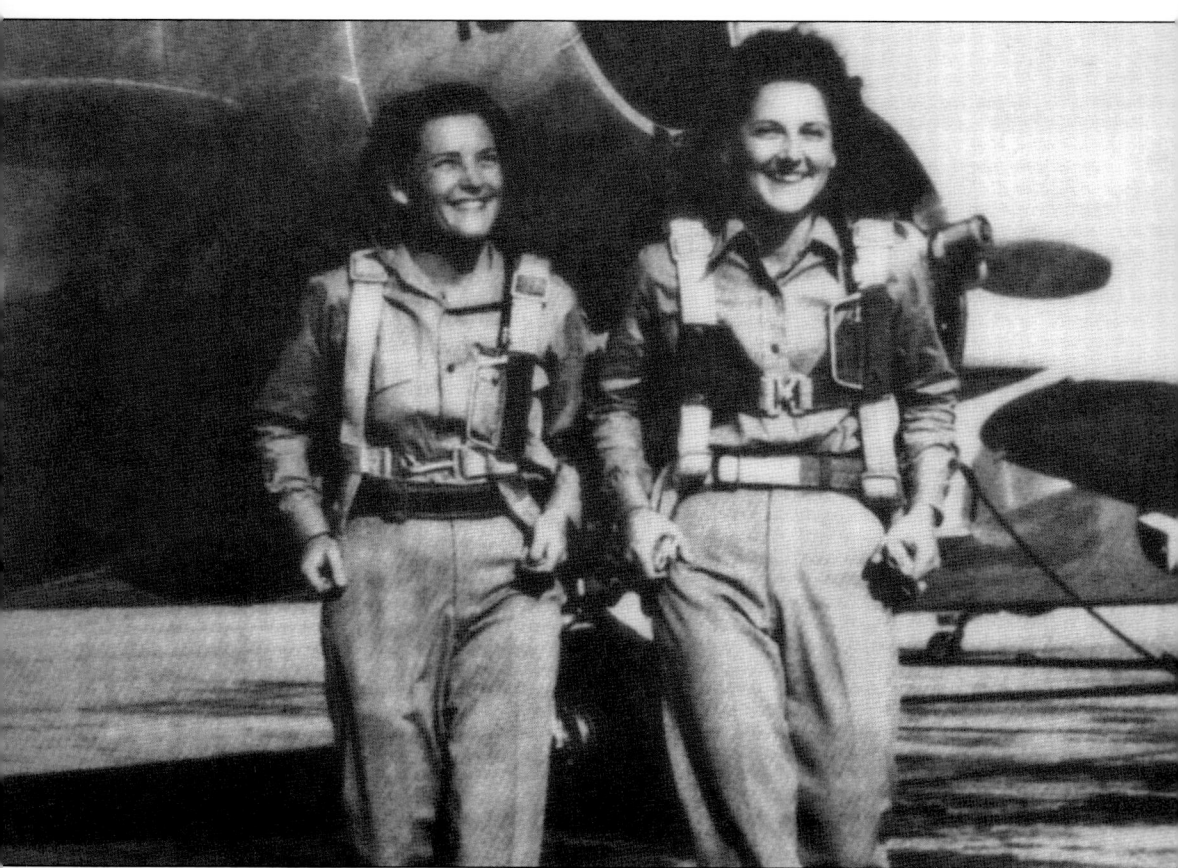

Women made amazing strides toward equality in World War II. The two women pictured were the first women to become test pilots. The woman on the left is unidentified; on the right is Betty Heinrich. Both of these ladies were stationed and photographed at Hondo Air Base (PL. 3G-562CF-3) in the 1940s.

On February 17, 1944, these famous navigators arrived at La Guardia Field. This was the first black officers unit ever known, and it was heralded all over the nation. The mayor of New York, Fiorello La Guardia (for whom La Guardia Airport is named), is shown as he shakes hands with Maj. Galen B. Price, commanding officer of the airmen, on their arrival on the steps of New York City Hall. This photograph is from the *New York Times*.

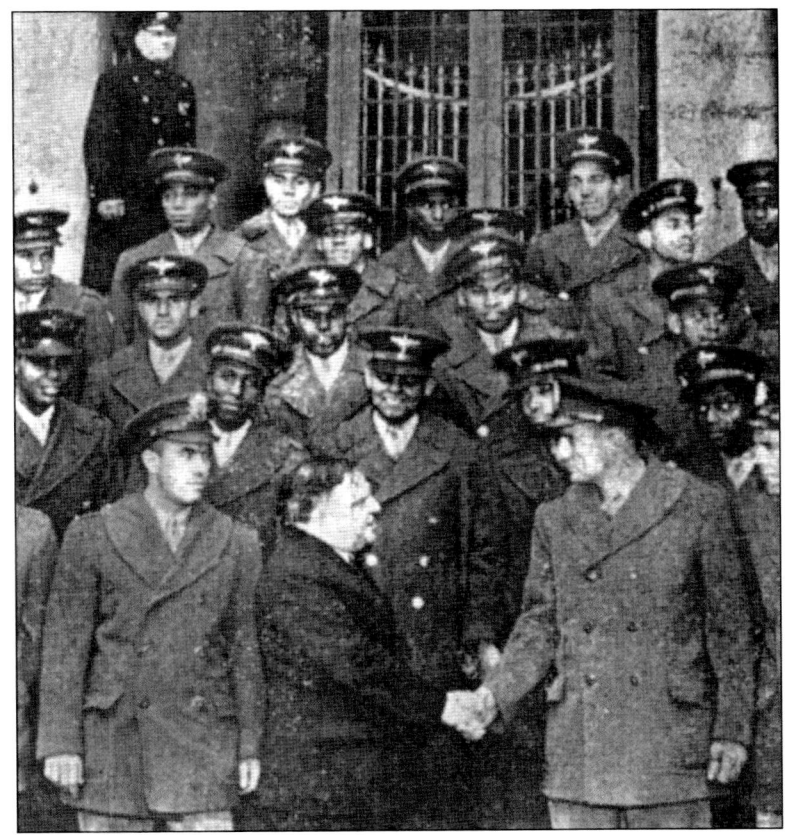

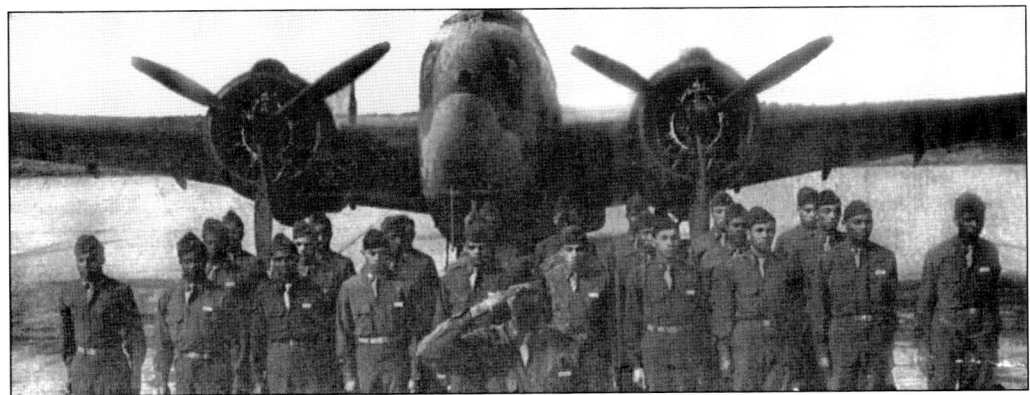

On their test flight from Texas to Chicago, Pittsburg, and finally New York, the "twenty four kids in the clouds" were lauded in the *New York Daily News* on February 19, 1944.

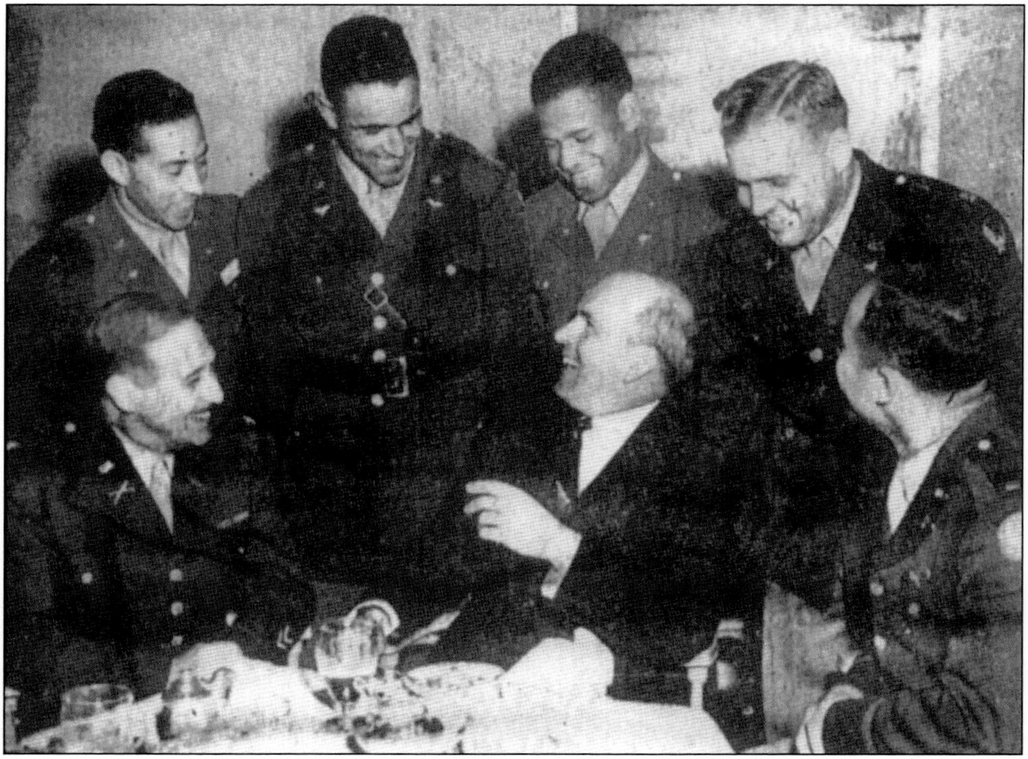

On February 16, 1944, air cadets speak to Assistant Secretary of War John J. McCloy after helping raise $1,192,000 for the war effort. These outstanding young men made their nation proud.

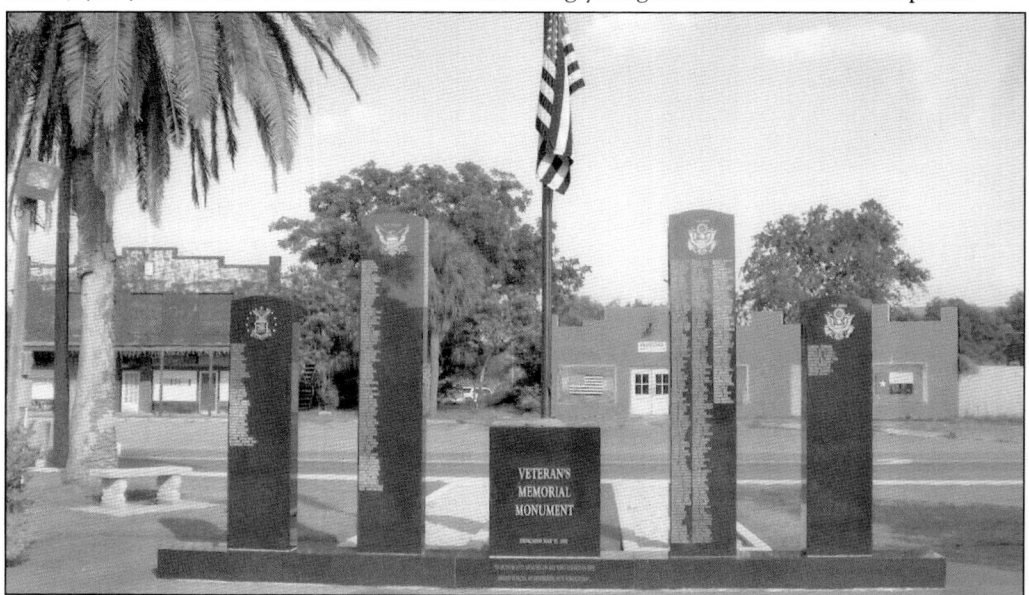

Pictured here in Natalia on Veteran's Day is the Veteran's Memorial Monument with the names of all those in Natalia who served. The American flag is at half-mast on Veteran's Day. (Courtesy of Ruby Vera.)

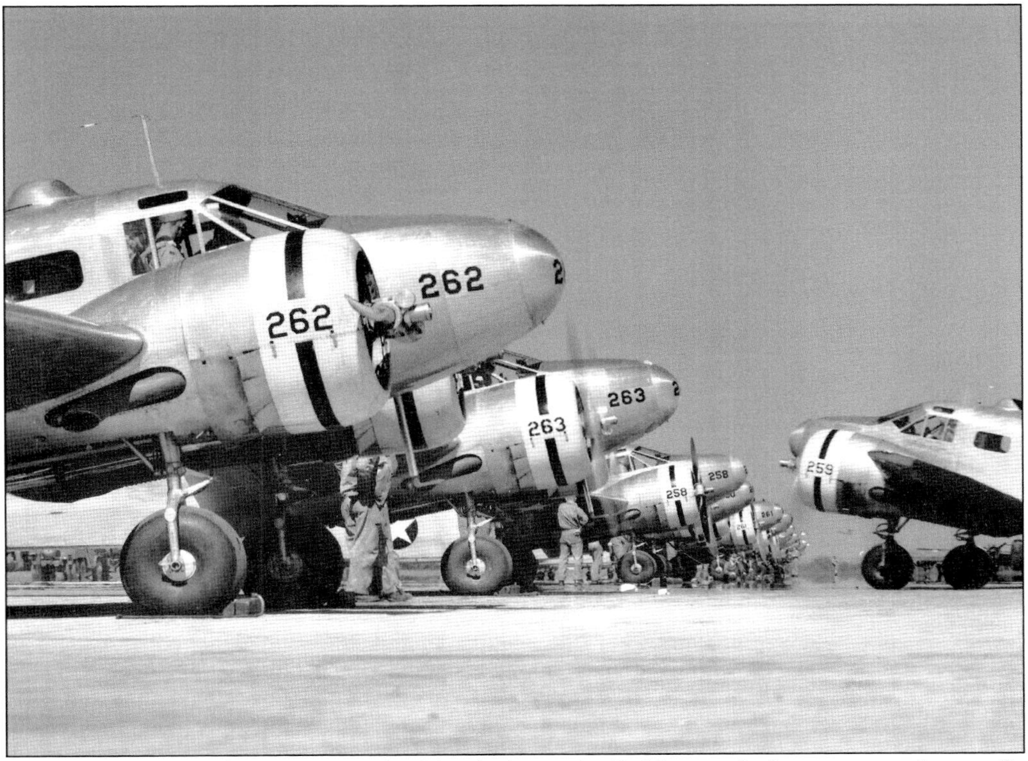

These twin-engine planes were used at Hondo Army Air Field to teach the navigators how to fly and navigate. The picture is from the 1940s.

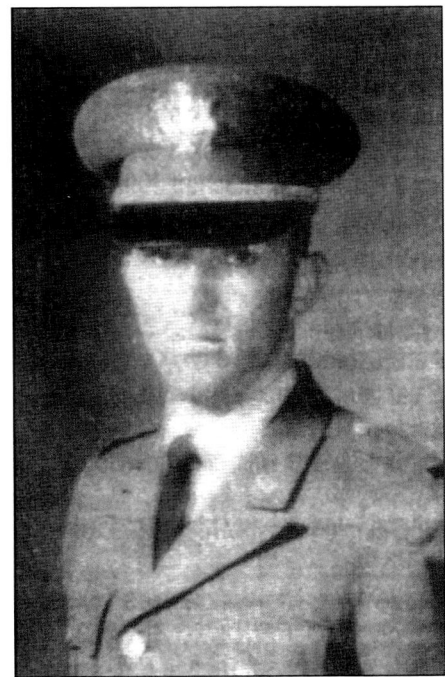

Army first lieutenant Larry D. Neumann of Hondo was wounded by a booby trap of grenades in the jungles of Vietnam. Hardly any part of his body escaped injury. He was awarded the Purple Heart for his brave service to his country. (Courtesy of the Mary and Henry Briscoe family.)

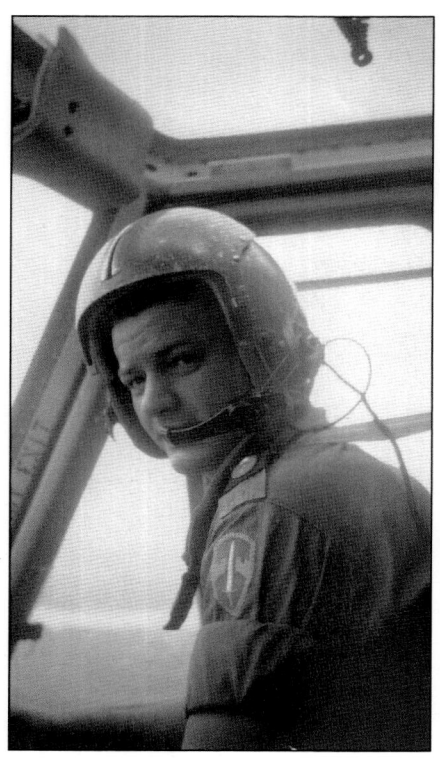

From Castroville, 1st Lt. Carl Joseph Mangold joined the Army after graduating from St. Mary's University. He flew a UH-1B helicopter. He was providing overhead cover for a convoy that was moving north between Phu Loi and Ben Cat when his helicopter exploded. Before he was shot down, he wrote to his wife and family, "If I must die in my tour here, believe me, I will always be proud to say that I am an American fighting man. We have to make a stand somewhere. This could very well be Castroville, Texas, instead of Le My, Viet Nam." Carl was awarded the Distinguished Flying Cross, Purple Heart, Bronze Star, and Air Medal with 26 clusters, as well as the Vietnam Medal. Carl left behind a young wife, Fran, three-year-old Shelly, one-and-a-half-year-old Jill, and five-month-old Christopher. He was also survived by his mother and his two brothers and two sisters. Carl was 25 years old when he was shot down. Also aboard the helicopter was his copilot, 2nd Lt. George Gutierrez Jr., also from Castroville, who had just joined Carl's group. Medina County lost two heroes at the same time. Two other US soldiers were lost in the crash, as were two Vietnamese army officers. (Courtesy of Paula Hoog Mangold.)

Col. Henry Bryn Briscoe served his country in the Air Force after finishing college. He got his wings after graduating from pilot training. He became a transport pilot and a C-54, C-124, C-141, and C-5 pilot and flew the Boeing 737. He was a squadron commander in Vietnam and flew many combat missions. Later, Henry served on the air staff at the Pentagon, was a wing director of operations, and was a base commander. After retiring from the Air Force, he became a farmer and rancher in Devine. Henry was eventually elected Medina County commissioner and stayed in this post for 12 years. He served 17 years on the Medina County Historic Commission and wrote a weekly column for the *Devine News* for 20 years as well as a monthly column on local history for three years. (Courtesy of Mary Briscoe.)

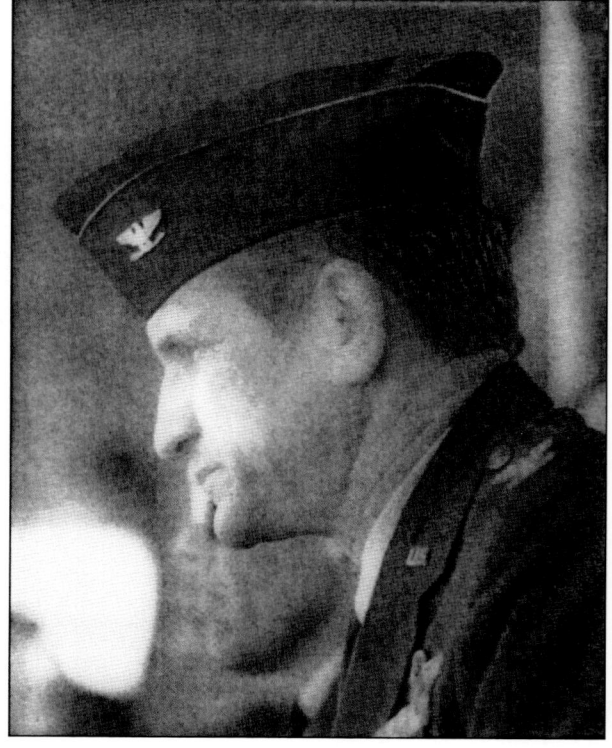

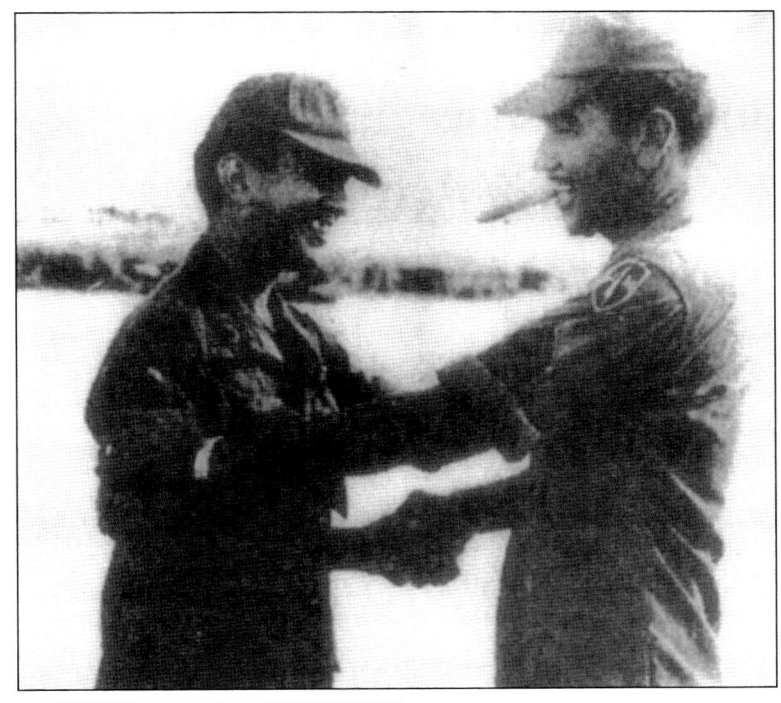

Pictured are two brothers of the Musquez family of Hondo. They continued the family tradition of serving in the military; through the years, this family has served in all branches of the military. Sfc. Ben O. Musquez (right) of Mobile Advisory Team (MAT) 102 met his younger brother, Spc. Angel Sr., at the Mekong River south of the city of Rach Gia, Kien Giang Province in South Vietnam in 1960. (Courtesy of the *Hondo Anvil*.)

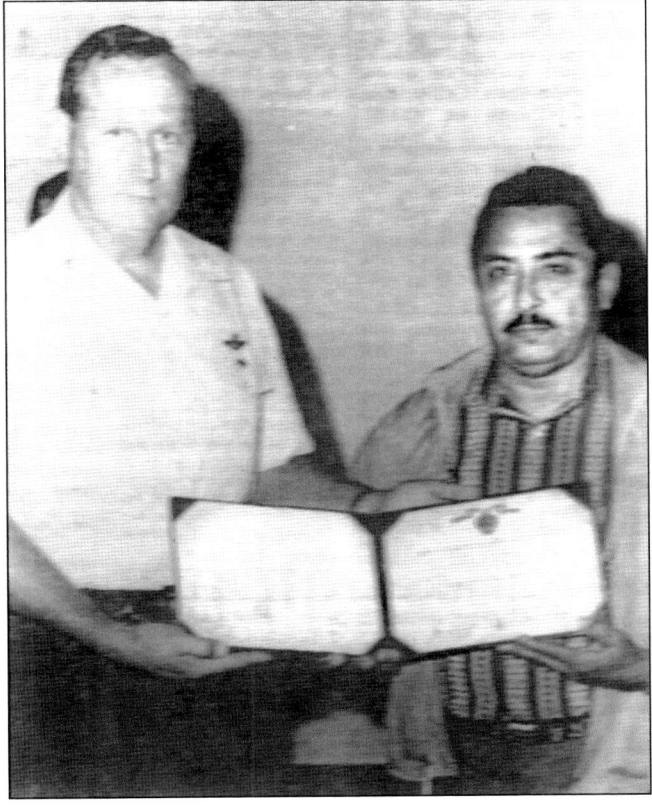

Pictured is Chom Pompa, son of Jose Anjel and Aurelia Costella Pompa of Devine. Chom joined the Navy after Pearl Harbor and worked as a beach master, helping planes land on the water in Pearl Harbor. He left Hawaii just as his brother Ruben Pompa arrived. He served in Johnson Island; Espiritu Santo; Brisbane, Australia; and Hawaii. A third brother, Richard Pompa, was also in the Pacific theater. In 1946, Chom married Alma Villarreal. Chom transferred from the Navy to the Air Force and received the Purple Heart when he was injured at Bein Hoa Airbase near Saigon, Vietnam. Chom retired with 33 years of both active and reserve duty. The family lost a bother-in-law, Juan Villarreal, in Korea in 1951. The Pompa family paid a heavy price for the freedom in which we live! (Courtesy of the Mary and Henry Briscoe family.)

Discover Thousands of Local History Books Featuring Millions of Vintage Images

Arcadia Publishing, the leading local history publisher in the United States, is committed to making history accessible and meaningful through publishing books that celebrate and preserve the heritage of America's people and places.

Find more books like this at
www.arcadiapublishing.com

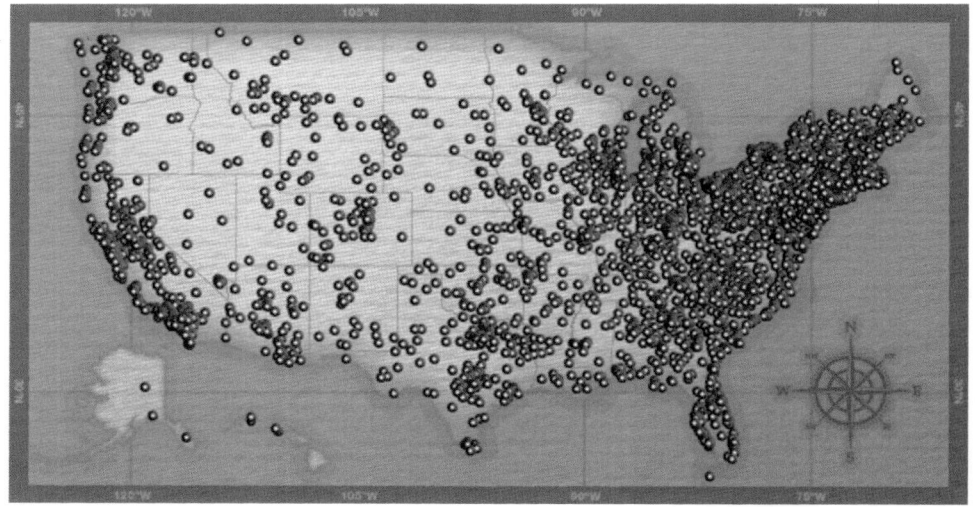

Search for your hometown history, your old stomping grounds, and even your favorite sports team.

Consistent with our mission to preserve history on a local level, this book was printed in South Carolina on American-made paper and manufactured entirely in the United States. Products carrying the accredited Forest Stewardship Council (FSC) label are printed on 100 percent FSC-certified paper.

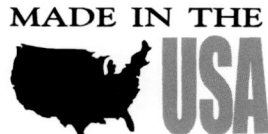